ANTI-INDIANISM
IN MODERN AMERICA

ANTI-INDIANISM IN MODERN AMERICA

A Voice from Tatekeya's Earth

❖   ❖   ❖   ❖   ❖

Elizabeth Cook-Lynn

UNIVERSITY OF ILLINOIS PRESS

Urbana and Chicago

Library of Congress Cataloging-in-Publication Data
Cook-Lynn, Elizabeth.
Anti-Indianism in modern America : a voice from Tatekeya's Earth /
Elizabeth Cook-Lynn.
p.   cm.
Includes bibliographical references.
ISBN 0-252-02662-4 (cloth : alk. paper)
1. Indians of North America—Government relations. 2. Indians in
literature. 3. Indians in art. 4. Indians of North America—Study and
teaching. 5. United States—Ethnic relations. I. Title.
E93.C76   2001
973'.0497—dc21   00-012723

Looking for a place to cross the creek
I hear a beaver splash and see him
hurry away in spirals of transparency
model busybody on his own
private journey to get home in one piece
alive and well. Like most translators
of these waterways, tributaries to the
vast Mni Sosa, he avoided
the great bluffs where I stood
and dropped into low waters
when he heard me intrude.
Predictable, sensible, he
feared the tread of humans,
probably learned he was no match
for the damn builders
whose turbid reservoirs could be heard
upstream for eight hundred miles.

Dusty trails along the tree-lined creek
turn to mud in shaded spots, cow
trails and horse paths lead to the
struggle for meaning of a hardscrabble
life, traditional values of the people
who lived here for thousands of years
displaced as easily as the river chewing
at its banks. Like a Muslim amid
the relics and ruins of any holy city
I weep for Tatekeya's Earth.

—COOK-LYNN, *I Remember the Fallen Trees* (1998)

Contents

PREFACE

In my lifetime the inexorable logic of Indian life in America has undergone deliberate diminishment. In my lifetime hundreds of thousands of acres of treaty-protected indigenous lands have been lost to Sioux Nation title, thousands of Lakotas and Dakotas have been forced away from their homelands because of anti-Indian legislation and poverty and federal Indian policy; and white Americans, by and large, have no more respect for or understanding of native cultures and political status than they did during Jefferson's time, though they continue, as he did, to collect bones and Indian words and delay justice. It is because of these losses that I write.

Today, America's tongue is cloaked in ignorance and racism and imperialism as much as it was during the westward-movement era; and "removal" is still the infuriating thrust of Indian/white relations. The tribal tongue of Nativism, by contrast, struggles to foretell a future filled with uncertainty. It is because of this reality that I write.

The agency town–military fort where I was born, *kudwichacha,* is nestled in the fluvial hills of Mni Sosa. It was famous as one of the guarded places of U.S. overseers of Indian policy, and its inhabitants were mostly ex-military, active missionaries, Catholic priests, merchants, public-health doctors and nurses, schoolteachers, white hangers-on, and, of course, Sioux Indians. About twenty years before I was born they took down the fifty-foot-high board fences that protected them from my people, whom they saw as the arrogant, mad Dakota Sioux who gave the country its name.

I am stunned by the natural beauty of that place, horrified by the destruction of it in my lifetime, and now I know that when I was a child I was never innocent as children are thought to be. I remember the silences of a people (the Santees and their relatives the Ihanktowan) made suspicious by past, untold events, the raucous intrusions of those who were not Dakotas, and the cautious tales told by those in whom we placed our trust.

I remember the mornings along the Crow Creek, where everything, in the beginning, centered around my grandparents, and the fog and the wet grass and the rattlesnakes and the berry bushes. A small wooden bridge rattled across the creek just a few yards from my grandmother's house, and on any late summer afternoon my sister and I could be found there, sitting grandly in the damp black sand rolling cigarettes with tobacco from a box of "kept" things our grandpa brought out only on ceremonial occasions.

I write because such days and places are unforgettable, and because the colonial dictatorship imposed on the very private lives of a very private people festers still and contaminates the life of a whole country.

This small collection of essays begins with a piece that attempts to define Anti-Indianism as a concept in American life and scholarship. The traits of Anti-Indianism are as follows: first and foremost, it is the sentiment that results in unnatural death to Indians. Anti-Indianism is that which treats Indians and their tribes as though they don't exist, the sentiment that suggests that Indian nationhood (i.e., tribalism) should be disavowed and devalued. It is anything in history and literature that does not invest itself in Indian audiences. Second, Anti-Indianism is that which denigrates, demonizes, and insults being Indian in America. The third trait of Anti-Indianism is the use of historical event and experience to place the blame on Indians for an unfortunate and dissatisfying history. And, finally, Anti-Indianism is that which exploits and distorts Indian cultures and beliefs. All of these traits have conspired to isolate, to expunge or expel, to menace, to defame.

These are the matters that have concerned Indian writers, including myself, for many years. After a successful career in teaching courses in Native Studies and writing about these subjects, I now find myself retired from all that, sitting in a small home office in the cluttered company of many books, papers, photographs, and memories, where I have been doing the work of a fulltime writer and have, in fact, written and published four books in the last ten years.

My grown children live successful lives: a son and three beautiful daughters. We are clustered in the same time zone and we revise our lives as our family matures: grandsons, new husbands and wives, new jobs, travel. I am continuously grateful to my children, who have taught me as much about growing up as I've taught them. And I am grateful to C. J. Lynn, who helped me raise them when my first husband, their father, did not.

A couple of summers ago at a tribal *wacipi*, I saw a stunning, tall Lakota traditional dancer in the circle of dancers. He wore a decorated Seventh Cavalry military hat over his long braids and carried a replica of a brass bugle at his belt and was otherwise resplendent in traditional dress, eagle feathers and beads and deer hides. One of my daughters, dancing beside me, poked me in the ribs and whispered surreptitiously, "Hey, what's with the bugle?" We laughed in admiration of the dancer's innovation and creativity, but in some mystic way we knew it was more than that; we knew this was a dancer who had just come in from the Battlefield of the Little Big Horn, a man who shared the victory dance with all of us; a man who knew our history and recreated it for us in the context of our modern tribal lives.

It is for the memory of such grace and knowledge that I write.

As a writer, I am one of the few who does not rail against Nationalism. I do not think Nationalism is a human defect. On the contrary, Nationalism is a vital component of Civilization. I do not deny the inchoate United States or any other entity its right to become a nation in support of its people. In that same context, I defend the right of the Great Sioux Nation, the Oceti Shakowan, to the same privilege. We are made up of the tribes of Santee, Oglala, Sicangu, Minneconjou, Yankton, Sihasapa, and Hunkpapa; we occupy hundreds of thousands of acres of land in the Northern Plains and *we are a nation of people.*

❖ ❖ ❖

The subtitle's Tatekeya's Earth takes its name from the protagonist of the author's first novel, *From the River's Edge,* and is a reference to the geography of the Sioux Nation. It is a place the author has known intimately, a place where she grew to know her life, a place where her relatives have always lived and are buried.

This collection of essays confronts themes of Anti-Indianism in the history and culture of North America and attempts to assist the reader in recognizing the wide variety of subject matters stimulated through the author's thirty years of working toward the development of Native American Studies as an academic discipline.

In the introductory essay, Anti-Indianism in America is defined in accordance with specific tribal experiences. Land loss and cultural diminishment, misguided governmental policy and faux morality are discussed in the context of the struggle for native sovereignty and survival.

In other sections, selected spokespersons, scholars, writings and theories are examined in order to shed light upon some of the trends of the last several decades of Indian/white relations in America. This work closes with two essays on Genocide, the historical phenomenon that follows the course of a bloody nineteenth century's progress to technology and winds its violence into the dramatic twentieth-century migrations. Genocide is known throughout the ancient and modern worlds. It is the unacknowledged and continuing human activity that characterizes the relationship between natives and colonists who attempt to live side by side in the Occupied Territories called America as well as in other parts of the world as they struggle to know their own histories.

PART ONE

ANTI-INDIANISM DEFINED

1

ANTI-INDIANISM IN ART AND LITERATURE IS NOT JUST A TROPE

Anti-Indianism is probably the foremost challenge to U.S. history and art, two major disciplines that often claim to be ethically neutral. Cultural critics of American social, intellectual, and political society have usually refrained from using the term "Anti-Indianism," though they have engaged in lively discourse in the last thirty years concerning the tragic relations between Indians and whites in this country, widespread racism, diversity, and multicultural interests. What this means is that the ubiquitous denial of Anti-Indianism in our lives and in our scholarship obscures our necessary understanding that there is almost always reason behind tragedy.

Obviously, many more disciplines than literature or history or art are implicated as participants in impulsive Anti-Indianism, now recognized by some of the more astute revisionist scholars as a form of discrimination and ideological bias in scholarship as well as in practical politics and mainstream thinking. Thus, Anti-Indianism, though the term is not widely used, is emerging as a major issue in recent cultural scholarship and deserves further examination.

This is a brief introduction to the term and a discussion of the traits of the phenomenon of Anti-Indianism in literary works as illustrated in specific generic examples of the writings using Indian motifs and themes.

Anti-Indianism in the American imagination, starting even before the time of such luminaries as Washington Irving and Walt Whitman, probably originated in religiosity. Like Anti-Semitism in Europe, Anti-Indianism in America raised its ugly head in specific places and in a variety of contexts but gained momentum as a fundamental element of American Christianity. Indigenous America was not Christian, therefore it was seen as an opposing force to be obliterated at any cost. This is not said to blame all Christians for the genocidal treatment of the non-Christian natives of this continent. Just as one cannot blame Nietzsche for Hitler or even Khomeini for Salmon Rushdie's plight, neither can Christian thinkers and writers be blamed for the killing of some say as many as 80 million Indians on this continent in fewer than a hundred years. On the other hand, neither are they blameless, because they built the institutions such as churches and schools and financial centers that mandated racist activity. Therefore it is sensible for scholars, and particularly native scholars, to examine the philosophical and political influences of Anti-Indianism in artistic expression.

Anti-Indianism, like Anti-Semitism, displaces and excludes; thus, its distinguishing purposes have been to socially isolate, to expunge or expel, to fear and menace, to defame, and to repulse indigenous people. Unlike Anti-Semitism, however, which has had enemies powerful enough to go to war against it and change the world, Anti-Indianism in America has had almost free rein; only occasionally and inconsistently have Indians and their allies fought back successfully against it in America. The writers of Anti-Indian texts have been numerous and popular, and today, even Indian writers have joined the producers of these texts. They have done so either wittingly or unwittingly, for one reason or another, but surely a significant reason has been to gain the acceptance of a mainstream readership.

Features of Anti-Indianism in art and literature should be examined carefully and at length by critics in order to understand that artists often make judgments in their works about Indians that are based in the Anti-Indianism of deep-seated American sentiment concerning self-congratulatory colonial knowledge and discovery and conversion. Most often this sentiment has not only worked to expel Indians from specific geographies, but it has also enabled its proponents or practitioners to see Indians and Indian tribal histories and identities as antithetical to the well-touted democratic ideals of the Founding Fathers of the United States; in other words, as Anti-American.

Forms of persecution of Indians have been perpetuated by an American society imbued with this inherent Anti-Indianism, and these persecutors will continue unless careful, insightful scholarhip critically examines Anti-Indianism as a concept with enormous impact on all Americans. Because Anti-Indianism began in religiosity, much as Anti-Semitism did, restrictions on Indian life and the deliberate killing of millions of Indians on this continent was undertaken. When that seemed slow and inefficient, during which time

Indians were thought to be impediments to progress, forced assimilation by law was instituted as a federal policy. This does not mean that Americans aren't good people. What it means is that they and their forebears, like the practicing Christians in Germany who participated in the Nazi extermination of the Jews in 1930 and beyond, have participated in a holocaust of major proportions. There is much denial of this crucial fact, and it is in this denial that the beginning of contemporary Anti-Indianism resides.

The contemporary authors and thinkers whose literary ethics allow them to create works that either insult or otherwise turn away sensitive readers through the use of Anti-Indianisms are many. In the following pages, brief examples of the work of three such writers are examined. Most Anglo-American writers like Walt Whitman, whose poem about George Custer is utilized here for the purpose of discussion, did not create an entire body of work that placed Anti-Indianisms at the service of his art. He simply digressed into Anti-Indian discourse now and then as this poem reveals, as is the habit of many writers who search for interesting topics to write about. Other writers like Adrian Louis and Louis L'Amour, however, whose examples are also examined here, have been able to place Anti-Indianisms as critical to the contextualization and wholeness of their art.

The long overdue critical analysis of anti-Indian works emerges at the close of the twentieth century at the same time that the genuine self-empowerment of native peoples in America emerges in politics and government. Indian self-determination is now a principle of law, and it cannot be dislodged from the sovereignty inherent in native history and experience. If writers through the use of deliberate inaccuracies and contemptuousness are allowed to usurp the inherent right of Indians and Indian tribes to self-empowerment and pride, native cultures will be forever deformed and tribal values will be supplanted. While this may have always been the aim of American thought concerning the indigenous populations of this contintent, its ethics are now under scrutiny.

Anti-Indianisms That Dare Not Speak the Name

Early American historical views in support of imperialism are Anti-Indianisms that have influenced literary form, a fact of art rarely viewed in early literary criticism as worthy of discussion. Imperialism, defined as the policy of extending the rule of an empire over colonies for reasons of conquest and profit, was a condition that clearly marked early Indian/white relations and continues today, on and off Indian Reserved Homelands throughout the country. It is the impetus for colonial praxis, which has become the basis for several centuries of oppression as well as the contemporary crimes of America that remain unlitigated.

The influence of empire-making on artistic expression was a "given" in early America but largely overlooked or ignored as simply too pejorative by critics and readers alike. It would have been thought an outrage to have called these expressions Anti-Indianisms during the earliest imperialist eras. Indeed, Herman Melville (1819–91) was, perhaps, the only early American writer who seriously questioned the Anti-Indianisms of his time. He called the phenomenon "Indian Hating" in his surrealistic novel *The Confidence Man,* and like many critics and artists who are ahead of their time, Melville wrote things people didn't want to hear, won no prizes, had virtually no audience for his most important work until long after his death, and even today illustrates the time-honored literary reality in America that prizes are never given to works by authors who, intentionally or not, exclude the readers.

Early American poets were often as much witting supporters of American expansionism and hegemony and, often, outright racism as were the criminal industrialists who exploited workers and resources for profit and colonists who stole Indian lands through legalistic strategies. Early writers were often Anti-Indianist propagandists, though there was much resistance to the idea that they should receive that kind of criticism. Even today there is resistance to the idea that any American works can be described as Anti-Indian. Just as the Anti-Semite Ezra Pound said of Karl Marx, "He is a Jew and has invented very little," so did the Anti-Indianist Teddy Roosevelt say in *The Winning of the West,* "The war against mercilous savages was the most ultimately righteous of all wars." This kind of Anti-Semitism and Anti-Indianism was and is adopted and accepted uncritically in all disciplines.

A rather obscure example used here to illustrate the point is a eulogy to an American hero, George Armstrong Custer, written by the quintessential American poet Walt Whitmen (1819–92) and published barely a month after the events called the Battle of the Little Big Horn in 1876:

A DEATH-SONNET FOR CUSTER

From far Dakota's canons,
Lands of the wild ravine, the dusky Sioux, the lonesome stretch of silence.
Haply to-day a mournful wail, haply a trumpet-note for heroes.
The battle-bulletin,
The Indian ambuscade, the craft, the fatal environment,
The cavalry companies fighting to the last in sternest heroism,

In the midst of their little circle, with their slaughter'd horses for
    breastworks,
The fall of Custer and all his officers and men.
Continues yet the old, old legend of our race,
The loftiest of life upheld by death,
The ancient banner perfectly maintain'd
O lesson opportune, O how I welcome thee!
As sitting in dark days,
Lone, sulky, through the time's thick murk looking in vain for light, for
    hope,
From unsuspected parts a fierce and momentary proof,
(the sun there at the centre though conceal'd.
Electric life forever at the centre,)
Breaks forth a lightning flash.
Thou of the tawny flowing hair in battle,
I erewhile saw, with erect head, pressing ever in front, bearing a bright
    sword in thy hand,
Now ending well in death the splendid fever of thy deeds,
(I bring no dirge for it or thee, I bring a glad triumphal sonnet,)
Desperate and glorious, aye in defeat most desperate, most glorious,
After thy many battles in which never yielding up a gun or a color,
Leaving behind thee a memory sweet to soldiers,
Thou yieldest up thyself.

Whitman had been a clerk in the Bureau of Indian Affairs in 1865, but was fired within weeks when it was discovered he wrote "obscene" poetry. One of the reasons to look carefully at this poem is to come to the understanding that poetry has always been a political matter, and Whitman as a journalist evolved into a defender of the Free Soil Movement. Despite the frequent claim of poetry as art committed only to aesthetics or beauty, politics and Anti-Indianism have had a broad range in the field. Who would think that Walt Whitman, that poet who nowadays is read as a defender of freedom by everyone from leftist politicos to those who call themselves citizens of Queer Nation to those who are readers of Victorian novels, could be accused of reducing poetry to a patriotic anthem? Well, it must have been a lapse of some kind, some readers might reason.

Probably not. This poem, written at the height of historical conflict, is a poem that accompanies empire-building. We should not be astonished to learn that much literature performs that function. The great body of Mayan literature, for example, functions to tell the greatness of Mayan culture and the powerful dynamics of Mayan peoples. Literatures all over the world have accompanied empire-building, but what have been called exemplary or classic literatures have rarely served to abuse others and breed hatred as is the case in some of the early American literary pieces.

The Anti-Indianisms in Whitman's poem have little to do with Whitman's desire to write a sympathetic tribute to a man he and others claimed as a fallen hero. These kinds of tributes abound in all national literatures, but ordinarily the classic writer uses reasonably accurate information, and when he does not, his work is contextualized within its inaccuracies. The issue in the Whitman poem is the use of a propagandist history concerning the *facts* of the battle, facts that are rarely if ever noted as dishonest. Custer was not ambushed, as the poet suggests in his second stanza. The Sioux and the Cheyenne Indians did not appear on the battlefield from concealed positions in a surprise and unexpected attack. Instead, quite the opposite was true. Custer and his Seventh Cavalry had the moving Sioux military and its accompanying villagers in its sights for many weeks prior to the actual engagement. Custer had pursued the Indians for hundreds of miles with annihilation in mind. This was hardly a surprise attack (ambuscade as the poet calls it) by Indians.

In ignorance or error or in a deliberate lie, the poet misuses the *facts* of this historical event in order to make Custer heroic (instead of just foolish or failed or unlucky) and, more important, to portray Indians as unworthy of their victory. They were (and are), of course, anathema to the American Dream of itself and what it might become. Whitman's dedication to the East and his emergence in New York as a major artist, his seeing the flowering of the Empire State Building and the flourishing of an immigrant population in making the city the most important city of his times would naturally put him on the side of U.S. Nationalism in the Indian/white struggle in the West.

The Anti-Indianisms in this poem are unmistakable. What ultimately happened to the people of the Sioux Nation, the eventual subjugation through legal fraud and the systematic brutal policy-making of America toward them that continues to this day, cannot be addressed by this poet's work or his readers unless the Anti-Indianisms are acknowledged. The failure to contextualize honestly the facts of history, then, must be identified as one of the main kinds of Anti-Indianisms in literary expression, creative strategies deemed acceptable as poetry-making, else it is merely and namely propagandizing.

Many paintings further developed the propaganda that Whitman indulged. One, by Casdilly Adams in 1896 called "Custer's Last Fight," became the most famous. It shows Custer, blond "tawny" locks flowing, standing alone, defending himself and the nation with his sword held high in the midst of carnage and death and hundreds of thrashing Indians. The painting was made into a lithograph and the Anheuser-Bush beer company distributed 150,000 copies nationwide.

The argument being made in this essay is not that nationalistic poetry about heroic figures always fails in artistic intent. Nor is it being said here that Whitman is a hateful racist. In fact, Whitman probably wrote his poem mainly because he desired to speak for the invaders of Indian Country and for the U.S. Army and his fellow Americans, and it is said to be a beautifully written poem by those interested only in his craftsmanship, not his historical perspective. The point here is that false information and flawed ideas were used by Whitman to injure groups of Indians and tribal nations, the Sioux and the Cheyenne, who had signed treaties in defense of themselves and, as a matter of modern fact, still today must co-exist in the American national forum. Intentional or not, nothing alters the fact that such creative work insults and turns away thoughtful Indian readers.

Indian Anti-Indianism—Louis

If it can be said that the failure to honestly contextualize historical event in poetry is one of the main types of Anti-Indianisms, there are probably many offenders, even contemporary Indian poets themselves. Anti-Indianisms, this discussion illustrates, often appear in the most unexpected places.

Adrian C. Louis, for example, a Paiute Indian writer who taught for several years at Oglala Lakota College in Kyle, S.Dak. on the Pine Ridge Sioux Indian Reservation, often draws imaginatively on American history for the vision in his work, which results in what can be called Anti-Indianisms. One does not know if one should give poetry a special dispensation in the Indian writers' case or if one should chalk it up to the theory that to satirize or ironize is the means by which poetry, often bad poetry, is made good. Unfortunately, the latter rationale is not always a useful criterion since satire or parody, which is supposed to communicate conflicts and confusion through a superficial level of humor, falls short when the piece is mean-spirited instead of humorous.

In a long discursive poem, "Earth Bone Connected to the Spirit Bone," which appears in *Ceremonies of the Damned,* one of the latest of Louis's nine collections of poems, Louis writes, without much humor: "Most of us know Sitting Bull wasn't bullshitting, but we still don't know which way to go. We are between two different worlds and between the past and the future. At least that's what we tell ourselves when we fail. *We never mention the fact that it was skins who killed Mr. Bull*" (emphasis added).

Contextualizing this sentiment in a book in which the poet calls himself and other Indians "damned" (which is, of course, an American stereotype) and entitling the poem with a line from a pop-religious song urging listeners to "hear the word of the Lord" places the poem in pop culture vernacular so that mainstream America can and will respond. In other words, these devices are used so that the poem will appeal to a broad audience of non-Indians.

Most Americans believe in the stereotypical assumption that Indians are "damned," vanished, or pathetic remnants of a race. It may be true that many Indians share in that stereotype. Most Americans have heard the Righteous Brothers or some other singing group render the song referred to in the poem and thus can add a whole myriad of images of their own in response to it. The song is very familiar to American audiences, may even have started as a negro spiritual, some say—"the knee bone connected to the thigh bone" and so on. But this alone does not make the poem an expression of Anti-Indianism; it merely contextualizes it in the language of popular culture so that it appeals to non-Indians.

What does make it an expression of Anti-Indianism is the *context* in which the historical fact of the killing of Sitting Bull in 1890 becomes the focus, an event that occurred just two weeks before the Massacre at Wounded Knee. As to this last phrase of the verse, there is no question that "skins" shot Sitting Bull, as the poet says. Sioux BIA policemen Red Tomahawk and Bull Head are generally regarded as the shooters. Tribal history, however, which the poet ignores in the poem, tells us much more. Tribal historians say that the U.S. government police force, made up of reservation-based Sioux Indian males, was part of an illegal occupation force much like the Jewish guard details at the concentration camps in Germany and Poland during World War II, who were hired and paid assassins and tormenters of their own people.

History now reveals some evidence that the killing of Sitting Bull may have been a political assassination engineered by the non-Indian Agency officials at Standing Rock Reservation. Like the Jews in WWII, forced by the Gestapo to starve and mistreat their own comrades in concentration camps, Sioux Indians were forced to beat and kill and otherwise menace their own people on their own lands in the nineteenth and twentieth centuries. Compulsory service of one kind or another was forced upon the Sioux on their own treaty lands during this period of extermination and genocide. It is largely white historians, and now Paiute poet Louis, who have interpreted the act of shooting Sitting Bull as an internecine act, rather than as the colonial extermination event that it probably was.

In "Earth Bone Connected to the Spirit Bone," Louis draws on this Anti-Indianism of American thought and by doing so condemns or at the very least blames the victims for this history. This is an example of Anti-Indianism in Literary Form because the poet uses the historical oppression and subjugation of tribal people, for which they were not responsible, against them in a contemporary retelling. Yet Louis has been praised for giving voice to "the virulent sad politics of America" (Chase Twichell), and is lauded as one who "channels the energy of anger into poetry with as much incendiary power as any poet writing in this country today" (Martin Espada).

Those who know the real history of Sitting Bull's assassination read the poem and the phrase adversarially. Indeed, many thoughtful Sioux readers will be offended at Louis's rendering of history, in which he blames them for the killing of Sitting Bull. Louis challenges the trust that Sioux readers want to have in him. This is not just a minor distraction. It is a real dilemma for those who would like to give this poet the benefit of the doubt. Yet because Louis discriminates between his audiences, an adversarial position between tribal readers and poet is the result. White audiences who can accept the misplaced blame in order to feel pity or contempt for the Sioux and compassion for their own histories read the poem with enthusiasm, and Indian audiences who refuse to accept a corrupted history and a misplaced blame read it adversarially. The Louis interpretation of this history is at the very least an apology for the white historical interpretation, at worst it is the tactic of a propagandist who does witting or unwitting harm to himself and fellow Indians.

Sioux readers, if they know the history of the event in tribal terms, may be offended by the poem because it does not seem to invest itself in them as participants in the audience. Indeed, it challenges unfairly the worth of Indian holocaust survivors and descendants rather than seeking an understanding of the complexities of a colonial history. There is no question that Indians should take responsibility for their behavior and their lives and their histories, which may be the point of Louis's vicious stereotyping of the Lakota, but there is a troubling self-disdain expressed by a poet who claims himself to be an Indian.

If irony or satire is the intent, the pervasive self-hatred that permeates the poet's vision of Indians in general and the Sioux in particular results in a failed attempt, because in its effort to circumscribe Anti-Indian sentiment, it adopts it. This bizarre irony does not teach the reader or listener much about the textual complexities of being a contemporary Indian living life on the homelands, an Indian reservation. It merely condemns these victims in what the poet sees as a dismal and hopeless postcolonial history. Is this technique of irony used in the ways that Louis uses it a rhetorical trope or is it a real way of seeing the real world? Is it a case of saying one thing and meaning another? Or is this one of the times when the poet forgoes literary device and very simply means what he says, that Indians are fools and deserving of their oppression?

This Paiute Indian writer calls himself "damned" and insinuates himself into a Lakota historical past that, perhaps, in no way reveals what the people he is trying to speak for think of themselves. He says the great spirit is dead. And, again using a Lakota historical figure, he claims a kind of simplification of Indian life:

> When Crazy Horse was
> murdered at Ft. Robinson,
> the last living free Indian
> died. Except me.

From that expression, one expects that his poetry has made him free but it hasn't. He is gripped in hopelessness and rage. One is reminded of the kind of self-defamation so useful to black comedians like Chris Rock or Eddie Murphy, who often disapprove of their fellow African Americans in parody for the benefit of appealing to non-black audiences. But it was Dick Gregory, two decades earlier, who had his black audiences in mind as he used humor to identify the real and significant racial problems of black communities in the United States. It was Dick Gregory who refused to manipulate his audiences simply for the purpose of defamation or the belly laugh. He, unlike the younger comedians, was not contemptuous of himself or his people.

In another instance, Louis's palpable rage seems based in contempt of self and his elected tribal leaders when he says:

> And, we're all the same, even our
> leaders, the tribal politicians.
> These chiefs are big, brown ants
> in panties. Flint-skinned mutants
> of the sacred song. Insects.

This invective against fellow Indians again blames the victims, as it overlooks all of the reservation population that has participated in an imperfect political system and government that everyone will readily admit deserves criticism. But the fact is, the poet holds no citizenship rights in this government that he condemns, and the reader, then, is either confused or unconvinced about his claim that "we are all the same." Is he speaking about "our leaders" on the Pine Ridge Reservation, where he is an outsider? Or is he speaking of himself as a Paiute? Or is he speaking of Indians in general, again the result of stereotype. His offering of himself as a major critic of tribal politicians is placed in a vague and ambiguous rhetorical mode that seems more inventive than authentic.

Louis's denigration of tribal politicians seems to give credibility to those white Anti-Indianists who want to abolish tribal government and the sovereign immunity held since time immemorial in tribal enclaves. His Anti-Indianisms are political statements that may be seen as indistinguishable from those expressed by the non-Siouxan residents of the state of South Dakota who want to be rid of tribal enclaves, the "let's get rid of Indian reservations" or "let's abrogate Indian treaties" voices. What is more puzzling than ironic is that Louis's hostile caricature of reservation-based political leadership in general is a form of contemptuousness toward the very tribal histories that allow him to influence and affect his white audiences. Jeering, scoffing insults directed toward Indians can pander to the tastes of one segment of the audience, but their political effect can be devastating to another. There is no question that the principle of free speech makes it possible for any artist to say almost anything, but what the reader or the critic of such works can make of it is important too. If we are to depend upon the artist as social critic, then the artist and his work must be examined fully, not just accepted without critical analysis.

For many Indian writers and readers, the poetry of an Indian writer like Adrian Louis is the invention of the genre called Contemporary Native American Literatures, and it seems almost untouchable to critics who want to be politically correct. To reject Louis is to reject Contemporary Native American Poetry, and we cannot disown him without disowning ourselves. There may be several reasons for this dilemma, but a major reason is that Contemporary Native American Literatures as genre or Contemporary Native American Poetry as genre is not tribal literature nor is it tribally specific literary work. While many writers and readers and critics are willing to engage in Contemporary Native American Literary Study, which is an invention of western cultural studies, they are unwilling or unable to engage in specific tribal literary studies, which would give greater contextualization to the work.

While this is not meant to be a broad-based critical analysis of the work of Adrian C. Louis, and certainly every poet's vision is sacred, there is the suggestion here that the misuse of tribal histories by writers can become a subversive technique useful to conceptualize and disguise Anti-Indianisms, which allow western literary study to seize control over the development of contemporary Native American literary expression. In general, this kind of usurping of fundamental native thought and history engenders hostility and misunderstanding in the relationships between Indians and non-Indians.

The observations of the past few paragraphs are not meant to argue for some kind of suppression, nor do they suggest that any such works should be dismissed as marginal or inferior. When Jean-Paul Sartre asked "What is Literature?" he wasn't defending the right or the responsibility of artists and critics to say what is "good" poetry, or what is "bad" prose, or what is "ugly"—or even "offensive"—art. He was intent on defending the right to write "without prejudice," and he felt the passion to do that in order to break away from the notion held by the culturally privileged, isolated western writers who talked only of "pure" and "good" art.

To ask What is Anti-Indianism in literature? is not to suggest that Indian poets or writers in general must say only good things about Indians, or that they must be something they are not, nor should one expect that critics, even thoughtful ones, can serve as arbiters of good taste in all things Indian. Certainly, all students of literature and writers themselves must feel Sartre's passion concerning the freedom of art to be what it can be. Furthermore, writers who consider themselves "political" applaud Sartre's influence, because in a major way he began in the 1920s and '30s and '40s to ask what politics and activism in artistic expression can contribute to human life.

Later, of course, Sartre answered his own questions in defense of activism vis-à-vis those purist critics and artists who considered politics and activism beneath them. Being a survivor of the European world wars of the twentieth century, Sartre wanted to communicate something distinctive about the symbiotic relationship between literature and practical politics. In addition, he was an advocate of journalism and understood its influence on the so-called fine arts. It should be noted that Adrian C. Louis, before he began his career as a poet, was a newspaper editor. It is a curious fact that many contemporary Indian poets have done and continue to do journalistic work. Journalism as prelude to poetry seems to be a profound reorganization of creative energy that may have more to do with audience than art.

In keeping with a generation of ubiquitous and changing contemporary scholarship, then, and influenced by thinkers like Sartre whether they have read him or not, most modern American Indian artists understand artistic expression as a function of philosophy, which derives from history and politics existing in the presence of a pervasive Anti-Indianism.

It is not just a question of politics or journalism, aesthetics or self-interest, militancy or culture. It is a question of whether or not we as readers and writers are willing to overlook what is harmful and insulting to Indian societies. Demonizing our own people as Adrian C. Louis does in much of his work does not connect our modern work to the traditional native artistic expressions of our ancestors that supposedly underlie it. If, on the other hand, contemporary work emerges inevitably from oppressive self-hatred or self-disgust seemingly inherent in contemporary Indian life, perhaps it can be argued that poetry can become a form of self-flagellation, and therefore can function to keep that self-hatred in check. Some people even believe that Poetry is to be written and published in order to avoid suicide. These are the Poetry-as-Therapy advocates.

It is one thing to criticize Indian political leaders, but to simply call them names in such hateful ways as Louis does is to reveal himself as an unreliable chronicler. Often, in contemporary literary studies, it is said that nefarious forces collide in the making of Anti-Indian discourse: an unhappy childhood, disappointments, illness and debilitation of one kind or another. This is said in order that a special dispensation be granted to art and artists; it is an expression of the so-called aesthetic alibi defense. Whatever slings and arrows Louis has suffered personally, he has had many professional opportunities that other native poets have not. He was one of the select Indian students of the past affirmative action era who was recruited to participate in elite university study at Brown University. As a writer he has won prestigious prizes. He gets to power through legitimate means yet de-legitimizes his origins through the subject matter of endless self-hatred and rage.

Not only does he de-legitimize his origins, he exploits his students: "she's drunk-rolled / a car and is dead, just like that . . . dead, / so I buy a new flashlight." A "ghost sighting" follows and they flip each other the bird.

In subsequent poems, Indians are "stumbling skins," "winging and whimpering," "mutant generations," "children have no respect." Expecting the worst, he is waiting for the following things to happen to his Indian neighbors at Pine Ridge: "dead in a car wreck at ten, room reserved at state pen, flunk out of college eight times in ten years, stab kids, dad and wife, stab himself, 6 children none from the same man, move to city and drink, write his own story and end it with no grace."

Making poetry out of Anti-Indianisms, Louis forecasts the dire endings of many of his own graceless poems, in lustful fantasy about his students even as his ailing Lakota woman of many years' duration, then in the throes of Alzheimer's disease, now in a nursing home, is at his side. He is as much a martyr to his ill partner as he is to his own meanness and despair. In these passages describing his miserable life as victim, he suggests that his readers should care that he can't live the good life as he once did, when he complains, "I'm trying to recall the taste of Tanqueray with a hint of vermouth and a cocktail onion."

A man with an elitist university education who is the winner of many poetry prizes, he manages no revelations and few insights. For Louis's writing, there is no hope, there are no children, there is no future for Indians, only self-loathing and Anti-Indianisms. One is reminded of the co-mingled pride and shame and self-revulsion of American writer William Burroughs, whose influences on this poet seem to be much more profound than the *lakota ohunkaka* he occasionally refers to, which brings up the question, again, of whether or not such lethal despondency as Louis expresses should rightly be called poetry or therapy. His misuse of the prayers he no doubt learned from the Lakotas, prayers to grandfather, grandmother earth, spirits and the wind, again excludes any meaningful participation by an Indian audience because of their placement within a spectrum of pervasive meanness. If this native poet believes in poetry as therapy, why doesn't he show us that he knows how to be doing therapy in regard to his own claimed Paiute roots?

Whatever else may be said about Louis's poetry (and some of it, though not profound, is quite filled with pathos), it is obvious that he is master of one of the major techniques of Anti-Indianism, which in its most obvious form is the *use and misuse* of historical events of Indian life and experience in order to blame, denigrate, shame, or dehumanize Indians. His belief that Indian tribes and Indian leaders are obstacles in the struggle for self-empowerment is on every page, and what this amounts to is anti-tribal propaganda that will ultimately damage Indian communities. Those who defend the Louis oeuvre do so by saying that he is simply being more honest than others who are writing about Indians, as they wish they were not as they honestly are. In other words, these readers say, Louis is one of the few contemporary chroniclers who is not "in denial," to use a therapist's term. He "tells it like it is," to use a contemporary phrase.

Most recently, Louis's poem "Announcing a Change in the Menu at Neah Bay, Washington" appeared in a regional publication called *The Temple:*

> The Makah Indians
> want to resuscitate their
> ancient roots, so they decide
> to assassinate a gray whale.

They hand-hew a canoe
out of cedar according
to primeval specifications.
News cameras capture
a highspeed boat towing
this canoe near a whale.
The mighty Makah warriors
harpoon the thrashing hulk
and then still the waters
by blasting it in the head
with a .50 caliber rifle.
A .50 caliber rifle can kill a tank!
Another goofy chapter in
the history of American Indians.
And for the Makah, there will be
no dreams of distant McDonald's.
For the next six months, maybe a
year, it's whale burgers for breakfast
and blubber pie for dessert. And
nightmares about the crazy whites
who march in a Seattle candlelight
vigil a few days after the hunt,
carrying signs that say:
Save the whales, kill a Makah.

This suggests that Louis may have moved on from the Lakota Sioux communities from which he has received much inspiration. His several books of poems have illustrated what may charitably be called the "tension" between this poet's self and his own native community. This "tension" is said to be a characteristic of "Feminism," but it clearly is a trait exhibited more broadly in the work of poets who define modernity in the genre. This poem uses vaguely political language (i.e., assassination, history, march) and must therefore be seen as a "political" poem concerned with the reasons for Indians recovering their traditions in a hostile and unlikely modern world to be viewed as fools.

No one is willing to contradict the Indian poet who identifies himself with the persecuted, even though he adopts anti-Indianisms to declare that we are writing "goofy chapters" of new history, the sacred circle is broken and the great spirit is dead, clichés that are simplistic and racist. The poet who uses "bad medicine" (another cliché) on Burt Reynolds and writes a backhand-ed eulogy to Jim Thorpe in which the great Indian athlete is said to be "dead of booze and stolen gold" gives evidence against himself as a poet of malig-nant intent. Yet his work goes virtually unexamined for its bias. No one is willing to say that writing a poem about Indians in order to use the word "fuck" forty times is probably as anti-Indianist as anything even the most dedicated racists have written about Indians.

Few people are going to condemn Indian poets like Adrian C. Louis for betraying the Lakotas to America, or even the Makah "warriors" or any of the people from other tribal communities he observes. Even the Creek poet Joy Harjo says, "Do not crack the pages of *Among the Dog Eaters* unless you are ready for the terrible truth of what it means to be Indian in the twenti-eth century." Such poems as Louis's, rather than offering truth, may simply represent a distinct moment in the contemporary avant-garde Native Amer-ican literary scene, when powerful people in the publishing and marketing industry of America once again discover Indians with the intent of publish-ing their work. Oftentimes, these publishers and editors are of little assistance to those scholars and writers who want to define specific canons of tribal lit-eratures, which would bring about new formal critical practices and theory.

Though this commentary is not meant as a total condemnation of the complete works of this poet, and certainly it is not to suggest that every In-dian poet must be a Wole Soyinka, winner of the Nobel Literary Prize for *his art*. But it does mean to suggest that it might be useful to ask why this poet-ry has won fellowships from the South Dakota Arts Council, the Bush Foun-dation, the National Endowment for the Arts, and the Book Award from the Poetry Center at San Francisco State University, as well as the very prestigious support of the internationally known Lila Wallace–Reader's Digest Fund. To ask this question is to come to a deeply offensive conclusion, i.e., that Anti-Indianism is as acceptable to public audiences today as Anti-Semitism has been during significant eras in Europe and the Middle East. The Anti-Indi-anism of novels and poems parallels legislative discrimination promulgated in the Congress of the United States, continuing theft of lands, and disastrous racial relations in a country that desperately needs racial understanding and tolerance.

Frontier Anti-Indianism—L'Amour

This white western prose writer has come under scrutiny for frontier Anti-Indianisms in recent years by educational reformers. This genre of storytelling in the West, which is almost entirely male, has even caught the eye of feminist critics and readers in the last two decades. And certainly this work has been denigrated by those literary snobs who have talked about the "high canonical texts" of Dante and Henry James. Yet because of the popularity of the works of western writers, still other critics have given the works of western prose writers in general and Louis L'Amour in particular a historical gloss that will live long after the authors are dead.

Millions of fans around the world have read the western books written by L'Amour and have watched as dozens of his novels have found their way to the silver screen. He is exemplar of the genre that has finally begun to gain the respect of literary scholars throughout the country in the last three or four decades. Indeed, the *New York Times* has said of L'Amour: "He is the most highly rated western writer in the country."

One of L'Amour's classics concerns the Sackett family, a Scots-Irish immigrant family that first settled in the Blue Ridge Mountains of Kentucky, North Carolina, and West Virginia, and ended up in New Mexico and Texas. It was said that prior to the onset of the devastating Alzheimer's disease from which he now suffers, Ronald Reagan, U.S. President and hero of Manifest Destiny politics, expressed some interest in playing the role of the elder Sackett.

On their way west, the Sackett family crosses Sioux country, and that's where they learn about Indians. One of the main characters in L'Amour's story says this by way of introduction: "Back in my Army days I heard folks tell of what a bad time the Indians were getting, and some of them, like the Cherokee, who settled down to farming and business, did get a raw deal; *but most Indians would ride a hundred miles anytime to find a good fight, or a chance to steal horses or take a scalp*" (p. 8, emphasis added).

At work here is the very useful technique of Anti-Indianism in literary form, expressed through punctuating the discursive prose with slanderous descriptions about certain kinds of Indians, descriptions usually based on quick, epigrammatic judgments of the author's own individual speculation. There are no facts given, only summaries of the writer's bias against Indians that amounts to libelous phrases having nothing to do with plot or event. Exposition, it is called in the literary vernacular.

The traits of going to war in defense of themselves, stealing horses, or taking scalps were traits shared by all peoples of that era on the frontier, and to suggest that this is something only Indians did indiscriminately is Anti-Indianism at its most succinct in western literatures. This narrative description of Indians has been so effective that these traits are often assumed to be genetically acquired, not just symptoms of recalcitrance or survival techniques.

Because of the effectiveness of such Anti-Indianisms, the argument is that this narrative technique justly empowers western culture. It has been so effective that Anti-Indianism in literary form is not thought to corrupt art. Rather, it empowers art in appropriate and sometimes inappropriate ways, often giving credibility in the process to biased thinking that even influences other disciplines, most obviously the physical sciences. Most writers of fiction and poetry ignore the results of such thinking because they know little of the educational, industrial, and economic establishments of the country, which exclude and degrade Indian participation in American life on the basis of Anti-Indianisms.

The Sackett characters devised in L'Amour suggest all manner of false theories concerning Indian behavior and life and should, perhaps, be analyzed in order to raise the standard of argument from what amounts to name-calling and angry retort to broad, professional scholarship. Concerning the theory of indigenousness that pervades all of native literary discourse, the narrative of the Sackett story says on page 56 of *Ride the Dark Trail:* "There are times riding in the hills when you know you are alone and yet you are sure you are watched. Sometimes I think the ghosts of the old ones, the ones who came before the Indians, sometimes I think they still follow the old trails, sit under the ancient trees. . . ."

Scientists worked furiously for generations, and certainly in the last 200 years, to prove that Indians came to this continent across the Bering Strait from Asia, and the L'Amour characters express that belief in fiction. In the latter part of this century Indians have been in a furious fight for ancient remains with anthropologists, ethnographers, archaeologists, and all manner of men of science, a tug-of-war claim concerning origins, the point being that fictional stories are pervaded with attitudes and beliefs concerning Indians that have little or nothing to do with truth or reality, and it may be in the bones that the "truth" lies. That seems to be the hope of Anti-Indian men and women of science. Recently, a major native scholar, Vine Deloria, Jr., has asked "Who are these paleo Indians?" and has said in defense of indigenousness that the Bering Strait Theory of origin on this continent is a "folklore belief with little or no evidence."

About the behavior of Indians, the Sackett fictional character says: "Personally, I found Indian people to respect. Their ways weren't our ways and a lot of virtues they were given credit for by white men were only ideas in a white man's head, and no Indian would have considered them virtues. Mercy rarely had any part in the make-up of an Indian."

As Anti-Indianisms have become more subtle, the "finding of Indians to respect" is a huge reason for white men to write about them in modern literatures and histories, especially in the works of the latter part of the twentieth century and the year 2000. In spite of these facts, though, white writers still find it difficult to rise above the stereotypes they have learned so well from historical Indian/white conflict stories. They still often suggest that as far as Indians are concerned, savagery is their major trait; thus, cruelty is biology, not warfare. What this means is that literary form will go its way fed unwittingly (or purposefully) by artists who fail to recognize and make amends for Anti-Indianism, offering, instead, only excuses. Those who try to make amends will be asked to provide "documentation," a tedious task to which few scholars are willing to attend.

When the fiction writer or poet identifies himself with the persecuted, as does Adrian C. Louis and even Louis L'Amour, who says his grandfather was scalped by the Sioux but he holds no grudges, one should question such specious and unfounded contradictions. The conclusions are forgone and the narratives and poems seem predatory to many readers, which means that anecdotal evidence will no longer suffice.

I once taught a class called "The American Indian in Historical Fiction" and used, among others, James Fenimore Cooper and L'Amour as examples of writers whose imaginations haunt the pages of fantasy about America and the American West, not the first but surely among the most influential writers of anti-Indian influence in fiction. Eventually, such courses were drummed out of so-called activist English departments because it was thought that "popular culture" writings were crowding out the study of the classics. "We must return to the classics," said the Dean of Arts and Sciences, and so, instead of making the case that the Cooper and L'Amour works *were* the classics of the West, which seemed too monumental a task at the time, we quietly went back to Eugene O'Neill and James Joyce and William Faulkner and Emily Brontë. And Walt Whitman.

Fantasy stories about Indians (produced mostly by the white, male American writer), while they are often harmless articulations about hope and deeply held personal convictions, become divisive and damaging works when they keep in the foreground false and damaging images of how it is that American Indians make history and live their lives. This fact, often unnoticed and unexamined by scholars as well as the like-minded public reader, is what makes them purveyors of Anti-Indianisms.

The white male repertoire is no better exemplified in modern readings at the close of the twentieth century than by the writings of the bland and blue-eyed, Harvard-educated Ian Frazier, a New Yorker born in Ohio who has succeeded in regaling his readers with what his reviewers call "colorful and always credible stories about Sioux Indians" in two travel books, *Great Plains* (1989) and *On the Rez* (2000). He is the envy of today's white male writers-of-Indians, often unconcerned or ambiguous about the undesired label for themselves as intrusive "wannabees" who have continued the tradition throughout the years. Frazier, for the last decade, has been traveling and imagining among the Oglala Sioux Indians of Pine Ridge, and in the process has produced works that are as popular with the mainstream reader as are those of Cooper and L'Amour of earlier times.

Inaccuracies abound in *On the Rez,* none more dangerous than his statement as he observes Germans and "other tourists" at a community powwow, and pays attention to "the sound of foreign languages on the streets," and concludes this: "It reminds you that Pine Ridge village is also the capital of a nation, one that receives emissaries from far away" (p. 176). Frazier's lack of understanding that the Oglala make up *one band* of the Sioux Nation (the others being Sicangu, Ihanktowan, Sihasapa, Santee, Hunkpapa, and Minneconjou) is an ignorance that permeates all of the stories of this popular work, and that's a shame because some of them are truly original.

Why do we need to care about this? Because political independence for Indian enclaves is not just a matter of "band" or "clan" or "moiety" histories, as anthropologists and journalists might have you believe. Political independence for Indian tribal nations held in poverty in colonial America for 200 years, the subject matter of all twentieth-century events written about by Dee Brown and Peter Mattheissen and Felix S. Cohen and Vine Deloria, Jr., and countless others, should not become fetishized and distorted by white male travel writers who hero-worship Crazy Horse; rather, it should be seen in the context of the Third World struggle of our time in which a very large field of learning must be explored.

How this deliberate ignorance translates itself into the popular will of the American reading public in the subsequent ways it deals with Indians (in public policy and legislation) should worry all of us. We should ask: What is the political influence of popular narratives written by such writers as Cooper and Frazier? Even more to the point, How does this storytelling ignorance and distortion translate itself into the popular will of Indian people themselves, who must develop future survival techniques? Perhaps Frazier's newest stories should be criticized as propaganda just as dangerous as James Fennimore Cooper's "vanishing-Indian" stories, which influenced a nineteenth-century American public toward public policies Helen Hunt Jackson and other thoughtful Americans called "dishonorable."

Native literary study, in the places it has been allowed to flourish, has taken up, uncritically, the works of very successful contemporary writers whose works explore Indian America. Seldom do these studies focus upon the Anti-Indianisms that not only insult and turn away sensitive native readers but influence and reflect mainstream stereotypes that are damaging. Some of these writers, under careful examination, can be said to belong to a cult of Anti-Indianists, yet they and their readers remain unconcerned about the ethical distinctions between Anti-Indianisms, Indian self-flagellation, and the writer's craft, and what this means to a multicultural society.

As an example of this unconcern, Ian Frazier, in an appearance in Missoula, Mont., in the year 2000, when an audience member asked what he thought about the criticisms by Indians of white writers writing about Indians, replied blandly and without insight, falling more into the tourist's gaze than one might have expected of him, "Well, I know that Indian writers have said critical things but I just have never thought about it."

If writers themselves never think about it, who will?

2

IS THE CRAZY HORSE MONUMENT ART?
OR POLITICS?

There is much evidence even in the most cursory readings in American literatures to give support to the idea that the assault on the public imagination about the indigenous peoples of America through the use of Anti-Indianisms has been relentless, politically motivated, yet often passed off as purely artistic and aesthetic expression, or even good works, or even immaterial. But because some say that all art is in one way or another political, it is useful to remind ourselves of the pervasiveness of art about Indians put into the context of modernity in order to say what it means to our present lives. From *Pocahontas* to *Dances with Wolves,* the sometimes resentful or romantic and always distractive role of the public image-makers has served to distort and disembody the realities of the native lives of those who have learned to live in a tribal way.

The most negative and damaging idea about native populations on this continent is the one that suggests they were or are mere sociological phenomena instead of nations of people with distinctive traits, languages, political structures, lands, and religions that differentiate them one from the other and differentiate them from any other so-called minority group in the country.

The reality is that from the beginning, the indigenous peoples in North and South America have behaved as nations among other nations, with complex governing and social systems, and a history of treaty-signing with the United States that has been largely ignored and dismissed by American and European scholars. There is historical evidence, though, even in such places as the Lewis and Clark journals, that while they called the Lakota Sioux the "vilest miscrants of the savage race," the travelers recognized, as they made their way up the Missouri River in 1804, that the Sioux were among the indigenous "nations" of the North American continent. Ordinarily, the nationhood status of tribal peoples was a threatening condition that the settlers of America were loath to acknowledge, because in doing so they would brand themselves as criminal invaders. If the Indians were just some kind of sociological, primitive population, then the presence of colonists and settlers could be justified and the taking of the land legitimized.

Only recently, since the middle of the twentieth century, has the broader mainstream society in America relented in its political and artistic assault on the First Nations, after years of deliberately and falsely regarding them as mere social phenomena. What this let-up has meant is that there has been a period of time provided here for the rise of the native voice, native imagination, and indigenous nationalism. Many Indians both individual and tribal have now begun to take part in the new dialogues, though their voices are still muted and often dismissed.

Since the publication of native works in recent times, the role of such works in scholarship and art have been seen by some critics and colleagues as an abrasive and annoying voice. The consistent references to tribal-nation sovereignty are often called silly, such manuscripts are said to lack scholarly purpose and substance, and native arguments concerning nationalism are said to be narrow in focus. In 1995, when the foremost Sioux intellectual, Vine Deloria, Jr., said in his book *Red Earth, White Lies* that the Bering Strait Theory of the origin of native peoples in the Americas was a "scientific myth" and that there was little or no evidence for such an origin story, critics said that he could no longer be taken seriously as a scholar.

Few non-Indian scholars of reputation have entered into a dialogue with any native written work that has as its real interest and focus the defense of tribal sovereignty and indigenousness, nor with the development of Native American Studies as an autonomous academic discipline to function as a defensive mechanism for the empowerment of tribal nationhood. Few have heeded the call for reform in fiscal and land policy, and the defense of treaties between the United States and Indian nations as the law of the land. But there is always hope that change is on the horizon.

Indian writers have taken up the essay form as a way, perhaps, of combating the hostility toward longer, more complicated works. There are several collections by such writers as Joseph Marshall III (Sicangu) and Leslie Marmon Silko (Pueblo) that have proven useful in adding to the present dialogue in the defense of native nationalism.

My undergraduate degree in journalism introduced me to the essay as genre, and as a result I have been enamored of the essay form all my writing life. While it seems to be the forgotten genre in literary study these days, it maintains a significant presence in the discussions of history. We are told that the essay was known to classical writers like Francis Bacon, for instance, who said, "The word is late but the thing is ancient." Bacon went on to describe essays as "grains of salt which will rather give an appetite than offend with satiety," which means, one supposes, that they are food for thought instead of gluttonous feasts, and somehow I find that comforting. From the French scholar Michel de Montaigne, whose first publication about repentance in 1580 was called "Essai," to George Orwell to Mark Twain to Zora Neale Hurston, who wrote "How It Feels to Be Colored Me," the essay is what newspaperman E. B. White said it was: "a relaxed form that imposes its own disciplines, raises its own problems."

I do not embrace the essay form so much for the reasons Cynthia Ozick gives in the September 1998 article appearing in *Harper's,* that the essay has the right to be self-centered and it must be a "vibration" that takes you in, like, she says, "a species of metaphysician" (p. 113). The essay for Ozick is "she," and it is a "warm body." How sexy! My view of the essay is all the things Ozick despises in its form. For me it is a rational, absolutist disputation. Its best examples are the work of political journalists. It is a tract. It is a polemic. But then, I say that about the novel, too. A polemical novel is my favorite kind. I'm not offended by those traits in novels or essays.

In a melding of Journalism and Literary/Art criticism, I have used this rather casual form, the essay, to take up many of the issues I believe to be significant in the Indian intellectual experience. As a recent example of how the essay form is useful in discussing in a personal way those things that are public and journalistic, a mountain carving in the Black Hills of South Dakota became the subject for one of my recent writings. I wanted to examine the meaning of the rock sculpture of a Lakota heroic figure being blasted into a mountain in the Black Hills. Its intent. Its influence.

I began by recounting what I thought of as recent modern history: since 1948, in lands now called the state of South Dakota, a European sculptor, Korzcak Ziolkowski, and his heirs have been blowing up with TNT a mountain in a place the Sioux have called the Paha Sapa, and they have done it, they say, in the name of the nineteenth-century Oglala Sioux war leader Crazy Horse. And, one assumes, in the name of Art. And at the behest of an Indian man named Henry Standing Bear, who claimed in 1939 to be a "chief" and who said, "This is to be an entirely Indian project under my direction." His foolish proclamation was, of course, mere puffery, but his letter is posted in the anterooms of the facility as evidence of complicity on the part of Indians.

This blasted monstrosity (I hesitate to call it a carving or a sculpture though sometimes I do) is now twenty miles from where I live in the Black Hills. The truth is I've lived in the Hills, as they are called here, two or three times during my past lives. I keep moving away and I keep coming back. This time I've bought a house in the Hills so I presume I mean this time to stay. The Crazy Horse Mountain Sculpture, I've come to believe, is emblematic of what is so wrong about this place. And it may even exemplify the reason for my seemingly unaccountable ambiguity concerning my life here in the homelands. The so-called sculpture represents quite obviously a failure to honor the values of Crazy Horse, who refused to have his picture taken during his lifetime because he believed such likenesses could kill the human spirit.

Human repositories such as the Guggenheim or the Museum of Modern Art in New York seem not to be enough for artists like Ziolkowski. Often, driven by hubris, they claim God's repositories as well, and they are notorious for coming into the sacred lands of the Lakota to express their strange ways, even claiming to be here at the invitation of Indians.

There are many white-man progenitors for such arrogance in this country, but Mount Rushmore is the epitome. It opens up what Indians around here call "the desecration tour." I once wrote a short polemical poem about that monument that some say represents democracy, and my poem appeared in an obscure little chapbook called "Seek the House of Relatives," published in 1983 by *Blue Cloud Quarterly:*

MOUNT RUSHMORE

Owls hang in the night air
between the visages
of Washington, Lincoln,
the Rough Rider, and Jefferson;
and coyotes mourn the theft
of sacred ground.
A Cenotaph becomes
the tourist temple
of the profane.

It's not a great poem. Coherence is its best trait. The kind of poem Audre Lorde might write. I haven't been able to write poems about the Crazy Horse sculpture and I haven't been able to say why. The first thing to know about the rock carving, though, is that it is ugly and absurd and obscene to anyone who knows history, because to know history is to know that the lands were stolen by the United States of America from the First Nation people of Crazy Horse, a genocidal holocaust occurred here, and we who are now called the Sioux are bare survivors.

"We are all Greeks," said the English poet Shelley once about Art, and today the relatives of those who stole the land from the Oyate are saying "We are all Indians" or "Indian is a state of mind," and there is supposed to be something comforting about that. Around here you see white men dressed in Indian buckskins, and you see white women in braids and beads, and they are all yearning for that vision about which Shelley spoke. In some odd contradiction, blowing up a sacred mountain in the name of Indians is what the Crazy Horse sculpture talks to them about. Unfortunately, Indians have heard it all many times in the last few centuries.

One supposes that Shelley was speaking as an art theorist when he made his statement, and it's hard to know what he had in mind that might be useful to us Indians. This much we know: all art and all creativity is based upon the observation of some rules. And the true artist knows how to depart from those rules meaningfully. For the indigenous peoples of this land, this has always been the case. We know the rules, and we learn how to depart from them, and that is what we call art. Innovation and originality have never been discouraged, but tradition is at the heart of it, always. For the Sioux Oyate it is not revolution or emulation that matters; it is, instead, culture and language and history. The rules that Crazy Horse knew told him that the land and the mountains were inviolate and that he and his people had a right to imagine themselves.

The way I see it, Crazy Horse has been a perfect victim for exploitation by whites. He was killed by them during his best years, and they've written more books about him than any other leader among our people. During his lifetime he allowed no photographic likenesses of him to be taken, no paintings, no drawings. He refused to go to Washington, D.C., and never spoke the English language. Neither did he, despite claims to the contrary, have any friends among the invading whites. Of all the Indians throughout history, he has, therefore, become their obsession. He has become a steakhouse in California (even a strip joint in Paris, France), and his name has been used profanely to sell everything from beer to poetry magazines and third-rate novels. And now, they blow up a mountain to invent his image in the stone that he knew as sacred. They do it because they must possess what they can not. It is why his language has always called them "fat takers."

Many artists have become hired guns for one cause or another. Money. Fame. Many Indians have sung the Christian Bible songs and danced for the tourists, sometimes for the same reasons. These are the realities of human life. Creative movements come and go and inspiration derives from many sources.

But the one distinguishing feature of modern white man–inspired art as it comes face to face with Indians is to reduce the role of art to absurdity. When that happens, social bankruptcy and despair, modern materialism, and mass media are all that is left.

There is nothing new about Europeans coming into the North American continent and calling it their own. There is nothing new, either, about artists telling us they are in tune with the times and that their art presents their own age. Ziolkowski consciously set out to look at the Indian world through the temptations of his own ruined society. He obliterates the sacred, and his work delights his fellows and they say to him: "If you build it, they will come. . . . if you build it, they will come." They are, I'm sad to say, right about that.

There is much irony in this story, which is told here only briefly. While the folks at Crazy Horse Mountain make much of getting "permission" from an Indian named Standing Bear for this project, world events may have had more of an impact than Indian thinking on the subject had. Between 1945 and 1949 the United States was getting ready to try the Nazis for war crimes at Nuremberg, Germany. These trials went ahead on the theory that the Nazis were men who "implemented policies which led to death, disease and starvation" (William Manchester, *The Arms of Krupp*, 1968), the same kinds of policies that led to "illegal appropriation" (theft?) of Sioux lands and the death of thousands of Sioux Indians from starvation during *this* century.

America was forced by public controversy to admit to the barbaric nature of its Indian policy. Congress even went so far as to pass the Indian Claims Commission Act in 1946 to hear all tribal "grievances" concerning land claims. Unfortunately, that act stipulated that stolen lands could not be returned, only paid for. Since 1980, when the Supreme Court called the "taking" of the Black Hills a "rank case of theft," the United Sioux have refused to accept the judgment monies and continue to press for land reform. This is the longest-standing land claim in the history of U.S./Indian relations. (For further reading on this subject refer to *Wicazo Sa Review* 4:1 [Spring 1988].)

In Part Five of my 1987 collection *Why I Can't Read Wallace Stegner and Other Stories*, I have joined those who have ridiculed this art form called the Crazy Horse Sculpture and have chosen to share a story, a joke, really, that I heard from tribal people who are confronted daily with such destructive imperatives of colonialism in their own land. It's a joke you can hear on the streets of Rapid City when Indians get together. I see it as an untitled resistance story by the suppressed people who are supposedly represented by the subject matter of the sculpture:

> No matter what happens in modern America, you know, nontribal people always think they have the last word. They are the ones, they think, who are in charge of time and history. In rejection of that idea, I'm reminded of a story we Dakotas tell about the mountain just a few miles from my home that "they" are blowing up in the name of the famed Oglala Chieftain Crazy Horse. It is a desecration, of course, evidence of the utter arrogance of whites coming into these lands. Beyond that, though, it's a way for whites to tell themselves they will have the last word. We've made a joke of it now.

> *Keyapi:* on the mountain, Crazy Horse is pointing to a place "over there, where my dead lie buried," in response to the white man sculptor's question: "Where are your homelands?"
> Just then the white man made a mistake. He set his dynamite under the pointing finger of Crazy Horse and, accidentally, he blew the finger clean off. Now, in response to the question, Crazy Horse simply lifts his chin and points with his lips.

The joke as it is now told can be described as performance art, and it is played out on the streets of contentious towns in South Dakota like Rapid City, where I live, and it is most often told in the tribal language by one Indian to another, a kind of secret coded message. But sometimes the story is told in English, and it is, therefore, accessible if one cares to listen to muted tribal voices. It is a little dramatic acting-out rarely seen or heard by the mainstream white American public that clusters in the streets of this tourist mecca. Indeed, it is created as a special tribal dramatic art—cloistered theater, if there is such a thing.

The language of gesture, the lifting of the chin and pointing with the lips, is filled with meaning. It is a custom among first-language Lakota and Dakota tribal speakers, taught from childhood that pointing is rude. At first glance in this case, the gesture of lifting the chin seems to be a gesture of indifference. It reduces the story, the history, the racism, the theft, the loose ends, the anger, art, and the hostility of land theft to the language of gesture, one far more grand than the pointing finger, which is more Lewis and Clark than Lakota in origin. In fact, the pointing finger of the sculpture is the first thing that is noticeably outrageous and ridiculous from the Lakota cultural perspective, and it forces the question, Can you conquer with seeming and studied indifference? Can hostility be expressed through a show of indifference? The joke suggests the genuineness of such an existential possibility. If it is possible, this small, symbolic gesture, then, seems grand in its improvisation.

The second thing to say about the joke is that it is an expression of contempt, something akin to "giving the finger," yet a more profound, deeply felt contempt with cultural and religious roots. According to the Lakota belief system, life is eternal and it is inviolate and it is *in the mountain,* not in the sculpture, not in the artist or in the number of white tourists who visit the site. It is known, too, that the sculpture, which performs as a popular tourist trap for the state of South Dakota as well as its foreign artists, brings further grief into the relationship between whites and Indians in the region, a grief based on several realities: first, this land was stolen and it remains a contested place; second, the whites will not return their ill-gotten loot, though they were informed by the Supreme Court in 1980 that it was stolen, indeed, "a rank case"; third, whites believe they can, instead, pay for their crime as colonists all over the world have done throughout the years; and fourth, there is no dialogue between whites and Indians, either official or casual, concerning return of stolen lands here in the place where the sculpture resides. This means that silence about and claimed ignorance of a criminal history are used as powerful tools of oppression.

Thus, Indians tell each other their own specific stories making fun of the monument and its defenders. Indians use stories like this as defense mechanisms against a callous artistic expression that does not take into account their feelings. It is necessary for Indians to tell each other this kind of casual, unwritten humorous story aloud because, while it does not express an extremist position that could be detrimental to them, it does involve a socio-critical point about art and language that lets them know the imprisonment of the Lakota imagination cannot be achieved even by the blowing up of a mountain with TNT. Moreover, it tells a real story suggesting that a significant reconciliation of history can not take place if crimes go unavenged, and if the criminal retains his fraudulent claim to innocence and ownership.

There are few here in this region to contradict what might be called a contrived and repulsive imagery of native existence. Many Indian people live in poverty, are poorly educated and inarticulate. Thus, native scholarly participation in publishing and in the media is meager and scant at best. In these instances, the oppressed often find their own ways of participating in mainstream culture and commerce. Some native craftspersons and artists have, of necessity, established an ambiguous relationship with their own contrived

artistic heritage by showing up for tourist occasions at the mountain, singing casual songs and dancing at media events that record another blast of
dynamite as the structure takes form. They bring their children to eat and
drink as guests of the widow of the now-deceased primogenitor of this art
piece. Indian saddle-bronc riders and bulldoggers come from all over the
West to participate in the "All-Indian Rodeo" every July, about the same time
the Independence of America from English rule is celebrated. Small academic
scholarships from tourist proceeds to native persons are awarded at annual
festivals around the state. There are many Indians, however, who refuse to
participate in the sculpture's tourist fetes, who would never take their children to see the monstrosity, and they are the ones, perhaps, who, cynical and
helpless to stop the mainstream art frenzy, have created the joke/story.

If it is true that the conventions of any artistic and creative period are more
often than not inherited or reinvented, we must ask what is being reinvented here in the sacred Black Hills, in the home of the Lakota, through the creation of the sculpture. It's hard to say. But to those of us who know less about
art theory than we know about Indian/white politics, it seems that surely this
is another conquest of geographical space, which began with the voyages of
Columbus and ended in genocide and broken treaties and poverty and subjugation of one people by another.

The Crazy Horse Monument in the Black Hills of South Dakota is dependent on the tourist trade, as well as on commissions from private donors as
memorials to themselves and each other, foreign, religious, transcendent,
though much of the funding for this enterprise is cloaked in secrecy. There
have always been circumstances of patronage that acccompany any kind of
artistic endeavor based on monarchy and revolution and conquest, and so
the patronage associated with this monument is part of what must be examined if we are to understand the underpinnings of what will be claimed as
artistic treasure.

The mind boggles at the exaggerated and belated show of respect this art
and its creators now attempt to direct posthumously toward a leader of the
Lakota people whose life as an Indian landlord so infuriated the invaders they
had to shoot him in cold blood, whose descendants are among the poorest
and least well educated in America's heartland and who occupy jail cells in
greater percentages than almost any other people in the world. Without an
acknowledgment of land theft and genocide, this art as an act of contrition
is outrageously cynical.

I am always astonished and outraged that we must all in this region of the
upper plains, Indians and whites alike, become victims of some kind of co-

lonial psychic pathology or damaging racist psyche simply because America refuses to acknowledge its criminality and return land to its rightful owners. Is that the fault of art? Is it the consequence or the rationale for such art? Is this sculpture, then, in artistic terms a-political, mere romantic irony? macabre parody? Or does it have as its intention an outright political statement of bondage, a cover-up of theft, a claim to ignorance and therefore innocence? If it is a political statement, who are its initiators? its consumers? its benefactors? its Indian collaborators?

It seems fairly clear to me that this art form, this sculpture of Crazy Horse in the Lakota sacred mountains, arises from a system that continues to empower the thieves of native lands, those who subjugated and killed Indians in the eighteenth and nineteenth centuries and got away with it. As far as I can see, this art does nothing to change the cliché-ridden or conventional notions of colonialism and the much-loved theme of the "vanishing Indian." Like the funerary monument to the Egyptian pharaoh Cheops, the Crazy Horse Monument declares Indians not of this world, but, happily, of the past one or the next. That seems to me a staggering blow to the point of view that Indians are modern and continuing participants in the lands from which they claim to have emerged.

If the question "Where are your homelands?" is asked and the answer is "Over there where my dead lie buried," it forever precludes the real answer Crazy Horse would surely have given had he not been assassinated and immortalized in faux art. He surely would have said, "My homelands have been stolen by white invaders who have condemned my people to poverty and then pretended their innocence." Surely he would have said what his people are saying at the beginning of the twenty-first century: *Stolen land must be returned.*

3

LITERARY AND POLITICAL QUESTIONS OF TRANSFORMATION: AMERICAN INDIAN FICTION WRITERS

Two of the most important ethical ideas concerning bodies of indigenous knowledge have had little chance for exploration in the academic world, mostly because there are just too few dissident intellectuals who want to go against the prevailing intellectual thought of a capitalistic democracy that holds to the idea that everything is for sale or trade and the only coin of the realm is the bottom line.

The ideas concerning ethics in literary study of Native America that are scrupulously ignored are: first, the idea that the intellect of an entire people is not property and therefore cannot be bought or sold or appropriated, a complex and troubling dilemma; and second, that the sovereign nationalism of tribal people is a humane trademark in native literary studies crediting those tribal people who presume to speak for their people with a unique coherency in the context of human ethos.

In light of a perceived academic lapse that ignores all this, Rigoberta Menchú Túm's reminder of it when she accepted the Nobel Peace Prize on behalf of the indigenes came as a surprise to many scholars and, perhaps predictably, has been ignored or vilified not only by large segments of academe but by the public in general. Menchú's reminder was this: "We indigenous Peoples attach a great importance to the Treaties, Agreements, and other constructive Accords that have been reached between the Indigenous Peoples and the former colonial powers or states. They should be fully respected in order to establish new and harmonious relationships based on mutual respect and cooperation" (*I, Rigoberta Menchú*, 1983).

Perhaps this ethical tenet, which seemed to get lost in the frenzy of the liberal public to accept or reject the "truth," or the "tragedy" of Menchú's autobiography, is the real reason for the present struggle concerning *I, Rigoberta Menchú*. The conservative public now, eighteen years later, has challenged the work, calling it fraudulent and untruthful. The ethic spoken of here by Menchú is still not on the front burner of intellectual and academic interest in native literatures, and it won't be any time soon if academicians (i.e., anthropologists turned literary critics) have anything to say about it.

Whether we are talking about economics or truth or law or literature or science or the native homelands or sovereignty, the call for respect for the past is a clear call for change on the scholarly borders where we interact as professors, writers, contemporary thinkers, American Indian novelists and poets. Menchú, whether every detail in her autobiography is "true" or not, whether every detail can be "verified," whether some details are even denied by others, means to tell us that the transformation of ancient societies into modern ones, as well as flawed colonial societies into honorable ones, will not occur unless the respect for the past is held dear by scholars and institutions across the land. Respect for the past is what is being talked about here. Not respect for the "truth."

This chapter will address some of the questions within the discipline of Native American Literary Studies as it exists in American universities that are at the heart of such a transformation, centering on issues of what I want to call, for the moment, *cosmopolitanism* and *nationalism* in contemporary Native American novel-writing. In this case, *cosmopolitanism* may be defined as the exploration in literature of the tastes and interests of the dominant culture, while *nationalism* may be regarded generally as a concept in the arts that argues for nation-specific creativity and political unification in the development, continuation, and defense of a coherent national mythos. All of this depends, quite obviously, on the First Nations definitions claimed by the indigenous peoples of this continent. Even before N. Scott Momaday's *House Made of Dawn* won the American Pulitzer Prize in 1969 and Louise Erdrich's *Love Medicine* received the American Book Award some sixteen years later in 1984, American Indian stories had a place in U.S. scholarship through work begun in the early 1800s, first in ethnology, later in anthropology. For the most part, this early scholarship was the result of non-native academics gathering and publishing tribal stories told to them by native "informants." In spite of the availability of those bodies of extrinsic knowledge (or perhaps because of it), modern American scholars were poorly prepared for the burgeoning body of fiction written by people who claimed to be American Indians that was to follow. Much confusion, unsettledness, irrelevance, and exploitation has been the result.

In the face of this flourishing contemporary art and the subsequent incoherence concerning it, the term Intellectual Property Rights, which may be defined as the right to own, the right to sell, the right to know (originating, not surprisingly, in western economics and jurisprudence), had been coined to form the groundwork for the discussion of everything from identity to copyright, from status and authenticity to money and profit.

In the decades since the publication of the prizewinning works of Momaday and Erdrich, the writings done in the accompanying discipline, Literary Criticism, largely undertaken by humanities scholars, have not centered upon the treaties, agreements, and other constructive accords spoken of by Menchú. Instead, they have focused largely upon issues concerning the dominant culture, issues of identity, authenticity, and purpose in the new stories called Native American Literature(s).

Little has been said of the function of art in modern native enclaves, nor of the intellect of a native nation of people in defense of its national character. Almost all of this subsequent western-style lit/crit scholarship has, instead, introduced two major questions. They are: (1) Who is an Indian? and (2) What about modernity? Not surprisingly, these questions have helped to create three categories of literary expression that are the foci of possible litigation in Intellectual Property Rights discussions. They are: first, oral literatures, some of which are owned by individuals or families but most of which are not, bodies of knowledge expressing a theory predicated on the idea held by many indigenous cultures that the intellect of a people is not property, therefore is not transferable in a market sense—a theory largely ignored in academe; second, the translated literatures that have made works public property simply through the untrammeled practice of scholars and researchers; and third, the stories, poems, and dramas created by people who publish their own work under their own names. In turn, critics suggest, these categories have made it necessary to talk of authenticity.

Recent books as diverse as Charles R. Larson's *American Indian Fiction* (1978), Michael Castro's *Interpreting the Indian* (1983), and Louis Owens's *Other Destinies* (1992), and many in between, have discussed authenticity in terms that meet the needs of publishers and scholars. The two political questions that have emerged (Who is an Indian? and What about modernity?) have been sanctioned by critical practitioners into dominant literary ones almost without challenge.

Who Is an Indian?

The seemingly puzzling question "Who is an Indian?," posed as though it were a literary question, seems to be interfaced with the agendas of groups who have mainly liberation interests, giving the questions themselves obdurance and influence in literary studies. Thus, a political question that has been nationalistic in origin becomes legitimized as a literary question, and those who engage in the discussion surrounding it are often accused of engaging in "identity politics" rather than in legitimate literary criticism. American Indian scholars who have sought to have a voice in the discourse have been described as illogical, resentful, and racist, and non-native scholars have felt defensive and abused.

The question "Who is an Indian?" is posed because American Indians are treated as colonized peoples, more specifically, because the autonomy and sovereignty of the First Nations of America has been thought to be incidental, i.e., occurring as a fortuitous or minor concomitant, the point being that Indians and Indian nations will in time cease to exist and their citizenship rights as citizens of their nations, therefore, are either nonexistent or disappearing. Since the beginning of colonization in America, its scholars, historians, and politicians have sought to define and describe the native populations in this "incidental" way.

The notion that First Nations are "incidental" has given rise to the idea that, first, they have nothing to say about their tribal citizenship and, second, these folks will not last long. Therefore, the "next generation" of native (Indian) writers and storytellers is described as a "mixed-blood" one, an idea that has been the major result of the academic discourse on "Who is an Indian?"

One must believe in two contradictory yet collaborative ideas in order for this discourse to take on substance. First, one must perpetuate the idea that Indian nationhood is not a historical reality, that Indians were and are just some mere sociological phenomena without consciousness of nationhood and sovereignty; therefore, Indianness is not a matter of legality based upon the laws of the people. This means that almost anyone can claim to be an Indian in America's present academic climate and there is no one to object except the Indian nations themselves, who argue for the sovereign right to say who their citizens are and are often told that there is no such thing as sovereignty and tribal citizenship (just enrollment) for Indians.

An example:

While Dr. Reyna Green of the Smithsonian, claiming to be Cherokee, has not been able to provide what doubters describe as suitable documentation of her claimed Indian heritage, and has seen her claim to Indianness publicly denounced by Indians and others as fraudulent, her standing as native folklorist, storyteller, poet, and scholar at that institution has not been jeopardized. This means that American institutions are unconcerned about this argument.

A more blatant case is that of a successful writer who, beginning in the late '60s, transformed himself from an unknown New York–born Greek or Turkish person, J. Marks, to Indian spokesman Jamake Highwater, with an undocumented "born and raised Blackfeet Indian" profile that convinced publishers of his identity acquisition but drew cries of fraud from native activists and scholars as well as Jack Anderson, the nationally syndicated columnist to the Philadelphia *Daily News.* Jamake wrote in 1996, "To escape things that are painful we must reinvent ourselves" and "I begin to think that our borrowed lives are necessities in our world filled with hostility and pain, a confusing world largely devoid of credible social truths." Because of the tendency of a modern American to feel compassion toward this point of view, Highwater continues to write and publish as an Indian. It means, too, that he has not denounced his fraudulent past, only rationalized it.

David Seals writes the successful *Powwow Highway* and is acclaimed as an Indian writer though he is not a citizen of any of the Indian nations of America. Ward Churchill, director of the Center for the Study of Ethnicity and Race at the University of Colorado, Boulder, claims credentials as a native scholar though he possesses citizenship in no native nation or homelands nor any such birthright. Recently acquired enrollment status in such cases has not quelled the public name-calling that has been the result.

These are but a few of the examples that have been publicly acknowledged to date, to illustrate the point that Indianness is not thought by academics in the field to be a matter of legal citizenship in an existing native nation. Further, the remarkable modern spectacle of writers and scholars who grew up white in America now scurrying about and rummaging into family archives to uncover a grandmother's secret possession of minimal Indian blood lays bare an embarrassing lack of understanding of the dynamic at the heart of nativeness, sovereignty, and identity. Example:

Hertha Dawn Wong, working as an innovative scholar in autobiography, which is both claimed and disclaimed by scholars as genre in Native American Literatures, says in the Preface to her *Sending My Heart Back Across the Years,* "When I began writing this book in 1984, I had little idea that I was part Native American, one of the unidentified mixed-bloods whose forebears wandered away from their fractured communities," and "according to my mother's findings, my great-grandmother was from a Plains tribe...."

Embarrassment aside, the endless confrontation and debate of all of this identity acquisition has derailed the important issues in Native American Literature(s), which should be the subject of much study and research, with a major focus the literary history of indigenousness on this continent. What about the treaties? The accords? How are these matters connected to the question of Who is an Indian? What about the old traditions, religious and secular forms, major figures, beginnings of drama, songs, genre development, languages, tribal nation history, and mythology? The truth is, the endless argument over Who is an Indian? is the poorest coin we trade with as responsible scholars in the disciplines because it is not our question to answer, not our commodity to buy or sell. It is a question that belongs to the First Nations of America, as it always has since the beginning of time, not to scholars, professors, agents, publishers, or self-proclaimers.

A concomitant thread of inquiry has been embodied in the subsequent question: "How much Indian is an Indian writer?" The bloodlines of Momaday, Erdrich, Silko, and others have been connected to the structures of a narrative, to the ideas and concepts of imaginative work as examples of fractionated Indianness. This seems to be a singularly American phenomenon, since no one asks how much Egyptian Naguib Mahfouz is, nor do they require that J. M. Coetzee provide proof that his identity is embodied in anything other than citizenship. Their realistic and fabulistic work in the novel form does not seem to carry with it much of this brand of western or colonizing scholarly baggage. What this means is that the mutual respect between nations that Menchú speaks of is at work in some scholarly circles and not in others, and, most important of all, is unsustainable by modern American scholarship in the study of Native American Literatures. In addition, those Native American Studies scholars who know that the function of their discipline is to struggle with the regulatory, defensive, and transformative strategies continue to be unheard.

The second belief about mixed-bloodedness that makes it seem to be a legitimate area of scholarly inquiry in the study of Native American Literatures, though it is probably not, is the idea that there is such a thing as "purity" of race. To adopt this idea in its fullest, most sophisticated sense makes hybridity a contaminant to the American Indian's right to authenticity. Ray Young Bear as recently as 1992 described the Indian version of this in *Black Eagle Child, The Facepaint Narratives* in this way: "We were in every sense a tribe but we made damn sure no one would ever prosper and succeed without first knowing their place," classifying tribal people in acronyms such as EBNOs (Enrolled But in Name Only), or BRYPUs (Blood-Related Yet Paternally Unclaimed), or EBMIWs (Enrolled But Mother Is White), or UBENOBs (Unrelated By Either Name Or Blood), and so on. And so on.

In spite of Young Bear's spoof, the idea of Indian mixed-bloodedness has lately been the armature of power in literature and criticism, the controlling idea, the framework of support that has singlehandedly put on the table the dilemma for modern Indians and existing Indian nations. They see that their ability to defend their intellectual property rights in the modern American academic climate will now be enjoined by skeptics engaged in the anti-nationalistic/anti-tribalistic study of Native American Literatures. What they can do about it is the question that draws scholars together. They ask: How can a defense be mounted? Most believe that until identity issues are seen as political rather than literary, as ethical rather than economic, as legal rather than sociological, the debate will rage, nothing will be settled, and the intellectual life of American Indians will continue to be trivialized, diminished, and stolen.

The idea of mixed-bloodedness has a strong connection to the anthropological and ethnological studies that began by putting in place specific tribal stories labeled "traditional," certain storytellers described as "authentic," and particular plots, motifs, and characters said to be "known" and therefore canonical and static. Following this line of thought, traditional storytelling must end. Almost everything outside of those patterns must be discarded, "fictionists" cannot be said to exist, and there is no sense of an ongoing literary and intellectual life. The new stories, should they somehow emerge, will always be lesser ones. There are no contemporary Homers, as in western literatures, no Shakespeares, no Isak Dinesens, no defenders of the faith, only pathetic imitators.

Almost all of this delineation of imagination and voice was done by nontribal scholars, who, if not directed by the "informant" who had the inclination to claim personal authority, at least had his or her blessing and knowledge. If "fictionists" did not exist, then novels could be said to be foreign to native societies. When American Indians wrote them, identity issues would co-opt one of the most important literary discussions of our time, the discourse on the function of the modern novel in modern tribal life and nationhood. Two contradictory dimensions of identity would take precedence: first, the native writer's right to authority would be challenged; and second, at the other end of the spectrum, his or her "expertise" would become orthodoxy. Identity would imply privilege bestowed according to western influences. The people themselves, from whom the stories emerged, would have no authority, no tribal-nation authority. Is this what the indigenes have in mind when they ask what the direct result of scholarship should be?

Because fiction in general, and the novel in particular, is thought to be imported from the nations of the West, and therefore concerns itself with originality, novelty, and a worldview in celebration of the merchant bourgeoisie ideals of Europe, the criticism that has accompanied all novel-writing, including the American Indian novel, rests on these assumptions. Thus, anyone writing novels in America or the West must be a novelist of America, and the Native Americans who offer an "insider's" view of primitive societies for the modern American reading public by complying with metropolitan literary tastes, emerge. Their work, often having little to do with nation-specific or culture-specific art, has been foisted off on an ignorant public as Native American literary expression.

The point I want to stress about the endless debate concerning Who is an Indian? and How much Indian is an Indian? is that it is not a literary question. It is a political matter, politics being that science that governs, at least to some degree. Making choices as a literary critic is much like making choices if one is an archaeologist: both must distinguish between contexts of discovery and justification. Personal interest or ideology are common directives and all politics has a chauvinistic air. Literary criticism, then, as it is practiced in the American academy on what is called the Native American literary voice, is very simply an attempt to claim authority over it.

As long as that is understood, we can begin the examination of the interests and interpretations of writers and their works with some degree of intellectual integrity. It has always been my view that authority lies in *nationalism,* not *cosmopolitanism.* The persistent political qustions that plague the study of the literatures of indigenous populations in America can be put aside only if the intellect of a people expressed in literary art is examined as the fabric holding a people together, not as the fundamental difference or similarity that either embraces or denies its colonization, or as a danger or threat to or collaborator in the eminence and aesthetic autonomy of American canonical thought.

What about modernity, then? What are the questions that must be asked of Native American novelists for appropriate nation-centered theory to emerge from praxis?

The cosmopolitan agenda in Native literatures, if it is said to be the same as that toward other "submerged" works, is illustrative of several traits such as the preference for novels, the use of European languages, i.e., English, anti-strident themes of colonialism, and the "like us" or modern aesthetic or taste, and is, therefore, more interested in establishing a relationship to Anglo-American society than in examining the relationship of the modern novel to First Nation reality. The cosmopolitan agenda does not critically examine the influence of the rise of so-called creative writing departments at American universities, from which many young native writers emerge, nor does it show how this phenomenon has shaped much of this fiction and its popularity among the general reading public. It says even less about whether or not these novels can assist in clarifying our tribal-nation sovereign conditions in a postcolonial world.

There is no more interesting possibility in the recent renaissance and popularity of Native American Literature(s) that have occurred since Momaday's breakthrough novel *House Made of Dawn* than the possibility that nation-centered theories of fiction may assist in the articulation of an ethic that would defend the authenticity of the native/tribal voice. The intellectual debate of how the American Indian novel may have theoretical importance for the Third World in the defense of indigenousness has not occurred, yet it may be the single most important debate in the intellectual property rights struggle. If we take Rigoberta Menchú's admonition seriously, foremost in this discussion will be the consideration that the reality of native nationhood, from which modern literary thought emerges, must be addressed by every critic, every writer, every poet who is a tribal-nation citizen. The 1994 work of native critic Robert Warrior, called *Tribal Secrets,* seems to be a singular, preeminent effort toward this end.

Here are some of the questions that must be asked of Native American novelists for appropriate nation-centered theory to emerge: How is the American Indian novel a formless genre that mirrors a native society, describes a temporal world of past, present, future? Are the self-conscious and confidential narrators, using the first-person "I," speaking in a tribal-nation timbre? Is the burlesquing of history a collaboration? Are we more interested in the artistic treatment of a subject than in the social function of literature, and why? How is style social attitude? How do native writers discuss the features of their homelands in an effort to make them a part of the "exotica" that is so much a part of the stereotype? How is the fantasist pimping to those stereotypes? How are American Indian writers, many of them schooled in America's elitist institutions, trained to lack a native conscience? What is the result of "creative writing department" influence? How do we generate Indian (native/tribal) history within the structure, style, plot of the novel? Is the "lie" of fiction (thought to be an obvious truth in literary criticism) dangerous to us as indigenous peoples? Are we as native writers rewarded for advocacy, and if so, how so?

National movements for independence emerged even as Momaday and Erdrich won American literary prizes some decades ago. To what end have their works addressed those movements? For American Indian writers the question of whether or not fiction can be accused of betraying nationalism is not just a question of adjusting to the American literary environment, it is a question of understanding that all art rises out of tradition, language, mythology, and politics.

No one should suggest that literary expression and literary study cannot find their own freedom, both personal and institutional. No one should suggest that the urge toward nation-centered dialogue is a call for separatist identity and conflict and monopolization of intellectual thought and scholarly inquiry. Do not confuse this call for nation-centered theory with the black cultural nationalism of Ron Karenga, who some decades ago declared that "all our art must contribute to revolutionary change and if it does not, it is invalid." Karenga's declaration is a compelling idea, and I just as often say to my fellow tribespersons, "All our art must contribute to the defense of our lands and nationhood and if it does not it is worth nothing," but in my heart I know that art must simply be free to be what it can be.

The truth is American Indian fiction and the American Indian novel, in particular, have been the unfortunate captives of western literary theory, and almost no scholar, writer, or researcher has addressed many of the questions of indigenous nationhood in fiction in any serious way. Instead, there seems to have been an agreement that the literary profession in its own cosmopolitanization has advocated that position for success by American Indian writers. Every work is looked at through the lens of a colonial aesthetic, not through the lens of the specific language of the specific treaty or accord or national history that Menchú holds dear.

Without speculating about what native/tribal nationalism means, then, the literary profession has become prisoner of an oppressive legal language and reading of rights that derives from a European-based, perhaps even male-oriented property rights tradition that institutionalizes knowledge not only as a commodity but as a possession. The profession plunges ahead with questions that cannot be answered in any meaningful way without a clear sense of the historical realities that formulated the contemporary American Indian literary voice in the first place.

The present state of the study of American Indian literary arts is very nearly unacceptable to Indian nations because it flaunts the right to institutionalize knowledge in accordance with its own American literary canonical interests. Everything, at present, can be used, appropriated, exploited, or surrogated for whatever reasons come to mind. As a woman's womb may be rented or used or appropriated in this modern world, mostly to serve anti-female interests, so may a tribal nation's knowledge, story, song, medicine be appropriated and/or corrupted to serve non-tribal peoples. Anything can be bought or used in the name of cultural freedom, the democratic process, and personal liberation, and no discussion of Who is an Indian? and What about modernity? will end the proliferation of exploitive deeds.

How would the development of a nation-centered theory of American Indian fiction and scholarship be in defense of Intellectual Property Rights? is an essential question. It must be asked. And we must begin to answer it. If we don't and if the past is any indication of the future, laws will be passed, collaborations will occur, books will be written, and the legally sanctioned appropriaton of the Native American voice will continue.

American Indian fiction writers, artists, and scholars who have stumbled into this remarkable debate about society and culture must not add to the confusion by failing to understand what is at stake. It is the very tribal nationhood invoked by the remarkable Quiché scholar Rigoberta Menchú that is being questioned, the very foundation of our origins that is being threatened.

4

THE IDEA OF CONSCIENCE AND A JOURNEY
INTO SACRED MYTH

When the writer in his own society can no longer function as conscience,
he must recognize that his choice lies between denying himself totally or
withdrawing to the position of chronicler and post-mortem surgeon.
—WOLE SOYINKA

This call for the writer to be encouraged toward conscience in his work should
liberate anyone who has considered him or her self a writer, and especially
those who claim to be Native Americans and tribal citizens. Wole Soyinka
said these words in an address at the Afro-Scandinavian Writers' Conference
in Stockholm in 1960 just before the Nigerian civil war. I didn't read a copy
of the address until at least ten years later. When I did read it I found it to be,
truly, a wise and essential piece of advice, but dangerous. Soyinka soon after
that time became estranged from his homelands, his works censored and his
life threatened.

Social and literary criticism of works by African and Native American
writers, or any of the writers who might be considered "Third World" rather than a part of the western canon, has been plagued by an adherence to the
principles that stand against the politicizing of literary study. Since much of
the life of colonized peoples such as American Indians is essentially politically inspired and has been for at least 400 years, much of the work that
American Indians have wanted to do has been considered politicized as well,
and therefore inferior or at the very least tainted. Soyinka's position seems
to suggest that if writers and scholars pay attention to the matter of "con-

science," a certain kind of liberation and understanding can occur and honest stories can be told without the fear of them being labeled propaganda. His position was not then naive nor is it now. More accurately, it is a realistic position on one of the important controversies of our time.

About the time Soyinka was speaking to these issues, I began to publish work that had been part of my professional and personal life for several years. Unlike much of the work published by Africans or Third World writers in other regions, the work of American Indians, who remain among the most powerless of colonized peoples these days, was not considered dangerous, merely irrelevant.

That was the case of a little story called "A Visit from Reverend Tileston," published in 1990 in a collection called *The Power of Horses and Other Stories,* printed by a New York book publisher, Arcade, Inc., and distributed by Little, Brown. This collection fell quickly into obscurity, as did my first novel, *From the River's Edge,* published by the same house the following year; but I found the experience to be my first real baptism into the milieu inhabited by writers who realize that someone outside of their own narrow world read their fictional and poetic works. I had, of course, a clear sense of my own narrow interests as a Native American scholar who published essays in very obscure journals read only by other like-minded professors and scholars, but I was fairly isolated from broader concerns.

One of the editors at Arcade then was Richard Seaver, and it was he who was interested in publishing my first work. He had published a marvelous collection of Indian stories called *The Man to Send Rain Clouds,* edited by Kenneth Rosen, some years before, and he was considered one of the "discoverers" of American Indian writers at a time when not many Indians were publishing their work. The only question he put to me in our one and only telephone call concerning the publication of *The Power of Horses* was "Are you a real Indian?," clearly a politically inspired question that was the beginning of the end of my innocence about publishing my work, and, more important, an expression of the precariousness of Indian literary effort. If I had expected a question about the work itself to be a foremost consideration, I now knew that questions of race, class, and gender were routinely a part of the dialogue as well.

The truth is, I've always thought the little collection of short stories published by Arcade and Seaver deserved a broader audience than it got, but I've only recently understood that a writer's conscience can sometimes build an audience for the writing but can just as often be a radical departure from what is ordinarily expected, and can therefore in some cases fail to find a substantial readership. The whole experience has brought up the question of how much "conscience" gets in the way of acceptance from a mainstream audience in America, where the likelihood of a death sentence is more a function of the bottom line than it is of political assassination or exile.

The little story I wrote, "A Visit from Reverend Tileston," makes use of a long-standing idea that the Lakota/Dakota/Nakota people (known in the vernacular as the Sioux) hold to be true but that few outside the culture recognize. Indeed, the story utilizes many features that are indisputably obscure. The story is based in a cosmology little known by mainstream cultures, its intent is to expose the natural opposition to an imposed Christian myth and religion, and to make fun of the white characters, who are plagued by beliefs in the old frontiers of primitivism and the Red Indian, whereby they think the Indian characters are a part of an impoverished world and treat them as such. In spite of all that, I think the story does not have as its major intent the exploration of any of those political realities, but instead examines the underlying mythic concerns that have informed the Sioux for hundreds if not thousands of years. These mythic concerns are also political concerns, since the theft of the continent from natives is treated as either inconsequential or unknown by the Christian intruders.

The point of the story is not to say something about the intrusiveness of Christianity, which is the way almost everyone reads it. The intent is to say that the Lakota religious view persists here in this geography and for these people even in the face of this aggression. The function of creation to be explored in this story is that before they were the Pte People (or Buffalo People), and before they were the Lakota/Dakota/Nakota, or the Sicangu, Santee, Ihanktowan, Minneconjou, Sihasapa, Hunkpapa, and Oglala, or even before they were the Sioux, they were the "Star People." For a tribal writer to take on this story in this traditional way is an expression of conscience, just as Soyinka has said.

The story itself was based on a brief and fleeting childhood memory, that of my non-English-speaking grandmother and myself, a bilingual but inarticulate and silent child, kneeling in our living room in prayerful repose with uninvited Christian missionaries who seemed to us to be acting on behalf of the truly loathsome and bizarre fundamentalist phenomenon called church ideology and proselytizing. An unabashed intrusion that dismissed—with utter contempt—us, and whatever conscience we might have possessed.

The idea of conscience in this story is that the Sioux were at one time a spirit people called the Star People, and they were made by the holy presence from water and were given the name *wicun* because they were supposed to be "little suns," whose job it was to light the darkness of the world. They were not to give out any heat, for the sun would do that, nor were they to cast shadows as the moon would do, so the purpose of their presence was mainly to look about and witness. They were to journey throughout the heavens during this risky time, when there were no known directions except the North Star and no one to accompany them except the Wind. One might say, then, that their journey was an exploratory one, a first stage, a trial-and-error journey into humanity, a creation meant to be amiable and salutary, reflecting mirror-like onto the earth. On the basis of this mythology the Sioux claim occupancy and possession of a specific geography on earth.

"A Visit from Reverend Tileston" is generally read as a satirical commentary on the intrusion of Christianity into a native enclave in contemporary times. It is thought to be a critique of Indian/white relations in America. It is, of course, all of those things, but it is also meant to be something more. It is an attempt to explore that vague, unknown thing called a native conscience. It is an attempt to "fight back," as Simon Ortiz, the Pueblo author, has always urged us to do, as he wrote and published his collection of stories using the title *Fightin'*, and more than anything it is an effort to move away from the destiny of which Soyinka warns, that of occupying the "position of chronicler and post mortem surgeon."

The story, as in the case of all *keyapi*, or "they say this" stories, begins with a long description of place and home, which is the now-abandoned place occupied formerly by BIA employees and situated along the Missouri River, the Mni Sosa. This description embodies both traditional and contemporary setting, signifying change and transition. The time of the story is in the 1930s. The family is gathered in the evening after supper. Uncle starts a smudge to keep the mosquitoes away, women clean away supper material in anticipation of an evening of storytelling. Full containers of wild plums and berries on the porch indicate that the women have spent the day berry-picking. Children play in the yard. Father and Uncle sit smoking.

Interrupting this scene, Reverend Tileston and his two sister missionaries, Bernice and Kate, arrive. Uninvited, they bear Christian Bible stories in the manner of all proselytizers known to native communities in the United States.

During the prayers a dog whines at the door, and when the Reverend waves his arms during the prayer, his action frightens the dog into lurching backward. The unfortunate dog knocks over the pails of berries, slinks under the porch, and wails amidst shouts of anger by the women berry-pickers.

As the family responds to this calamity, the Youngest Daughter watches the Christians take to their car and drive away. She turns toward Uncle, the Dakota storyteller, and is reminded of a star story about a journey into the unknown, about *wic'a ak'i yuha(n) pi,* the star constellation called "man being carried in the sky." The substance of the star story that concerns the Big Dipper is not retold in "A Visit from Reverend Tileston," since it is as well known to the Sioux as the Joseph and Mary story of the Bible is to Christians, and would be redundant and repetitive. Youngest Daughter does not speak out loud her vain, childish hope that the Reverend and the Sisters will be helped along their homeward journey by the mythological spirit people who are so much a part of her lifeway. It is an ironic ending, of course, because her civilization, the Dakota way of life, was alien to and of course vilified by Christians who came into native communities with conversion in mind.

Wic'a ak'i yuhan pi is a constellation that has four stars situated at the four points of what the non-Siouxan world knows as the Big Dipper, along with three stars that make up the handle, seven stars in all. These four plus three points in the constellation are thought to be "carriers," defined with sacred status. They are carriers of the seven sacred rituals of the people, and therefore are repositories of religious knowledge. Further, they are considered to be four spirit people who often assist other humans, sometimes carrying them, in the journeys across the skies during the *ohunkaka* (creation) period, toward humanity.

This act of assistance is often recreated in a modern Lakota/Dakota/Nakota dance ritual known in English as "the blanket dance," when four dancers (usually traditional dancers) hold the four corners of a blanket and make a journey around the dance arena asking that donations be placed in the blanket for the singers, who, it is always said, "have come from a far distance" and need assistance on their homeward journey.

As for the dog in the story, his presence is foregone. "Sacred Dog" (*shunka wakan*) is a primordial figure who has accompanied the Sioux people on their journeys in the present world. There was a time when he could speak to humans. His presence in the cosmos appears to occur after the Star People period. There are many stories telling of the function of the Sacred Dog, who got his instructions from *tokahe,* the first man, a creator, during the primordial period. Shunka follows, protects, and guards. He is a carrier as well, and is obedient. It is said in the oral tradition that Shunka carried *tokahe* out of the primordial world so that no one in the present world except the Sacred Dog knows of *tokahe's* whereabouts and no human being has seen *tokahe* since that time. In that sense, Shunka is essential to the continuing journey into myth and humanity.

It is no accident, then, that the whining dog of the story "A Visit from Reverend Tileston" saves the people from the Christians, who have been known in history to desire complete conversion and assimilation of the Sioux people into the Christian cosmos. These folks will be spared that ignominious fate almost by accident but more probably by a miracle performed by the dog. The disruption caused by Shunka, they would think, is a miraculous event meant to affirm the myths of Siouxan creation. The old traditions and myths have fused with the new.

It is not surprising, either, that Youngest Daughter, a child, knows the ideals of her people and insists upon their authority. It is in the children, after all, that a culture places its future. If she has been told the stories of the stars, where a life of goodness and respect exists, she knows that it exists in her own *tiospaye* (extended family) here on earth as well, because it is a tenet given by the religious people of the Sioux that what is in the stars is on the earth and what is on earth is in the stars. Thus, even though Youngest Daughter has been witness to the invasion of the sacred by the Christians, she does not fear them nor is she angered by their imposition. In other words, she has confidence in her Dakota *wicho'an* (lifeway), and life goes on as before.

The nature of Sioux mythology is both sacred and pragmatic, mysterious yet accessible, communal yet individualistic. It is a body of knowledge not attributable to any narrator, yet noted for illustrating an authenticity concerning the earth's generative powers and the concept of human beingness. This authenticity sometimes transcends observable reality but almost always is informed by an imaginative force or urgency that originates in culture and language. It is the source of religion and lifestyle, ritual and the arts. It is the source of the imagination.

In the tribal literatures, in what are often called the Oral Traditions of the Lakota/Nakota/Dakota, traditional plots and characters and themes were and are known by the people. There were generic constructions to these literary traditions that developed throughout the many centuries of life on this continent. Contrary to popular scholarship and belief, however, wherein anthropologists and ethnologists sought out the validity of the Oral Traditions only by how many times a story was repeated by various informants, therefore classified as traditional or known, there were always fictionists among the Sioux, those persons who invented new tales and new characters out of the fabric of individual imagination and tribal experience. There were always persons who told variants of old stories, embellishments of one kind or another. Whether or not these fictive inventions became a part of the tribal literary canon depended upon their authenticity and connection to what tl people knew as observable, real, possible, or useful.

Fraud in this imagined world of mythology, religion, science and the arts was generally acknowledged in terms of exploitation, destruction, and injury to the people. In spite of the possibility of that risk, those persons with superior imaginations were always highly valued by the Sioux, and after proving to be authentic, they were incorporated as the intelligentsia of the people, the storytellers and keepers, historians, artists and artisans, carriers and physicians and priests upon whom the people could depend.

What needs to be acknowledged, then, about the writer in America who claims to be or who is "labeled" or who is thought by critics to be a American Indian Writer, is that he is not an artist unless he knows the myths, mores, experences of his tribal society and knows how to depart from those records in the fashioning of his own artistic vision. This is what is called *conscience* and it is what Soyinka implores writers to uphold in their work if they are to produce real literatures and not become mere "chroniclers" or propagandists or "post-mortem surgeons."

5

TENDER MERCIES AND MORAL DILEMMAS

No matter what one thinks about race relations in America as the century turns, Amerindians have tried to come to grips with the reality that *the return to a* moral *world as they knew it is no longer possible.* This is the challenge for the indigenes, who knew this country before it became America and before their nations suffered colonization.

Because the return to a moral world isn't possible, there are today only "moral dilemmas," to which Indians and whites (or the indigenous populations and the invading colonists, if you prefer) rarely have solutions. Morality seems to be a complex thing, and often moral differences are irreconcilable. *One of the definitions of a moral dilemma is to want two incompatible things at the same time, which for Americans means that there are many conflicting versions of what is thought to be "decent" and/or "moral."*

What America wants in its race relations with American Indians is to steal and occupy land, to kill and otherwise destroy the land's inhabitants, and yet provide an ethical example throughout the world of a democratic and "good" society developed for the purpose of profiting from that activity. This means that America rarely engages in useful discussions of morality and ethics as it applies to race relations. It only engages in popular rhetoric concerning what it thinks of as "contemporary issues," such as "What can we do?," "Who am I?," or "What does it mean to be me?"

The tribes on the North American continent who have claimed nationhood and occupancy for thousands of years have lived in regret for the loss of a moral world since invasion and colonization. Perhaps since 1500, when the

Mayans might have said to themselves: If we want to live in the ethical world as we have always lived we must kill all the invaders, we must kill all of the plants and the animals the Spanish have brought here, all the chickens and beef cattle. So the Mayans named every species they knew that had been introduced artificially into their lands in preparation for such a killing, but as we all know, it did not occur, and the chance to recover their moral world was lost forever.

Inherent in what is now imagined as that failed Mayan wish for a return to precolonized life is a theory of Indigenousness based on a morality unknown to the people now called Americans, who, having completed their invasion of the globe as gladiators, Puritans, homesteaders, colonizers, imperialists, and immigrants of all manner, now look forward to the invasion of space and other planets and even other "unoccupied" universes.

What this might mean for Americans and their ancestors is that idealism and morality have nothing to do with concepts of originality or domesticity or aboriginality, as the Mayans may have imagined a moral code of unacquired-ness and innate-ness and inborn-ness. Americans, on the other hand, have come to know that they specialize in the unnatural making of new worlds, the making of borders and the crossing of them. Invasion, colonization, Christianizing (often the surreptitious baptism of unbelievers for their own salvation), capitalism, and democratization is what border-crossing is all about, in American thinking and experience.

Hardly anyone these days believes these specializations in the American experience to be a bad thing. It is not perverse to make borders, cross them, and democratize everyone in sight including their assets. It is certainly not criminal, say those of what we might say is conventional wisdom. In fact, discussions of these matters and contextualizing them as perversions of history or "crimes" of the past, as many American Indians have wanted to do, offends many of those who listen and read and contemplate history.

What we may need to do is to reexamine our cultural experiences concerning legal and moral dilemmas, something we as citizens who occupy this planet do not do very frequently. The first thing we must agree on is that empire-building and the hating of indigenous peoples have gone hand-in-hand in the making of America. Why would Thomas Jefferson have talked about "Indian Removal" long before the "removal" and "dispossession" of Indians from their homelands really happened, if he had thought Indians had a moral or legal right to be there? Or Frederick Jackson Turner of "savagery" in a thesis that has become the basis for methodology and theory concerning the settling of the West and the ridding of the continent of Indian nations? Suffice it to say that endless examples of such history exist. These are, indeed, the examples that have fed the storytelling of America, which has, in turn, led to the destruction of Indian lives and the theft of Indian home-lands. *So, first we must agree on the premise that Indian-hating is a reality for Americans and it is America's moral dilemma that it has wrongly killed the indigenes and put a legal and moral system in place to provide justification for that crime.*

It's stories like my previously mentioned one about the Reverend Tileston that can be used to illustrate what may be called the "moral dilemma" of America and become a basis for further dialogue. What the Reverend Tileston has wanted is what America has wanted: to invade the world of a people native to a given land for "good" reasons, to make them forget who they are for "good" reasons, to obliterate native origins in that land for "good" reasons, to call themselves "good" in the process of this dispossession, and then to claim their lands to make them productive in a "good" way.

Why can't this history be called a moral history? After all, America has become the richest nation in the world. It is a small enough sacrifice for ris-ing to such heights that colonization, Christianization, and subsequent de-mocratization have resulted in chaos and grief, death and disease, and star-vation and poverty for millions of indigenous peoples in North and South America, an ongoing system of racial injustice well documented in poverty and early death. It is a small enough sacrifice, the thinking goes.

America requires that the new history of the New World be described as a decent history, "good" and "moral." America wants itself to be considered "good" because it has become the richest, most technologically advanced civilization in the history of nations, and almost everyone believes this ra-tionale to be acceptable.

American Indians, on the other hand, do not agree. They want their own histories as the indigenes to be contextualized in the land they have claimed from time immemorial. They know this land in terms of relationships long standing, they claim to know the stars of the universe as their relatives, as well as the rocks and natural creatures. It is a religious view of origin and occu-pancy not shared by colonists.

Americans, as colonists, want to be "citizens of the world and the globe," explorers of *empty* places that can be claimed and renamed in their honor, immigrants to far places bringing the good word of the Christian Bible. American Indians, on the other hand, as indiginists, want to be tribal, paro-chial tenants of the land of this planet, which they say has been occupied naturally by all those to whom they are related in Creation, the stars and the wolves and the water and every creature. These conflicting desires are inherent in the land of America, and because it is impossible to be an indiginist and a colonist at the same time, a dilemma exists in which the defeat of colonialism both as a reality and as a dream is the only answer. This means the return of lands and the return of assets and the return of the symbols of social order (education, police) to those from whom they were stolen.

Because of this enormous conflict it has been difficult and sometimes dangerous for those who have dared to imagine that they could defend the compelling, consummate, and consensual traditions of a native people and the natural world. Their work has confronted the kiss of death from editors and publishers and other scholars simply because it is not in the service of the national interest. As Sicangu writer Joe Marshall has told us in a 1995 collection of essays, *On Behalf of the Wolf,* "The first peoples of this continent and wolves have certainly faced the same difficulties." Wolves have not served the agrarian interests of an economic system based on domestication, just as the Indian's failure to disappear has not served the national myth.

A Moral Dilemma and Theory

Moral dilemmas in this country are often grounded in theories that have risen out of the need of Americans to deny that anything worth anything ever existed here before Europeans set foot on the continent. Even the land, while rich and compelling, had to be changed to meet European specifications, plowed up, made productive or "worth" something. The farming population living in the floodplain of the Red River in North Dakota in 1997 learned, albeit belatedly, why it was that the natives of that country did not reside near the rivers on a permanent basis, but rather used that land as God had given it to them. Their practice of moving away and returning, moving away and returning just as the river had always done was described by the invading populations as "nomadic" behavior. It gave credibility to the longed-for rationale for land theft that Indians did not really own or possess lands. The morality, then, or the "ethic" of the newcomer settlers, whose predecessors set down brick and concrete and plowed up thousands of acres of the land to make it "worth" something and to make it "permanent," should have come into question during the 1997 flood catastrophe, but, to be honest, this morality did not become a part of the "disaster" dialogues that followed the event.

In addition to these practical matters, "the theory of the first predecessor in interest" has been and continues to be an implacable principle by which decisions and economic distributions are made and history verified. This theory has been used in curious ways when applied to the thinking useful to the undermining of indigenous claims to specific geographies and the conflict of ownership, and the actions of the newcomers.

One of the primary arguments made by many historians and politicians in the region of the Northern Plains, and even by legal scholars who make and interpret law, against the claims of the Sioux Nation to the Black Hills, for example, has been discussed in the context of this legal phrase. Though Sioux mythology suggests a very ancient tenancy in the Black Hills and a knowledge of the Northern Plains and how to live there, that legacy is challenged by others.

It is purported by some scholars and lawyers that the Sioux did not occupy the Black Hills until very recently. Non-Siouxan history says that there was a "migration" that took place as the Sioux first crossed the Missouri River between 1750 and 1755. This history places the Sioux in this area about the same time that the French fur traders arrived. Therefore, this reasoning goes, the Sioux are no more historical or indigenous "possessors" of the lands than other casual wanderers or nomads or migrators. The Sioux "interest" is not, therefore, a given interest that precedes all others. Moreover, since their Indian "reservations" were not established through the treaty process until a hundred years after that so-called migration, their possessory rights to the Black Hills and other contested lands throughout the region are said to be neither sacred nor indigenous. This is the theoretical argument thought by some historians and lawyers to be a valid one.

For dissenting scholars, though, tribal possessory rights have been said to exist as indigenous rights, inherent in geography and myth and occupancy and language and treaty agreement; otherwise, why would any nations, among them the United States, Holland, England, and France, have signed these treaties with them in the early years of occupation? In spite of the reasonableness of this dissenting view, the rights called indigenous rights have been notoriously manipulated for profit by white men and colonizers throughout history and even in present time to accommodate non-Indian and anti-Indian interests.

In 1989, the centenary year for the northern states, as an example of the continuing stance that Indian nations aren't what they say they are, the state of South Dakota began another dispute in the courts about "rights," arguing that the Cheyenne River Sioux Tribe had no jurisdiction in regulating area game and fish populations in South Dakota. The case was litigated by the attorney general in U.S. District Judge Donald Porter's court in the capital of the state, Pierre, S.Dak., but little attention was paid to tribal-court input.

Without regard to the fact that the tribes signed treaties with the federal government decades before the state even existed or had any relationship with the federal government, the state of South Dakota has argued its point based upon a congressional act that they say precludes treaty stipulations, that the tribe's claim to jurisdiction is to land acquired by the U.S. Army Corps of Engineers when the Oahe Dam was built starting in the 1940s. This kind of confusion and ignorance, which attempts to dislodge the principle of sovereignty inhering in Indian nationhood, has now become legitimized in the corrupt legal systems that Indian nations confront.

"When the land was conveyed to the United States," says the attorney general for the state of South Dakota, "they [the Minneconjou Sioux of the Cheyenne River Tribe] lost the ability to regulate hunting and fishing on it. When it lost sovereignty over the lands, it lost sovereignty over non-Indians on that land."

There are so many wild assumptions in this argument, one hardly knows where to start a discussion.

First of all, lands "conveyed" to the United States for this twentieth-century Missouri River water project (which, not incidentally, destroyed more fluvial landscape than any public-works project in the world, to say nothing of the 550 square miles of treaty-protected lands that were confiscated even without declaring public-domain regulations) illustrated a clear method of coercion by the federal government. The U.S. Congress even told the Indians what they would be paid for their losses. Because the U.S. government claimed "trusteeship" of Indian populations through its flawed interpretations of treaty agreements, it as buyer could tell Indians what to sell, how much, where, when, and even what the price would be. If anyone thinks this kind of transaction, often called "conveyance," is an ethical way for nations to deal with each other, they clearly do not understand the nature of colonial rule on Indian reservations. The tribal nations opposed this transaction from the beginning and throughout.

More recently, the attorney general of South Dakota told the court that a 1978 U.S. Supreme Court ruling said that Indian officials "have no authority to prosecute non-Indians for any reason." He referred, of course, to the issues raised in a Northwest Indian case, the Oliphant Case, which resulted in a serious legal loss of rights of tribal nationhood. What Oliphant has meant to tribes is that states have predecessory rights but tribes do not. How did this happen west of the Mississippi, where there were clear tribal-nation predecessory rights established in treaties prior to the establishment of any status of statehood in the West? It has happened through the collusion of the

U.S. Congress, the U.S. court systems in the land, the federal government and its many bureaucracies, and the "token" tribal governments, which were established in 1934 for reasons of collusion.

The Oliphant Case is a deceptive one. In 1974, a Washington state senator, Slade Gorton, notorious as an anti-Indian legislator, and a member of the Gorton family fish empire of the East Coast, came to the aid of Mark David Oliphant, a white man arrested by the Suquamish Indian police for assaulting a tribal officer during the Chief Seattle Days celebration held on Indian lands. Gorton and his client argued that the tribe possessed no criminal jurisdiction over non-Indians. Astonishingly, the Supreme Court agreed, even though it acknowledged that Congress "had never expressly removed tribal criminal jurisdiction over non-Indians." The evidence used to come to this failed conclusion was a long-buried 1834 report from the Congress to itself that "with the exception of two or three tribes, the Indian tribes are without laws." These kinds of reports had long been seen by the courts as biased and prejudicial, though many state governmental and legal officials have found comfort in that report and others like it. Indeed, the state of South Dakota's taxpayers paid for much of the Oliphant litigation, some $20,000 or $30,000, and twenty-one other states joined in, either as amica or in whatever political ways would advance the state case. This deliberate and contrived case, put in place to affect all tribes, not just the Suquamish, has for thirty years been the power behind many of the struggles for tribal jurisdiction across the country, and some say is a major cause for continuing failure in law-and-order issues on tribal homelands.

Felix Cohen, in his *Handbook of Federal Indian Law*, clearly disputes many of the interpretations occurring in the Oliphant matter, though, indeed, these issues have been made complicated in the courts and by the courts over the years until the present tribal regulatory systems rarely get a chance to do anything but defend themselves, and the federal courts must gear up to straighten out lower court decisions and the work of legislative bodies, usually years after the fact. No one is sure about whether or not predecessory rights and jurisdictional issues are the same thing.

Cohen says in Section E, "Against Whom Protection Extends," "Tribal possessory right in tribal land requires protection not only against private parties but against administrative officers acting without legal authority and against persons purporting to act with the permission of such officers" (pp. 308–9).

Action taken by the Department of the Interior concerning the entire Missouri River Hydro Power Development has had far-reaching consequences and has been seen by some as negligent in protecting what Cohen has called possessory rights of the affected tribes. Since Cohen has said "Indian possessory rights are enforceable against state authorities as well as against federal authorities," one wonders at the failure of the courts to uphold these principles (*Danforth v. Wear,* 9 Wheat, 674-1824). This case is clearly a digression from the focal matters of this discussion, but is brought up here merely to show how it is that the interests of the so-called first predecessors are often used against tribes even in the face of acknowledgment of their indigenousness.

The Paiutes Displaced

Though the Sioux dilemma is most often cited in my discussions about justice, there are many Indian nations that can recount these kinds of experiences. Among the First Nations in North America who have had considerable experience in defending their possessory rights, and who know this corrupted "theory of the first predecessor in interest" best, may be the Paiutes of Nevada, for it was this theory and subsequent legal tenets that were used against them for a hundred years.

It started when the Paiutes tried in the 1940s to evict white cattlemen, whom they called "squatters," from the Pyramid Lake area. The situation was this: whites apparently took up lands in this Paiute country in Nevada in 1864, 1865, and 1866, or sometime during the Civil War years, and just after, on their own in the "squatter" tradition. They later called themselves "pre-reservation pioneers," the West's version, one supposes, of the Plymouth Pilgrims, or the African version of the Boers.

Some generations later, in 1924, Congress passed a bill that allowed these "squatters" to buy up the land at woefully inadequate prices. It is probably no accident that this bill was passed at the same time that the Congress passed a bill magnanimously "conferring" citizenship upon Indians, many of whom objected and refused to accept citizenship. It is important to note that the Paiute Indians did not consent to the agreement of the "squatter" activity, just as many Indians did not consent to citizenship, and the irony is that in most cases they were not even asked or consulted.

The Paiutes, in particular, were sovereign peoples who did not come into any kind of cooperative legal position until some time after the squatter activity was well entrenched. Prior to this, the Paiutes were without U.S. federally recognized legal status, and they therefore did not even exist in the minds of the squatters and the U.S. Congress. In contradistinction to this lack of status with the United States, the Paiutes had an ancient residency in their country and considered themelves sovereign peoples.

By 1936 the land still had not been paid for by the "squatters," and the Department of the Interior, in the absence of any mechanism allowing the Indian nation to proceed with the eviction process, in the midst of great pressure from the Indians, called the whole deal off. By now the whole country was in the middle of a Great Depression, and the "squatters," who were now farmers and ranchers, were hard pressed to survive.

While the controversy broiled, the Indians fenced off the land in contention, and the whites, who had by now developed irrigation projects, cut off the water to the people downstream. By now the original "squatters" no longer occupied the lands, and for the most part large livestock companies claimed possession. In these decades, numerous bills were introduced by anti-Indian interests to "authorize the Secretary of the Interior to issue patents for certain lands to certain settlers in the Pyramid Lake Indian Reservation, Nevada" (First Session on S.840, 1937). The "successor in interest" or "predecessor in interest" theory was invoked in all of these bills thusly: "At the time that these lands came into the possession of these whites, there *was* no reservation for the Paiutes." The new occupants made these claims through a battery of lawyers. Indians, by way of defending themselves, said, "We may not have been on reservations but we lived here thousands of years prior to statehood for Nevada."

There were actually five white claimants at the time of this proposed legislation in Paiute country. One, Mr. E. C. Finney, who was Acting Secretary of the Interior in 1929 at the time the controversy was smoldering and before some of these bills were introduced, wrote: "As to the equities in the matter, originally these Indians were nomadic, obtaining their living chiefly by hunting and fishing. Essentially they were not agriculturalists and knew nothing of the art of irrigation. As to the lands immediately here in controversy, the equities in favor of the Indians are far from strong."

In writing this he states the reasoning subsequent to the "theory of the first predecessor in interest" with which we are all familiar: The Indians have never been in actual possession of any of the lands in controversy and accordingly have done nothing toward the development of the lands as agriculturalists. This reasoning articulates the "Manifest Destiny" theory, which says they are unworthy because *they* do not farm and irrigate the land and *we* white immigrants are worthy because we do. This is the theory that in the whole of the nineteenth century perpetuated a federal policy of denial of justice to Indians.

In applying this theory of "first predecessor" and the subsequent notion of "Manifest Destiny" to the Black Hills Case, a regional historian from the Black Hills State University at Spearfish, S.Dak., David Miller, said: "Star charts, petroglyphs and pictographs notwithstanding, there is abundant evidence to indicate that those Sioux Tribes identified as those to whom the land should be returned *came fairly recently* to the Black Hills region. They displaced other peoples," he says, "the Cheyenne, the Crow, and perhaps the Kiowa, perhaps others."

David Miller, a longtime professor of history at Black Hills State University, received posthumously the Governor's Award in 1997, an award promulgated through the work of the South Dakota State Historical Society. He was given the award as an exemplary interpreter of history and historical figures and for his work in popularizing history. He wrote a text for middle school students called *The South Dakota Story* and a book on Rapid City, S.Dak., titled *Gateway to the Hills.* Throughout the years, Dr. Miller was active in opposing any Black Hills legislation for the return of lands to the Sioux Nation. He was one of the organizers of the Open Hills Association utilized to fight the Bradley Bill, legislation calling for land reform in the Black Hills, and he had the support of many politicians including South Dakota Senator Tom Daschle (D).

The views of Dr. Miller are buttressed by the many local historians and politicians who promote the theory that the Teton Sioux moved into the Missouri River country and eventually the Black Hills area by *displacing* the Arikara, Mandans, Hidatsa, Arapaho, Omaha, Ponca, Crow, Cheyenne, and countless other groups. This theory is based on the historical description of the Sioux as an aggressive, warlike people, as well as on the denial of indigenous theory contextualized in Lakota/Dakota history and myth.

The argument of the "theory of the first predecessor," then, can be used to render moot any discussion of indigenous rights and can ignore the historical reality that Indians knew and called their own (not in competition with but in cooperation with many other cultural groups) the entire area from the Wisconsin Dells of Wisconsin to the Big Horn Mountains of Wyoming. The question of how these arguments and theories are being used to delay justice to a people whose lands of their sacred origin were stolen through flawed U.S. legal reasoning, as has been said by the Supreme Court concerning the Black Hills Case, is rarely taken up.

Sometimes, however, justice is served, and such examples should be regarded as reason for hope. In the case of the Paiute Pyramid Lake controversy, for example, the Supreme Court ruling of 1973 said that the taking of the lands and water from the Paiutes was illegal and that the "fiduciary" responsibility of the Department of the Interior had been breached. This eventual ruling, however, hardly makes up for the years and years of deprivation, poverty, and defensive litigation the Paiutes experienced when they could have been developing a tribal-nation economy and improving their lives as citizens of their communities.

There is no question that Indian rights to property ownership have been severely limited in the centuries since European invasion. But possessory rights have been invested in Indian nations throughout the legal history of this country, and we shouldn't forget that. As early as 1821, in a case of the Cherokee Nation, the Supreme Court affirmed this right (*Holden v. Joy*, 84 U.S.211, 244-1872. Accord: 1 Op. A.G. 464-1821):

> Enough has already been remarked to show that the lands conveyed to the United States by the treaty were held by the Cherokees under their original title, acquired by *immemorial possession,* commencing ages before the New World was known to civilized man. Unmistakably their title was absolute, subject only to the pre-emption right of purchase acquired by the United States and the successors of Great Britain, and the right also on their part as such successors of the discoverer to prohibit the sale of the land to any other governments or their subjects, and to exclude all other governments from any interference in their affairs [emphasis added].

Similarly, the view of Indian possessory rights were affrmed in a Seneca land case (*The Seneca Lands,* 1 Op. A.G. 465-1821) when the attorney general said:

> The conquerors have never claimed more than the exclusive right of purchase from the Indians, and the right of succession to a tribe which shall have removed voluntarily, or become extinguished by death. So long as a tribe exists and remains in possession of its lands, its title and possession are sovereign and exclusive; and there exists no authority to enter upon their lands, for any purpose whatever, without their consent. . . . Although the Indian title continues only during their possession, yet that possession has always been held sacred and can never be disturbed but by their consent. They do not hold under the States, nor under the United States; their title is original, sovereign, and exclusive.

There are dozens of such references in U.S./Indian case law. Some will argue that the writing of such decisions has an air of ambiguity about it and that the interpretation of these ideals by judges and legal bodies has muddied the waters irreparably. It is true that cases subsequent to these early declarations have put forth a succession of ambiguous opinions concerning the Indian possessory right and the limitations of that right; but some interpreters of history such as Helen Hunt Jackson and others suggest that it was never the *intent* of early newcomers to this land to institute policies of genocide. Those theorists say: Without intent there is no genocide.

Whether or not one agrees with the matter of genocide in Indian/white relations, it is certain that the man-made law of this country prevents the return of lands stolen from Indian tribes even when it is proven in court that the land was stolen, that such theft can only be "compensated" for, which means that a monetary value is put on it and taxpayers pony up the money. Paying for criminal theft of Indian lands is treated in the courts as recompense for "sin," as it would be in the Catholic church, which since medieval times has engaged in the buying and selling of indulgences. In spite of pious denials by the clergy and the powers that be, paying for pardons is historical in the life of the church, as is paying for stolen goods and lands in Indian country in America.

Defenders of American legal systems generally put forth the argument that the intent was never theft or genocide. My speculation on these matters does not convince me of the benign status and intent of the law and its interpreters. What can be said is that elementary principles of possessory rights and sovereignty were established through early treaty-making, litigation, and judicial opinion. In light of that beginning, the "first predecessor in interest" should be a theory that clearly works to affirm Indian possessory rights rather than oppose them.

In conclusion, this discussion takes a very limited view of the entire legal and historial matters concerning a specific reference, the Black Hills issue. It reveals, some will say, only a limited manifestation of the "theory of the first predecessor in interest" in Indian law, and gives limited examples of the ambiguous nature of such thinking.

It is clear, however, from this brief discussion, that the interference by local and regional interests in matters sovereign to Indian nations only delays democratic ideals and contributes to the weakening of the political, cultural, and social strength of Indian people and nations in America. It weakens, also, the U.S. claim to world leadership in controversies involving Third World issues of the modern twentieth and twenty-first centuries.

American Indians are not the only colonized peoples to confront empire-building. Indeed, issues in Ireland and the Middle East and South Africa and countless other regions around the world bear marked similarities to the controversies inherent in the relationship of the U.S. government to the Sioux Nation. To see the Sioux Nation and American Indian nations, in general, in bondage to the self-serving interests of whites who run the oppressive state and federal agencies that the above-mentioned cases exemplify, suggests a pettiness and selfishness unbecoming to one of the most powerful nations in the history of the world. The failure to recognize flaws in thinking or deliberate strategies in thinking concerning these tribal nations within a nation and to set in place ongoing methods to weaken them challenges the U.S. claim to a place of honor in the family of nations. It will forever be seen as racist and hegemonic.

According to Helen Hunt Jackson, in *A Century of Dishonor* (1881), the law of the land has rarely stood for courage in dealings with American Indian nations. Congressional and statehouse bureaucrats, carriers of the briefs, politicians and do-gooders of every stripe, put in place to defend what is often described as the greatest democracy on earth, were, in Jackson's time, dangerous to indigenous life and limb, to say nothing of rights and estate. Jackson pointed out that the United States made and broke treaties with Indians with some regularity, a fact of history which she said "convicts" a powerful democratic nation that "outraged the principles of justice" (p. 29). A brief look at a couple of recent issues show that their behaviors have changed very little in the subsequent centuries.

In this century the historic theft by the U.S. Congress of the Black Hills is, perhaps, the best example of the kind of moral dilemma that plagues the United States as it continues into the modern world. The latest court description of this dilemma is expressed when the court calls the "taking" a "rank theft," putting it into another legal category, yet the crime goes unavenged because the return of the stolen lands will not be the punishment. As another example, the flooding of 550 square miles of treaty-protected Indian lands through the damming of the Missouri River for hydro power is treated in the courts not as an act of eminent domain or public good, but as an act of progessive economics. No principle of law was ever evoked in the deliberate flooding of these lands. The only requirement was the "trustees'" agreement and even that was belated. These actions may be described as dilemmas because the United States, in its relationship with the tribes, constantly describes itself as just, democratic, and benevolent, not as uncaring or greedy. Yet these actions have condemned the Sioux to poverty and extinction.

The resurgence of states' rights occuring at the close of the twentieth century presents further dilemmas. The state of South Dakota, already revealed to many but unacknowledged publicly as an anti-Indian entity in competition with the tribes for resources and rights, files one jurisdictional suit after another in what it sees as defense of the people of the state. It is obvious that state officials react to what its white citizens want and need, not its Indian citizens.

In 1995 the state attorney general's office believed itself to be on the right track, finally hitting pay dirt, when it received a ruling, in *South Dakota v. U.S. Department of Interior,* that declared the tribal reclaiming of lost lands for trust status to be unconstitutional. Momentarily, this ruling rendered another devastating blow to tribal sovereignty and economic development, but the Sioux Nation will withstand even this awful event because there is the sense that this ruling was the result of an outrageous crusade on the part of the anti-Indian state officials, who refused to take into account not only that the tribal economies would suffer, but that the whole case was simply further moral corruption of the historial rights of the tribes.

The tribes wanted this case to be dealt with in the appellate process. Sioux land-law watchers knew that even that wish would be a disappointment to those looking to the courts for fairness, and they were right. The U.S. Supreme Court in the year 2000 refused to hear it. Sioux Nation land and jurisdiction cases in particular are perfect examples of Anti-Indianisms in the law and the lack of morality concerning historical precedence. Land grabbers often overreach themselves, and sooner or later someone will have to write laws in indigenous America that make sense to those who know what justice means.

Moreover, the recognition of Anti-Indianisms in legal reasoning, the displacements, the exclusions, the defamation and isolation from reasonable protections ordinarily expected, give evidence of their own ravages even as natives and tribal nations continue to put together resistances as best they can, knowing that their resistances are, at least in part, formed out of the colonial degradations of the past centuries.

PART TWO

A NOVEL CLASS
OF SPOKESPERSONS

6

LETTER TO MICHAEL DORRIS

January 1990

Michael Dorris
Native American Studies
Dartmouth College
Hanover, New Hampshire

Dear Mr. Dorris:

It gives me no great pleasure to write this letter to inform you that we will no longer include your name on the masthead of *The Wicazo Sa Review* as an editor/consultant/reader effective at the time of the issuance of our Fall 1990 edition. You had been invited as such a participant in our project on the basis of several things: (1) the recommendation of a colleague, (2) your position as director of Native American Studies at Dartmouth College, (3) the notion that we shared certain philosophical and ethical ideas concerning Native American Studies and our individual and collective participation in the contemporary development of the discipline. I am sorry to say that I am no longer convinced of your suitability to serve as our consultant.

As you know and as you, perhaps, have read my recent review of *The Broken Cord*, I find myself as an editor of what we at Eastern think is a significant journal in Native American Studies in the unhappy position of being forced into making a decision about what we may term ethics. I am enclosing the publicity blurb I recently received in the mail concerning your upcoming public reading in the Tri Cities in which you claim to be an anthropologist, even "a respected anthropologist," one who apparently has the academic credentials to work with health care professionals and communities throughout the nation. So far as I am able to determine, you possess a Master's of Fine Arts but no "terminal" degree in anthropology, psychology or the social sciences. Please correct me if I am wrong.

I am adamant in the view that we must not disguise ourselves as scholars in any discipline we choose in order to become influential in non-Indian communities, the commercial world, or academia. Indian Studies, especially at this time in its development, cannot afford such an attack on its integrity and it cannot afford the criticism which will be directed toward it from an already intolerant epistemological base as now exists in most universities.

Basically, three things motivate me to remove your name from our editorial list: (1) the integrity of the *Wicazo Sa Review* as a journal that people can feel tries to be honest, but, more importantly, (2) my certainty that your position on the matter of FAS among the Sioux will, ultimately, work to do even more damage to us. Your "study" is flawed for many reasons but, certainly, for the anecdotal nature of it, and the fact that your personal sorrow has made it possible for you to humanize inhumane policies toward us. You do not speak for the Sioux on this matter and you and I both know it. But, because of the nature of your so-called study and no matter how often and how frequently or infrequently you disclaim that role, no one else will know it and, finally, (3) the belief that those of us who desire to become public policy makers should work through our own tribes, leaders, politicians, elders. I realize that this is not a commonly held view in commercial America but, it is my view.

Please understand that I am not critical of your commercial success, nor am I critical of your imaginative writing(s). Anyone is free to imagine anything he/she wishes!! We all do that as writers and, god knows, I would be the last person to deny anyone his or her imagination!!! But, writing a "movie-of-the-week" is one thing. Being billed as having expertise in Native American Studies, Anthropology, Sioux Alcoholism and Drug Studies, Health Care, Parenting, Reservation Life (what reservation were you born and raised on and where are you enrolled?) and Sioux Feminism is entirely a different matter.

It is my hope that you will understand my position though, of course, you are also free to tell me to go to hell.

Sincerely,
Elizabeth Cook-Lynn

❖ ❖ ❖

In answer to this singularly unfriendly letter, Dorris, ever the sweet-talker, answered me on January 29, 1990, and I keep the letter in my personal files. He said, "No, I won't tell you to 'go to hell' as you suggest I might; I wouldn't say that to another Indian author no matter how much I disagreed with her. Back-biting and holier-than-thou attitude have no appeal. May your journal and writings prosper."

It was a two-page letter in which Dorris defended his anthropology credentials, pointing out that he had an M. Phil. degree in anthropology from Yale, not an M.F.A., and explaining that at the time he was in graduate school the M. Phil. was considered a terminal teaching degree at Yale and Berkeley (where it was called a Doctor of Arts, or D.A.), as opposed to the "research-oriented" Ph.D.

As for being a "respected anthropologist," he explained that he had earned tenure and a full professorship in anthropology and Native American Studies (which program he said he founded in 1972 and chaired for a dozen years) at Dartmouth College. He said he taught courses in both disciplines for sixteen years, until he resigned in 1989 in order to write fulltime, at which time his title changed to adjunct professor. He identified himself as the author or co-author of a "couple of well-received books in the field" and a number of published articles. He mentioned that in 1981 he was "extremely honored" to be voted the Indian Council Fire's Indian Achievement Award, and that he made a point of noting in his acceptance speech that he was not enrolled, though his late father was half Modoc.

Dorris dropped several important Sioux names in defense of his work and said it wasn't meant to be a "study," simply a personal account and memoir.

7

A MIXED-BLOOD, TRIBELESS VOICE
IN AMERICAN INDIAN LITERATURES:
MICHAEL DORRIS

The correspondence discussed in chapter 6 shows that quarrels break out not only in governments and courts and schoolyards, but also sometimes between writers in the pages of their work and in their assessments of one another. These quarrels are often quite fascinating, and readers are drawn to them as I was when I read recently the story told by a man who had been a long-time friend and protégé of V. S. Naipaul, the East Indian novelist. The storyteller ended a friendship by calling Naipaul uncomplimentary names in a book published to good reviews, but at this writing Naipaul has not responded, and critics have had to defend or expose the writers and take sides in the quarrel. Most of us go on, reading and writing, hoping for the best, which is a common reaction to these kinds of unresolved quarrels.

The world of the American Indian literati is no different from the more mainstream examples, though in the Indian world we are thought to be in agreement about everything. An Indian is an Indian is an Indian, to rewrite that famous "rose" quote of Alice B. Toklas's friend. Michael Dorris, the man who was called a major Native American scholar/writer for two decades, and I, though we refrained from the public mudslinging that sometimes accompanies disagreements, quarreled about his book concerning the Sioux (*The Broken Cord*), and for at least a decade avoided each other. Sadly, he tired of his self-defined and anguished and public world and ended his own life in a small hotel room in Cornish, near Dartmouth University in New Hampshire in 1997. He needed "peace," his last note to either his family or his public said. It was a disturbing event, as all suicides are.

Dorris's anguish was expressed in the *Hungry Mind*'s issue on Race in 1994:

Growing up mixed-blood is, for many of us and for too long in our lives, growing up mixed-up. Dual identity may eventually be an advantage for empathy, may greatly benefit us if we become a psychiatrist or a writer or a counselor, but while it's happening it's usually not much fun. It demands wariness, humility, patience, and the lonely nurturing of a self-image strong enough to stand up to all challengers, whether intentionally malevolent or merely stupid. It inspires our jealousy toward those who don't seem to face the same problems we do because they look the way we feel, and simultaneous guilt because they often suffer or are discriminated against for that otherwise enviable quality. It engenders instant recognition for and psychological bonding with another person of any age going through a similar trial. It wears us out even as we tell ourselves it builds character. It insists that we create an independent model for who and how we need honestly to be, then follow it because finally and forever, for better or worse, mixed and stirred up is who we are.

At the New Hampshire memorial service in May of that year for suicide victim and contemporary author Michael Dorris, an aunt from New York City and many relatives from Kentucky attended. Dorris's estranged wife, novelist Louise Erdrich, sent a fax from her home in Minneapolis, promising that the following year she would be on campus, where her husband was a charismatic professor, to do a traditional "give-away" to express her grief and consolation and that of the children and others.

The president of Dartmouth College, a man who had been a personal friend of the suicide victim since his own Iowa days, when he wrote a fan letter to Dorris, spoke at the memorial service as though Dorris were a son. A western historian of the Dartmouth faculty who became provost at the college spoke of his own conversion experience with an Indian medicine man on a hill in Nebraska and how that connected him to Dorris's work and life. This historian is described by some of his colleagues as a "Black Elk Speaks fundamentalist" who claimed a deeply and profoundly personal connection with Dorris, the famed self-identified Indian writer.

On this occasion, which had a dual purpose as the twenty-fifth anniversary of Dartmouth's NAS program and quickly arranged memorial for Dorris, all spoke in recognition that this tragic event was even more tragic because it was clouded with unknowns. They referred to the accusation that Dorris was at the time of his suicide under suspicion as a child molester and in the last few months of his life under investigation by the Minneapolis police. There was speculation that these unbelieved and unbelievable charges were the reason for Dorris's taking of his own life, though his widow claimed depression as the cause.

The legal investigation/accusation was in the beginning of primary importance to those involved, to those who are considered friends and relatives of
the unfortunate man, to his surviving children, three of whom made the
awful accusation of abuse. And was denied by several important people in
the victim's life. But the legal inquiry into it has probably been stopped forever by Dorris's suicide, and we may never know the truth of that part of his
personal life.

It was reported in the newspapers that the night before Dorris killed himself, he knew Minnesota authorities were going to charge him formally with
the sexual abuse of his two biological daughters. Four of the five living children of Dorris told authorities that he sexually and physically assaulted them
or sexually abused them, and that his estranged wife, Louise Erdrich, had
knowledge of it, a report from the Hennepin County attorney's office has
revealed. The children reported that he kicked one daughter down a flight
of stairs, choked another, and frequently struck them. These charges against
a man respected as a writer of children's books, a scholar in children's health
issues, a novelist and an expert in Indian Studies were shocking to the people gathered in New Hampshire, for Dorris had kept hidden for over twenty
years these darker aspects of his life and personality. Many simply did not at
the time of the Dorris suicide and do not today believe that the charges have
any validity.

In cases like these, it seems legitimate and necessary for critics and literary professionals to assess the influence of the personal life of a writer/scholar
on his work, and to say what his professional contribution has been to literary studies in an era of unprecedented development of Native literatures.
Dorris will forever be remembered as the most successful self-identified
Native American writer in the country, a family man who was allowed to
adopt Sioux Indian children, a person who, along with his successful novelist wife, won the acclaim of the contemporary literary world. Yet he was also
a man charged with acts that suggest he may have lived a life of deception.

Writers and scholars are not expected to live exemplary lives. There are literally thousands of examples of those who do not and have not lived un-
flawed lives. William Burroughs is one well-known example, a man who died
in 1997 at the age of eighty-three in Lawrence, Kansas, who was known as a
significant contributor to the so-called Beat Generation of writers, along with
Allen Ginsberg, Gregory Corso, Lawrence Ferlinghetti, Jack Kerouac. In 1959
he wrote *Naked Lunch,* which included homosexual fantasies, drug use and
abuse, strange visions of all kinds, and the development of the unforgettable American literary character Steely Dan, a fictional icon of all manner of

vices who also, according to his creator, had a perpetual erection. Burroughs's work, some twenty novels, was considered obscene by some and was often banned, and many critics called him a pervert, yet he also was given membership in the very select American Academy and Institute for Arts and Letters. His life was a life of agony, yet his significant writing career rose out of that agony.

There is a huge difference between Michael Dorris and William Burroughs, of course. Clearly one of the significant differences is that William Burroughs did not lie about who he was. He often called himself a pervert, was a dedicated drug addict and alcoholic, a man who had moved on from the Midwest Protestantism into which he was born to the weird social upheaval of the sixties. His literature reflected who he was and who those around him were, and his writings broke new ground for the American literati. It was the honest, authentic work of an honest wordsmith, and some say it suggested that his visions and symbols had connections to the genius of previous literary work, like that of writers such as the French Symbolists Rimbaud and Baudelaire and European scholars such as Kafka, Nietzsche, and Spengler.

The honesty of one writer and the dishonesty of the other, then, is a crucial matter both in the lives they lived and in the art and scholarship they created. The professional life of Michael Dorris should be assessed now in the context of his suicide and the new charges made against him, which show the extent to which he, unlike Burroughs and others whose personal lives were flawed, was dishonest about who he was and what his work reflected. It can be argued that it is the obligation of those who shared his interest in the emerging discipline called Native American Studies that an assessment of his work and his influence be begun.

He was probably not a brilliant novelist, no Tolstoy, not even Ernest Hemmingway. Nonetheless he was considered a competent writer with a broad audience in the American mainstream. The *Boston Review,* the *Hungry Mind,* the *Bloomsbury Review,* the *New York Review,* and dozens of other high-profile contemporary literary journals respected his work and published glowing critical reponses to it. His didactic and hopeful children's works, some now say, could have risen out of a denial of the actual relationship he had with his children, revealed after his death as unsatisfactory, but even that work was acceptable to his growing readership.

Dorris was for more than a decade the director of Native American Studies at a major American university, Dartmouth College, said to be one of the foremost NAS centers in the country. He was described in the media as a foremost native scholar/writer and was considered an Indian in the professional world, possessor of critical authority and identity. He was in the company of major native writers like N. Scott Momaday, (Kiowa), winner of the Pulitzer Prize, and James Welch (Blackfeet and Gros Ventre), Leslie Silko and Simon Ortiz (Pueblo), leaders of the Native American Literary Renaissance since 1965. And he was the husband and, some say, the Svengali of the literary career of his brilliant and talented wife, Louise Erdrich, winner of numerous American literary prizes.

It will no doubt take years for the literary community and the Indian communities around the country to absorb the social and scholarly ramifications of the brief literary career of Michal Dorris. But for those who take literary art seriously, the Dorris legacy must be examined within the context of Native American Studies, the Native American Literary Renaissance, colonial and postcolonial studies, and multiculturalism. Because of Dorris's claim to be an Indian person, scholar, and writer, and because he claimed an exemplary family and marital life in order to enhance his professional reputation, the task of looking at his career within the realm of American Indian Studies and Culture must not be relegated to silence or rumor vis-à-vis the nature and circumstances of his unfortunate death. Instead, the Dorris influence and the career of what now seems to be a cleverly disguised voice in literature and politics must be examined within the guidelines of an emerging discipline.

The so-called Native American Literary Studies Movement, or Renaissance, as it is called by some, in which Dorris became a major star, began in the late 1960s, and its trademark was the claim of its practitioners to Native American heritage. In the same way that Black Studies in American colleges and universities and Black Literary Studies were said to be initiated by the desire to hear the "authentic" black voice, so was the Native American literary voice said to be "authentically" Indian because those who produced it were Native Americans. Race and culture were the visible catalysts. The critical matter of authenticity has been a major focus ever since.

Books by Michael Dorris are as follows: *Native Americans: Five Hundred Years After* (New York: Thomas Y. Crowell, 1977); *A Guide to Research on North American Indians,* with Arlene Hirschfelder and Mary Lou Byler (Chicago: American Library Association, 1983); *A Yellow Raft in Blue Water* (New York: Henry Holt and Company, 1987); *The Broken Cord* (New York: Harper & Row, 1989); *Morning Girl* (New York: Hyperion Books, 1992); *Rooms in the House of Stone* (Minneapolis: Milkweed Editions, 1993); *Working Men* (New York: Henry Holt and Company, 1993); *Paper Trail* (New York: HarperCollins, 1994). He collaborated with Louise Erdrich on *The Crown of Columbus* (New

York: HarperCollins, 1991) and *Route Two* (Northridge, Calif.: Lord John Press, 1991).

His last novel, *Cloud Chamber* (New York: Scribner, 1997), a fictional story that begins in Ireland and suggests that races in the world simply blend into one another, seemed to be, as one reviewer put it, "a haunting reflection of Michael Dorris's humanitarian concerns," but as a whole it just "doesn't come off." "As a compelling story about believable people," the reviewer in the *Times Literary Supplement* said, "it does not succeed. All of its voices sound the same . . . earnest, vague and sentimental."

Because of the tribelessness of the Dorris voice, his work was often said to be eloquent but unconvincing. Yet its influence in the entire dialogue concerning Native American Literatures was enormous as well as controversial. In a recent essay, "Who Stole Native American Studies?," I wrote this: "Unscrupulous scholars in the discipline *who had no stake in Native nationhood* but who had achieved status in academia and held on to it through fraudulent claims to Indian Nation heritage and blood directed the discourse." This sentiment could very well be applied to Michael Dorris as writer and scholar.

By "stake," I presumed to mean investment or commitment. In that essay I meant not to focus the discourse on who the messenger was, or, as it is generally stated, who has the "right" or "authority" to speak for Indians. Rather, I meant to *challenge the message* brought forth by those who had no real stake beyond personal interest or individual involvement or the desire for fame, fortune, and status.

In that essay and in this one, I suggest that the use of the word "unscrupulous" as it applies to behavior refers to deceitful and exploitive actions. One may also say that the message brought by unscrupulous persons may be skewed, falsified, and largely irrelevant to native populations in America, who at the close of the century still seek self-determination, the defense of homelands, their rights, and their resources.

The message, I said then, has seemed to me to have been a message to America of the personal experience of its victims, not a tribal-nation and historical message to the America of Indians and nation states. A tribal-centered message, I said, would have to include tribal-nation solutions, and undoubtedly should exclude the pretense of many culprits, scenarios, venues with no future potential. The function of art and literature and scholarship that can call itself Native American must clearly have two approaches: a corrective approach that goes beyond criticism to reconstruction, and the expression of an inevitable tribal consciousness that acts to assure a tribal-nation people of its future.

At the time I was writing these things I had no notion of Michael Dorris's private and personal nightmare, marked by his alleged secret and criminal behavior toward members of his own biological family as well as those native children he was allowed to adopt. In light of this newly speculative knowledge, however, his tragic case, which ended in March 1997, when he killed himself with pills, vodka, and a plastic bag over his head in a motel in Cornish, N.H., after a twenty-year career as a Native scholar and as many years of publicly claiming to be of Modoc or Klamath Indian ancestry, may be a foremost example of unscrupulousness and dishonesty in literary studies.

It can be argued that Dorris's suicide was the direct consequence of deceit and exploitation. The first issue is the issue of Indian "identity." It is important, I suppose, to say that Dorris claimed "ancestry," not citizenship of an Indian nation. However, in substance this is a man who, along with Louise Erdrich, was accepted by the literary world, the media world, and contemporary America as one "of the most prominent writers of American Indian descent we have, of the very few to have found a significant audience out in the larger world" (*Conversations*, p. ix). And it was his role on many occasions and in hundreds of venues to speak authoritatively of the Indian presence in America. The rumor that he was not really an Indian, that he was fraudulently claiming to be an Indian, followed his career but did not interfere with his ascent to stardom and his purported legitimacy.

"Neither the Modoc Nation in Oklahoma nor the one in Oregon has any record of Michael Dorris's ever having been enrolled," Eric Konigsberg wrote in "The Suicide of a Literary Star" in the June 16, 1997, issue of *New York*. Patricia Trolinger, the Modoc tribal historian, told Konigsberg that "Dorris was probably a descendent of a white man named Dorris whom records show befriended the Modocs on the West Coast just before and after the Modoc War of 1873. Even so," she told Konigsberg, "there is no record of a Dorris ever having been enrolled as an Indian citizen on the Klamath rolls." And, clearly, being a descendant of a white man does not make Dorris an Indian.

If he was not a citizen of an Indian nation and if he had no ancestors who were, what was Dorris's claim? According to his own admission, his claim was to "mixed blood." To be "mixed blood" in America you do not have to prove "citizenship" in an Indian nation. You don't even have to prove ancestry. To be "mixed blood" you can cite all manner of probables. There are many instances, particularly in the American Southwest, of an assertion or claim to Indian heritage on the basis of remarks and inferences made in family discussions, vague and ambivalent assertions carefully cloaked in a kind of secrecy that rises out of prejudice. Dorris's claim to mixed blood, like many others, seemed to be that kind of a fantasy predicated on the basis of what little he knew of a deceased father. The possession of any Indian blood of any quantum, in cases like this, is often mere imagination.

People who are legal citizens of Indian nations like the Sioux Nation or Pueblo Confederacy or Navajo Nation or countless others, on the other hand, aware of the U.S. historical process that has fragmented and debased them for hundreds of years, are often loath to confront people who make fraudulent claims to "Indianness," just as often as they do not confront those who deny being Indian, and often just accept the stories and the storyteller without public comment. Yet in the last few years, native scholars are beginning to analyze the identity phenomenon in a more critical vein, using the terms "cultural transvestites" to describe people who fraudulently claim native identity and "cultural pirates" to describe those engaged in cultural thefts of various sorts.

It doesn't help that the so-called citizenship or enrollment process developed through U.S. and tribal government processes is held in low regard by much of the native population, and thus simply ignored as often as it is claimed. There is no evidence, however, that any of the tribal nations of America who survived a massive holocaust (some say eighty million Indians were killed on this continent in less than a hundred years) have given up their right to claim who their citizens are, nor is there any suggestion that such a course of denial will be taken by the tribes. Citizenship in Indian/tribal specific nationhood is a national right retained by native nations in America even as other national citizenship rights are claimed and defended by nations throughout the globe.

Who is given legitimacy in speaking for the indigenous peoples of North and South America is crucial to the development of economic and social life on native enclaves and to Indian nation status and Native American Studies. It may be crucial to the very survival of Indians, since it is clear that the exogenous scholarship and imagination that have been the norm have failed to strengthen and develop Native American populations in any substantial way. Indeed, while the twentieth century has witnessed the bare survival of Indian nations in America, it has also brought an alarming continuation of land theft and erosion of indigenous rights. These matters are not just rhetorical or academic. The real question of who speaks for these native populations in a democracy like America should not be just a function of literary star-making by the media or by colonial and business and educational institutions or through an ignorant American romanticism. The cultural capital of native and Third World intellectuals is dependent upon an understanding of its inception, its sources, its descriptions.

An example of how it is that native intellectualism is disavowed or ignored or belittled in academia can be found by studying a 1996 publication from Duke University Press, a collection of essays called *The Real Thing* written by individual non-native scholars who call into question the entitlement of the literary hybrid *testimonio* as it applies to Rigoberta Menchú. She is ordinarily considered an authentic spokesperson for Guatemalan native populations and won an international prize for human rights, yet in this collection the scholars suggest some ambiguity concerning that authenticity because of her acquisition of the Spanish language and her worldliness.

The issues of cultural heritage and identity, racism and ethnocentricism, history and marginalization, difference and impersonation in Native American Studies have been on the margins of scholarship for as long as the discipline began identifying itself within the dominant power structures three decades ago. This has been so not so much because the messenger (scholar) may not be an Indian, but because the message (scholarship) may not be authoritative. Authority, then, is just as often a function of subject matter and methodology as it is of racial identity of the scholar. It's subject matter rather than subject that is crucial here.

Native American Studies has tried to distinguish itself for at least three decades from the related and established disciplines of ethnography and anthropology not because the scholars in those disciplines were Indian or white, but because the scholarship brought about by disciplinary methodology of such social sciences as anthropology and ethnography was often thought to be engaged in a distortion of Indian-related issues.

It is essential, then, that authority within the discipline of Native American Studies be at the forefront of intellectual discourse. One of the major thrusts of Native Studies methodology is to refute the rigid acceptance of "outside" and therefore purportedly unbiased knowledge-gathering based solely on exogenous methodology. Methods of knowledge-gathering from *within* the culture have been the focus of research and curricular development in the discipline of Native Studies. The claim to be of Indian heritage, then, the claim to possess "insider" knowledge of culture and language and experience, followed as one of the useful criteria for the production of authentic research and scholarship.

Even as he claimed to be Indian, though, Professor Dorris illustrated some ambiguity in these forms of expectation. He often expressed frustration that he and his writer wife, who has relatives on the Indian tribal citizenship rolls in North Dakota, were being identified as "ethnic writers rather than writers who happened to be mixed bloods and sometimes wrote about American Indians" (*Conversations,* p. 195).

This frustration was part and parcel of the imagined Indian world created by Dorris in an effort to establish identity, and he often spoke of it and wrote of it as what might be called his burden to bear. Now we suspect that he had many burdens, but this was one he wrote about publicly. This identity issue became such a burden that the scholarship he engaged in was almost entirely personality-laden and self-centered, in contradistinction to the tribal-nation scholarship that is expected of American Indian intellectuals participating in the emerging discipline of Native American Studies.

Yet in spite of these complaints, Dorris "became fascinated by his Indian background," according to Konigsberg in the *New York* article, and "took eagerly to the spotlight" to sell novels and foster his reputation as an Indian Studies expert. He accepted credit and acclaim for starting the Native American Studies program at Dartmouth College, which was at one time believed by some in the field to be one of the most influential Indian programs in the country.

Moreover, Dorris took a leadership role throughout the country in the growing national controversy over the use of drugs and alcohol by pregnant women and the resulting Fetal Alcohol Syndrome, which is said to be responsible for massive infant-deformity issues on Indian reservations throughout the country. He did this because of his adoption of an Indian child afflicted with Fetal Alcohol birth defects, and his subsequent adoption of two more Indian children who he said were also Fetal Alcohol–affected, though these afflictions were unknown to him at the time of the adoptions. In his book *The Broken Cord* he put the major blame for these deformities and the social breakdown in Indian life on Indian women, and, astonishingly, he advocated incarceration of them during the nine-month period of pregnancy. He tells us in his book that he testified before Congress, and his testimony seemed to advocate a legal response to the health issues described in the book rather than a medical response. In his desperation, he urged the passage of laws to prevent FAS, even intimating that incarceration and eventual sterilization might be the answer. On page 208, Dorris couches a vicious remedy in stilted language for prospective Indian mothers: "This issue inevitably seemed to return to law, to external coercion in the absence of self-restraint, to deprivation of liberty as a last resort. Again and again people to whom I've talked, especially those on the front lines, face to face with the innocent victims of maternal drinking, came to the sorry conclusion that no arbitrary freedom was worth the cost in lives that FAS entailed."

He quotes, among others, Immanuel Kant, the eighteenth-century Austrian philosopher, and invokes, without a hint of irony in terms of the history of the tribes, the Christian saying "Do unto others as you would have them do unto you." "That is the rule," Dorris intones, "the 'categorical imperative' as Immanuel Kant termed it, at the base of all cultures. It is the necessary condition for survival, but perhaps in its subtle permutations it is not part of our natural instinct; perhaps it must be learned, imposed. When that primal impulse does not flow of its own accord, *laws have to be written to mandate it.*"

Yeah, I thought as I read on, why didn't someone think of that, do unto others as you would have them do unto you, 500 years ago, before European pioneers and colonists invaded the native homelands to murder and plunder, to promulgate racist laws and place Indians at the lower end of justice in America. A bit late, I thought. Those who have read the complete writings of Kant, *Observations on the Feelings of the Beautiful and the Sublime,* know that the specter of unenlightened eighteenth-century racial theory raises its ugly head in the scholar's work. In 1764, as just a quick example, Kant claimed: "So fundamental is the difference between races of man, and it appears to be as great in regard to mental capacities as in color." Like many later European scholars, he conflated "color" with "intelligence" and promoted the view of racial inferiority. Some twenty years later, Kant stated unequivocally in his published writings: "American Indians and blacks are lower in their mental capacities than all other races." For a major writer on American Indian topics in the twentieth century, claiming himself to be an Indian, to suggest that a philosopher who held to these views would have something relevant to say about the origins and solutions to an important social problem on Indian reservations in South Dakota in our time is profoundly troubling.

In one of many newspaper interviews, Dorris said about feminist criticism, "I resent Katha Pollitt [a feminist writer for *The Nation*] and people who take the purist view that it's no one's fault that prenatal exposure to alcohol causes such sadness in so many people's lives." Pollitt had made the point in a March 26, 1990, essay in *The Nation* entitled "A New Assault on Feminism" that Dorris "unfairly blamed" Adam's alcoholic birth mother, a woman who died of alcohol poisoning a few months after the birth of the child Dorris adopted. "I found Pollitt's misreading of that book reprehensible and irresponsible," Dorris said publicly.

Criticism of any of Dorris's books was rare, and that was particularly so of the nonfiction book *The Broken Cord.* Dorris publicly ignored the review essay that I published in the *Wicazo Sa Review,* though he sometimes suggested that Indian writers should not criticize one another since there are so few of us, a view shared by many native artists. I, like Pollitt, was troubled by the misogynistic tone of *The Broken Cord*. It seemed to me very much like an out-and-out male attack on Lakota womanhood, yet very subtle in its deep-seated hatred of women.

Women, I said in my review, are often the first victims of social upheaval and poverty, and while no one suggests they should not take responsibility for their actions, alcoholism for both men and women has been diagnosed as a fierce disease among Native Americans just as often as it has been thought to be a lifestyle choice or deliberate recalcitrant behavior. Dorris's blame directed toward women seemed to me rather more mean and vicious than helpful, if the reader is to think in terms of decent solutions.

As the writer of *The Broken Cord*, and as the father of adopted children who were sometimes unable to cope with their lives, Dorris seemed simply unable to enter into a reasoned discussion concerning the themes he introduced in the work. Though he said nothing publicly about my views, he wrote the defensive letter earlier discussed after my book review was published and I removed his name from the list of contributing editors to the journal, saying that Indians who criticize the work of other Indians are "back-biters," and suggesting that since there are so few Indian writers and scholars such criticism as mine was damaging to Indians.

I did not answer this letter, so no further dialogue occurred between us. Two weeks before he committed suicide, though, he was interviewed by a woman journalist at Minnesota Public Radio in St. Paul on his new fiction, *The Cloud Chamber*. When the interviewer, in an off-the-air query, asked what he thought about my criticism of *The Broken Cord*, he said, "Well, what you have to understand about Liz Cook is that she is a very unhappy woman." The interviewer was shocked at this dismissal of my work and told me so. We agreed that this kind of response is often a classic method used by males to belittle the work and opinions of women scholars, a little like saying, "Well, it's that time of the month, you know." Yet Dorris's remark haunts anyone who is even marginally privy to his own hidden unhappy life and his apparent depression, and is aware of his subsequent suicide.

The issues brought to a public forum in Dorris's study concerning the social disintegration in Indian communities and drug abuse by Indian women are weighty. They are profoundly important. It is certain that the study has had an impact in communities all over this country, and the book remained on the *New York Times* bestseller list for nonfiction for months. Most native practitioners in the fields of health services, however, do not agree with Dorris's methods for alleviating this problem, nor should they. No one should

believe that the incarceration of native women is the answer to this dilemma. The truth is, native communities use the Dorris book to call attention
to this enormously dangerous dilemma, but I know of none who seriously
advocate the further victimization of women. This does not mean, however,
that such further victimization is not a real possibility.

The message, in this case, is far more influential and dangerous to Indian
communities than whether or not the messenger was a Modoc Indian as he
claimed and could not prove, or whether he was a "mixed blood" as he often stated, or whether he was neither of those things.

The message that Fetal Alcohol deformities among Indian populations can
be avoided by focusing exclusively on the drinking habits of Indian women
and incarcerating these women for nine months is a shortsighted and foolish message, based largely in the messenger's self-pity and frustration rather
than in reason. It ignores tribal solutions to these kinds of social dilemmas,
which must include the empowerment of tribal societies, governments and
courts, nations and families that have faced continual subjugation for far too
long. Social calamities are often the result of poverty and oppression in any
case, and certainly in studies on Indian populations these factors are not
summarily dismissed as causal.

The message concerning women's roles in tribal communities and health
issues of young children, then, presented by a scholar who has no stake in
tribal nationhood and is himself charged by his own children to be a violent
abuser, is a message that must bear the scrutiny of all of us in tribal communities, not just the mainstream publisher or the sympathetic public.

The complications concerning authenticity of the American Indian message and what it amounts to in the long run is nothing new to either the
American narrative legacy or the American academy. The profound nature
of the genre of oratory by Indian leaders was a fact of historical life and literature at some time in the distant past. But who spoke, who listened, and
what its consequences were is largely a postscript to the hegemonic reality
of American nationalism. What we know of Dorris's professional voice in his
imaginative and scholarly work is that it was thought to be authentic, that it
was largely respected, and that it was, perhaps, ahead of its time. What we
didn't know was that it was very probably based in a personal life of lies and
deception.

Some of the important questions that would have led to the theoretical
understanding of authenticity were seldom posed toward Dorris's fiction:
What literary strategies are used by Dorris to preserve and communicate
culturally specific or tribally specific meanings? What analytical rules and

regulations might be promulgated for the understanding of imaginative works that claim "Indianness"? Are there experiences that are inaccessible to "others" that Dorris expresses as a Modoc/Indian writer? Is the essentialism of race or culture a concept that can be analyzed in the Dorris oeuvre?

The question of the authenticity of the Indian voice and its reference to the voice of Michael Dorris is crucial to the understanding of mainstream thinking on this issue. Today, if you are to believe the brief publicity brought to bear on this case, some might conclude that the Indian voice is, in some general way, the Dorris voice. By that I mean the contemporary Indian voice may be one that is not conducive to asking and answering the above questions, but is, simply, personality-laden and self-centered and tribeless.

Perhaps we should not be surprised at this assessment in native scholarship, or in scholarship in general, since the popular television series "Seinfeld" reached into every nook and cranny in the world, including Indian reservations, for nearly a decade, and is said to have been totally self-referential and self-regarding. And it proved to be the most watched series in the history of the small screen especially because it exhibited those very modern qualities of personality-laden self-centeredness.

This sitcom was described by the economic news magazine *Business Week* in 1996 as one of the "most important shows in history." There is nothing more important, one supposes, than the imagined personal quandry of the individual who is not accountable to anyone, the heartfelt quibbling and whining of the self-centered and the physically attractive, the art of smirking for the purpose of making money out of banality and easy solutions and *the art of living a lie.* Seinfeld ultimately defines our age as an age without significance in the same way the personality-laden Indian voice defines our times as irrelevant to the political reality of Indian-nation survival in America, the struggle to postcolonial autonomy. One cannot discount the influence of the media. Indeed, a popular Indian novelist and scriptwriter has suggested that "the Brady Bunch of Indians" will be the storytellers, i.e., moviemakers, of the future in Indian Country.

If this is an accurate description of how native issues are presented and how they are perceived in the mainstream, the American Indian voice produced during the decades between 1960 and 1990 and on beyond to the turn of the century is, in large measure, less intellectually honest and more irrelevant than at any time in our history. Considering the lies that have been perpetuated in the name of Indian History and Culture throughout the past centuries, this is a frightening conclusion to reach and one that I resist.

It is one of the ironies of this time period that this intellectual dishonesty also coincides with the years during which Native American Studies attempted to become the single most important educational determinant for native-nation empowerment, for Indian peoples' engagment in academic acts and discourse, and for taking its rightful place in the academy as an autonomous discipline.

The Michael Dorris case is crucial to understanding the future of the work claimed by Native Studies. Dorris's mastering of the art of self-deception and duplicity and fakery must be exposed before the disenchantment of our twentieth-century progress in education and scholarship sets in. During this period and the decades following, those who tackle the tough issues in Native American Studies, such as Sovereignty, Jurisdiction, Law, Land Reform, and Economic Development on the Homelands, expect that the discipline will achieve maturity, stewardship, and justice for its constituencies, the First Nations of America. We must not misrepresent our goals nor ourselves in the process and we must not fail to examine the symptoms of failure.

The real question of how Native American Studies can do what it has set out to do when it exists within a public milieu in which dishonest scholars and writers are rewarded for their deceptions is the foremost challenge of those scholars who know an illusion when they see one. Rewards often are not available to those Indian writers who tell the real stories that matter to the people, withheld from those native writers who tell America about its own real non-illusionary past. Two excellent examples illustrating that annoying fact in recent times are the voices of Leslie Marmon Silko (Pueblo), who published her long-awaited novel *Almanac of the Dead* in 1991 to mostly dismal reviews, and Vine Deloria, Jr. (Sioux), who wrote *Red Earth, White Lies* in 1996 and was set upon by angry scholars defending their own long-held biases.

Far from receiving the acclaim afforded Dorris in any of his previous work, Silko was called all sorts of names by reviewers who did not like what she had to say. She was accused of being "a very angry author" unable to create "a single likeable or even bearable character." "More than her novel needs remedial help," said one critic, indicating, as Paul West of the *Los Angeles Times Book Review* suggested, "She has the shattered mind of an atavist." Others, unable to take the Silko message that America is now and always has been corrupt and Indians will rise up to prevail in a futuristic world, talked about her "inadequate craft." There is evidence that rhetoric and literary criticism and the study of language and literature become the scholarly art form used to discredit the voice the academic community does not want to hear.

The truth is, Silko is one American Indian fiction writer who tells stories America does not want to hear. It is one thing to read fiction that visualizes spinning off into the technological future or gives fantasy to a world of harmony and romance, or suggests that we will all converge, raceless and tribeless, into one world; but it is quite another to say that such a vision signifies death to humanity, and America is responsible. It is one thing to write stories suggesting that white men are outcasts from their own souls, but quite another to say that we can no longer keep under control the horrible things that result from that loss.

When Deloria wrote that the Bering Strait Theory of the origin of American Indians on this continent has been a fraud and a "scientific myth" perpetuated by neocolonial scientists who create mythologies for public consumption, he was immediately set upon by those white scholars defending their turf who responded to this heresy by saying that he would no longer be accepted among them as a viable scholar. They said these things because Deloria told the world, and America in particular, that there is little or no evidence for a theory of origin that white Europeans have husbanded for hundreds of years.

His recitation of Indian stories concerning floods and lakes and earthquakes that flow into and accelerate the meaning of thousands of years of experience of natives on this continent emerge into belief systems of tribalism and origin theory that have remained coherent far longer than anyone can remember. This scholarship reminds people that Indians had their origins on this continent millennia ago, not just the 12,000 years or, more recently, the revised 30,000 years ago that scholars have grudgingly admitted to as they talk of indigenous migration to this continent from elsewhere. Deloria's narrative is a story that America, the great invader and colonizer, does not want to hear, because to accept indigenousness as a principle of origin makes the invader forever an alien and the colonization of the last 500 years a crime against humanity.

Unlike Dorris and many other tribeless voices, Deloria is a man who hasn't always been an academic, and this may account for some of his practical ideas concerning scholarship and art. He was once the executive director of the National Congress of American Indians and the only Indian attorney in the early Wounded Knee trials. He assisted not only his own people, the Sioux, toward renewal during this twentieth century, but he helped the Nooksacks, Tiguas, and Payson Apaches get federal recognition, and one could go on and on with the practical achievement of this tribal scholar. He has not spent his time whining about his own Indian identity, nor has he blamed Indians for their own oppression.

Today's popular Indian Voice, on the other hand, self-centered and self-referential, mixed-blood and tribeless, takes many forms, and authorial impersonations abound. A persistent example occurred in 1973 as Asa Forrest Carter, a member of the Ku Klux Klan, was identified as an Indian author who wrote a "true story" of a child's return to his Indian roots called *The Education of Little Tree*. It is still on the most-wanted list of the University of New Mexico Press's titles, and remains immensely popular with the American public and in its educational institutions.

Identity theft and confusion in the literary world is far-reaching, and it seems to me that the blame lies with presses and editors in the mainstream whose intentions are unexamined. *African Atto*, a story taken by publishers and readers alike to be an authentic story of racial identity and struggle, was written by ex-Klan leader David Duke under the nom de plume Mohammed X. A WASP from Yale University assumed the name Danny Santiago and wrote *Latino*, a story of the streets, and it was, for a time, accepted as a new addition to the developing genre in Chicano literary studies. In 1996 a Japanese poetry hoax was perpetrated by Kent Johnson, a forty-one-year-old professor of English and Spanish at Highland Community College in Illinois, who professed to be Yasuada, a Hiroshima survivor. It mixed avant-garde poetry with Japanese sensibility, called itself a "poetry of witness," and was praised by the *American Poetry Review* and university presses. A vicar from England named Toby Forward pretended to be a South Asian woman named Rahila Khan and wrote a collection of short stories in the 1980s published by Virago. Patrick O'Brian, who wrote *The Hundred Days* (W. W. Norton, 1998), was an Englishman born Richard Patrick Russ in London, the son of an English mother and a German father, in 1915. For more than forty years he maintained that he was an Irish writer, raised Catholic, born in the west of Ireland. An unwitting critic in *The Observer* reviewed *The Last Pool and Other Stories* in 1950, saying, "This charming book by an Irish sportsman is a genuine collection of tales of the Irish countryside." O'Brian was said to have a fetish for privacy. Such deceptions in the mainstream literary world are unremarkable, apparently.

Indeed, the mainstream literary world seems incapable of condemning the baseless and contrived imaginations and the weird fantasies of its practitioners, and maybe that's a good thing. But to fail to define them and examine their rationale and consequence is, in my view, unacceptable. Michael Dorris wrote in an essay called "The Thin Line," published in *Northern Lights* (Spring 1991): "A writer of fiction is in disguise, wearing the clothes and speaking the words of someone else. A story or a novel is an elaborate puppet show where, if the ruse works, the enlivening hands are invisible."

It is one of the hazards, though, of our profession that as we try to achieve the magic of another world we apparently fail to distinguish between sensations and associations, fantasies and dreams, history and sociology, identity and desire, and we should at least acknowledge that reality. If we fail to do so, it means that we should not take ourselves very seriously as artists, since we end up saying nothing real, we merely entertain and escape. There is nothing wrong with entertainment and escape, obviously, but as fictionists (not fantasists or fabulists) we should also be trying to say something real about the world we imagine.

The pretense to identity other than one's own reality can be seen as merely a trend in contemporary American literary studies or it can be seen as a "hoax" with damaging consequences. By claiming to be an Indian, as in the case of the author of *The Education of Little Tree,* the author and his publisher are lying to the reader concerning the authenticity of the work in order to make his "reminiscences" reliable. I can't help but think that the consequence of such publishing is to skew the academic dialogues so that they are irrelevant and dangerous, in a time when the appropriate focus of racial dialogue is crucial to the people who need to understand each other.

My purpose here is not an exposé. Rather, it is to call to the attention of scholars the possibility that the relationship identity has to scholarship and the imagination might point to unreliability inherent in the work itself. Is it possible that we can learn something from this kind of social criticism concering identity and literature and art and aesthetics? I don't know, but I am sure that contemporary works must be contextualized within a reasonable history, both personal and tribal, a known and verifiable History.

As for Michael Dorris's legacy, the PI News Services reported this a few months after his death: "Louise Erdrich says she will not contest the will of her late husband, author Michael Dorris, which provides for their three biological children but excludes his two adopted children and her. Dorris, who committed suicide, said in his will that he omitted Erdrich because she had 'commenced an action for dissolution to our marriage.' He did not name her trustee of his literary estate."

Dorris, "one of the first bachelors in the country to adopt children" according to the PI News Service, and in the end a rich man by most native standards, legally adopted two American Indian boys and a girl from the Sioux Indian reservations in South Dakota, yet cares for none of them in his legacy. His apparent anger toward his wife, without whom he could never have created an ouevre with lasting consequences in the study of Native American Literatures, also casts her out from the care and comfort of his earthly rewards.

These seem to be unnecessarily cruel actions coming from one who throughout his professional life claimed a commitment to humanitarian concerns. Literature and writing, it is said, is supposed to be the connecting thread of civilization, but too often successful writers and important intellectuals are overcome by human smallness.

8

INNOCENCE, SIN, AND PENANCE

Identity searches in individual lives in America are ubiquitous, and readers of history often suggest that it is America itself that is searching for identity. There are some ideas, facts, and myths about America's beginnings that are simply false, and the confusion about these matters makes it possible for America to continue its unceasing but futile search for its national identity, as well as its relentless defense for America's killing of millions of indigenous peoples who had lived here for thousands of years. Attempting to write about the confusion, I published a book of essays in 1996, but to some readers and reviewers, like Ruth Bayard Smith of the *New York Times* "Books in Brief" section, I was simply "castigating" Wallace Stegner for writing that "Western History sort of stopped at 1890."

Bayard Smith's narrow view of what that collection of essays attempted occurred to me as I was reading what I consider the exemplar of a very bad book on Indian affairs, called *Killing the White Man's Indian,* by Fergus Bordewich, published in 1996 by HarperCollins. In many ways it serves as another attribution of Stegner's influence. This book looks like a novel but reads like a polemic in which the author agrees with Stegner's earliest works by saying "the physical extermination of Indians was never an *official* policy of the U.S. Government," and in all other ways it resembles the western story for which Stegner is precursor. It is apologetic, repentant, and wrong. There are many references that efficient and thorough American scholars can point to but rarely do. For example, in U.S. Miscellaneous Document #1, 40th Congress, 2d Session, 1868, [1319], there is this sentence: "Indians are to go upon said reservations. They have no alternative but to choose between this Policy of the Government and Extermination." These references are so numerous in congressional writings of the time that it is difficult to say why it is that scholars utilizing the historical archives have rarely made reference to them.

There is a difference between classical historical writings and modern journalistic ones, yet it is difficult to come to terms with such inaccuracies and omissions as in the Bordewich book. I suppose the key word in Bordewich's statement is "official," since Bordewich declares that there is simply no evidence of an "official" policy. Even if we cannot say what this journalistic writer means when he refers to an official policy, I dare say there is much evidence in the legislative record of the U.S. Congress, as a starting point, that refutes his blatant assertion. Often such policy statements are cloaked in an official language for the purpose of obfuscation, yet in just as many instances it is written in language plain enough for even the most obtuse of readers to understand. Genocide, though always intentional, premeditated, and willful, is hard to prove, as there are few witnesses willing to come forth, and often no smoking guns that can't be hidden or ignored. As we moderns can testify, the Bosnians and Serbs, in the last decade of "ethnic cleansing" in Europe, did not write many documents either, to leave as evidence for their inhumanity as they killed each other off in massive numbers. That omission doesn't mean that the genocide has not occurred, nor does it mean that it was not the "official" policy of those powerful murderous regimes.

The Bordewich statement is one of those "myths" about America's beginnings that pervades the western story. Writers like Forbes and Berkhofer and Thornton and Deloria and Debo and others have written prolifically of the deliberate holocaust, and say outright that this denial is simply a false mantra of apologist American historians.

The foremost idea concerning America's beginnings that obscures intent is the idea of Conquest, defined by colonist nations as a principle that gives such nations the right to steal land—not just occupy it but actually own it. How this idea and the subsequent principle have been implemented as far as American Indians are concerned is another example of historical manipulation that has been fairly well utilized in historical writings in order to put the best face on an ugly reality, and it, too, has become myth. Usually "conquest" means "defeat in war." The truth is, the Sioux Nation in the Northern Plains, as just one example, was never defeated in war. On the battlefield, the United Sioux won more wars that it ever lost. So this interpretation of "conquest" is another falsehood, a myth concocted for public consumption and the legitimization of land-theft.

But there is another idea about "conquest" that is particularly American. It's the idea of conquest as ownership of land, property rights, and a literal form of benign and inevitable economic growth. This is a trait of capitalistic democracies, in particular, and it is a self-serving definition of "conquest" promulgated by American scholars in defense of America's success in exploiting resources.

The point that is often neglected, when the discussion of "conquest" is undertaken in American history, is that "conquest" everywhere in the world including America has meant genocide, deicide, and theft of lands. It really has meant the slaughter of millions of Indians in the case of North and South America—a holocaust of enormous impact. "Conquest" means the spilling of blood of innocent victims and the theft of lands belonging to others. This is sometimes and in some places in the world called "criminal" behavior, but in the case of America's attempt at ridding itself of its indigenous population, it is not. Conquest and Genocide in America seem benign, not the premeditated strategies of criminality.

American Indians who have become academics have had the opportunity in the last several decades to speak publicly on these issues. This dialogue through the work of certain intellectuals who make up the middle class is a work-in-progress. A major source since 1970 for this dialogue has been the work of native novelists, who seem to have bought into the system to make up the middle class, which, it is said, is the power base of any democracy.

In America, as happens elsewhere, a native elite is developed, and this is, perhaps, what has happened in the instance of the development of a Native American writers' class, a novelist class of spokespersons, one might say. Promising writers and their works have been put into place in order to speak to the public and in order to speak for their own people. They are sometimes rewarded, and if you read Fanon and Camus and such works as *The Wretched of the Earth,* these spokespersons run the risk of becoming, as Fanon suggests, the "dogs that bark but don't bite"; they learn the vocabulary of postcolonialism, postmodernism, and diversity and begin to serve as the ideal democratic assimilationists. There is a black man by the name of Keith Richburg who shows such promise, a journalist for the *Washington Post,* who has written a book, *Out of America,* about modern African politics and life as well as history, saying, in so many words, "Thank god I'm an American so I don't have to put up with the chaos inherent in my African heritage."

Some Third World critics like Fanon would call these writers "colonized laureates," people who speak for the tribe or the race but condemn both in the process of assimiliation and missionizing. There is little or no defense of native heritages and beginnings in the writings of such tribal or non-tribal laureates who have come to prominence in the last thirty years.

Since America rarely admits to its crimes and since many of the major scholars both Indian and white do not analyze as criminal the events of a history of colonization in America, another major false idea about America's beginnings has, therefore, to do with America's "innocence." The western story, in particular, describes America's good intentions, America's innocence, nobility, grandeur, naiveté, trust, optimism. America is, according to this false idea, a new and empty land, a land of hope and endless opportunity, a land of grand possibilities whose indigenous inhabitants have been and are willing to sacrifice themselves for the new order. This theme of innocence and hopefulness is pervasive, but it says nothing about the fact that Indians are exempted from this hopeful vision. Indeed, Indians are often recognized—when they are recognized at all—as the "have-nots" and "the vanished."

There is, occasionally, some lamenting over these facts.

Even Wallace Stegner in his old age, say his biographers, realized that the American dream "twisted our lives and corroded our values and spoiled the land." He hated to give it all up, though, much like another American writer, William Faulkner, who had to take into account what had happened in the South as he wrote with regret about the failure of the southern aristocracy, so too does Stegner regretfully take tragedy and failure into account in the West. Even as he looks at the failure, he says that the West is still a decent place, it has a "shine" on it, it is the "native home of hope" because it is "new."

Ken Burns, the latest western documentarian, follows in Stegner's footsteps by saying in his television series "Journey" (1996), "The great thing about this country, America, is that it started at zero." It is "new," say these makers of myth. New is, of course, a synonym for "innocent."

The West is not new. It is, instead, very old. It is not a new seedbed into which something new must be planted for the sake of the future, because it has already grown and nurtured cultures that are thousands and thousands of years old that *must* be taken into account in the continuing American story.

The concept of the West as new, as seedbed for new growth, is very strong, yet it is a concept that must be challenged as we go into the twenty-first century. The western concept as a new place urges us toward discussions by conservationists, wilderness advocates, community organizers, bio-regionalists, nature writers, ecologists, philosophers, conservation biologists and planetary biologists and ethno-biologists and on and on. They ask themselves "What shall we do?" and "We have sinned against the land," and again "What shall we do?"

A major recognition here is that the central myth of the West, as Stegner, Bordewich, Burns, and others see it, is a Christian myth: Innocence followed by Sin and Penance and, finally, Redemption. This is the myth implanted in the New World by Christian colonizers that must be reexamined and eventually discarded, because, as anyone knows, the reward at the end of the line in the Christian myth is to *go out of this world.* If you are a believer, you will go to some other place, heaven. It does not matter what solution is found on earth, then, the scientific solution, the biological solution, the philosophical solution, because the reward is not an earthly one; rather, it is to leave this world and get to heaven. In contradistinction, native mythologies offer no such incentive, and therefore it might be surmised that native mythologies are loath to adopt the facile or expedient solutions of other worldviews.

Other myths, lesser ones perhaps, have to be given up too. It might be a good idea to get rid of the Custer myth in the Northern Plains, for example. Get rid of Buffalo Bill and Kit Carson. We must get rid of Mount Rushmore and the newest violation of the sacred Black Hills, the Crazy Horse Monument, because these are symbols of the known, historical criminal behavior of one people toward another, in violation of earthly accountability. They are the colonial imaginings that become the strategies for possession of land.

Speaking imaginatively, or mythically if you prefer, Dakotas say *wi yoh peyata* in reference to the West. It is a very old word that refers to the sun, the wind, the placing of the sun in the universe. It is so old, perhaps, that it refers to the time when the Dakotas were the Star People, a time when there was only water and the darkness and the wind and our relatives, the stars. The wind had four sons and one of them was *wi yoh peyata,* where the sun sets. It is the kind of language that establishes relationships in the universe. Dakotas are relatives in the west to the sun and the wind; and the stars of that period are Dakotas. The West, then, is for the Dakotas not a newly specific geographical place that is set off from everything else in the universe. It is old and significantly tied to everything else in the cosmos. And the myths are hardly so trivial as the romanticization of a third-rate general, Custer, or even the idealization of a young Lakota man called Crazy Horse, who was shot to death at thirty years of age by invaders who stole his homeland. Considering the morality of mythmaking, the blowing up of mountains in the sacred landscape is hardly the appropriate behavior of human beings who are part and parcel of an enormously old and grand cosmos.

One of the most important themes of the white man's West was expressed in a PBS documentary narrated by Robert Redford when he interviewed Stegner just a few years before the writer's death. Stegner said then that he learned about the West as a child, when he was sleeping under a wagon in Saskatchewan, Canada. It was during a terrible storm, he said, and he was cold and frightened. He found out then, he said, that "the Universe doesn't have any obligation to you." This is an incredible admission to the Sioux, an outrageous idea to the indigenous people, who know that, on the contrary, the spiritual presences in the universe love us. They hate us, too. They are often jealous and unpredictable. But, after all is said and done, they know us and have regard for us. The universe is, therefore, obliged to us, according to Sioux legends, because of the interrelatedness of everything in the cosmos. It is not that there isn't danger here in human life and heartbreak and misery. There is. But to suggest that there is not reciprocity between the spirits and the universe and humans is an indefensible idea.

The idea that the universe is not "obligated" to humans may be the most important idea, myth, or concept rising out of the white man's western story, and it may be the most dangerous idea of all; for the Sioux believe in reciprocity, and they will tell you, even today, that what goes around comes around. They will tell you that what is in the stars is on the earth and what is on the earth is in the stars.

And they will admonish you: if the universe has no obligation to you, as white westerners suggest, you have no obligation to it, either. This is the essential dangerous idea that newcomers from Europe have brought into this country. They have acted on it. This concept has allowed them to act as though the universe and human beings are not bound together morally and legally, that there is not a binding promise here, no penalties. Nothing could be further from the truth and nothing could be more dangerous to the planet and the future lives of our children.

9

NEWS OF THE DAY AND THE YANKTON CASE

As the previous essays suggest, Anti-Indianism and Genocide stem from a deep uncertainty about what America really represents in the family of nations and who Americans are in the context of their fear, hate, ignorance, and self-absorption. When the politically inspired American Indian Movement recently celebrated a twenty-five-year memory here in South Dakota on the cold prairielands, those uncertainties became obvious, and the public spokespersons of the area once again discovered that Indians are alive and, if not well, at least surviving.

"Legacy of a Standoff" read a February 1998, newspaper headline in South Dakota as the members of the American Indian Movement slogged through the snow and ice to commemorate the 1974 "takeover" of the tiny village at Wounded Knee. This has come to be an annual remembrance, recorded in the media and talked about on the streets and prairies where people of good will gather.

"American Indian Movement's 71-day occupation of the historic village of Wounded Knee in 1998 is a remembrance of the 1890 December massacre of over 100 Lakotas at that spot," proclaimed the local newspapers.

"Indian Views Vary Wildly on Wounded Knee," said the smiling television newscaster.

The newspapers and television image-makers showed an old photo of a chimney that was the remnant of a trading post, then owned by whites, burned to the ground during the early days of that occupation.

Pros and Cons were examined, and there seemed to be a grand effort to play on people's emotions.

"It was like a war!" said those interviewed in the blowing snow.

Those who were here during the times being commemorated focused on the political, economic, and historic reality faced today by Indian peoples whose Indian nations survived the holocaust of 1490 that spread across the country, concluding, some say, with millions of native deaths on this continent. Make no mistake, said those who were here twenty years ago at the site of one of the most infamous of those many massacres, a holocaust happened to Indians on this continent. And it happened again. And again. That is what Wounded Knee symbolizes, they told others.

It seems to be the charge, burden, and privilege of those AIM people, in the midst of the constant controversy and ambiguity that follow them everywhere, to remind the people not only of the holocaust but of the subsequent history, loss of land, theft of resources, poverty, inadequate colonial governing systems, what America did, and what America might do again.

The Sioux at Wounded Knee seem to be the bare survivors of this holocaust. Oglalas at Pine Ridge, Minneconjou at Cheyenne River, Santees at Sisseton, Hunkpapas and Santees at Crow Creek and Standing Rock, Sihasapa at Standing Rock, Yankton and Yanktonnaise at Yankton, and Sicangu at Rosebud and Lower Brule are sovereigns and all are bare survivors. They possess hundreds of thousands of acres of land, vast water resources, resources of all kinds, and a longtime treaty relationship with the federal government. This relationship, this "trust" or "fiduciary" relationship, has undergone various descriptions in the courts, few of them anything but pretenses.

It is not only massacre that is talked of here as historical remembrance. It is also land theft. As the wind blew on that day of commemoration by the "militants" of Wounded Knee II, a federal case called *Yankton Sioux Tribe v. South Dakota* made its way through the legal system. The Yankton Sioux Tribe, like the Oglalas at Pine Ridge and their relatives everywhere on this plain, has had a very long history in the region, signing treaties with the federal government in the 1850s, some forty years before the state of South Dakota came into being in 1889. Even though a principle of Indian law has been defended for over a century, i.e., that Indian treaty rights take precedence over states' rights, Indian lands are still being confiscated for one reason or another, and the Yankton case demonstrates that reality.

Treaty Rights Precedence is an important principle that has been defended in the West for many decades, and that defense was one of the reasons for the uprising at Wounded Knee in 1974. The Boldt Decision in Washington

State in the 1970s clearly defined the rights of tribal fishermen as preceding the rights of others, and there are many other such cases, and the American Indian Movement assisted in the articulation of that history in recent times.

It may be important to say here that since 1858 the Ihanktowan (Yankton), the people of a middle tribe of the powerful Dakotapi (the Sioux Nation), have attempted to articulate their nation-to-nation relationship with the United States, and they have been particularly traditional in seeking to solve land disputes. They have always pinned their hopes on the U.S. legal systems. Their treaty of that fateful year, 1858, 140 years ago, was a landmark case because it established one of the the first of several "native homelands" on the traditional Sioux lands adjacent to the Missouri River, in accordance with an agreement reached between the Yanktons and the Americans.

Within four years of that fateful year, the northern Dakotas, the Isianti (Santee) relatives of the Ihanktowan, would be at war because of the failure of their treaty with the whites, and within ten years, the western Lakota relatives, the Oglalas led by Red Cloud, would declare war with the United States to oppose the opening of the Bozeman Trail, which was another clear violation of tribal-nation treaty rights by the United States. When the treaty disagreements resulted in war, the Yankton Sioux Tribe stood aside from its allies and its relatives, isolating itself from the the Sioux Confederacy, and they clearly expected that because they did so, the federal government would honor its commitment to them. This turned out to be a vain hope and a mistake.

During pre-settlement times it was a fact that the Yankton Sioux Tribe had possessed 13 million acres of land between the Missouri River and the Des Moines River. This was true not only because of the traditional relationship between tribes, it was a well-known fact of the region even as white men began to trespass up and down the rivers. The treaty of 1858 resulted in the giving up of much of that traditional estate, but it was done by the Yanktons so that they would continue to hold more than 400,000 acres as their reserved homelands in making way for the inevitable white settlement. The official survey has indicated that the exact number of acres was 430,405.

Since the time of the establishment of the state of South Dakota, however, in 1889 (just a year before the terrible massacre at Wounded Knee), almost constant disagreement and litigation has resulted. The state of South Dakota and Charles Mix County seem to reveal in their dealings with the Yanktons that their settlement around those reservations, those boundaries and possessions of the tribe, entitles them to more and more land and resources. The scholars and lawyers and historians who write about the Yanktons often suggest that after the signing of the 1858 treaty agreement, the U.S. Congress (in cahoots with state and county development) changed its mind about the so-called reservation concept, and the intent was to "diminish" the reservation into oblivion (i.e., disestablishment), that the Yankton people would soon cease to exist as a people, and that their lands could be subsumed. This is seen by many non-Indian scholars as a nonviolent way to progressive democracy. At least that's the way it is described in many of the histories that have been written.

In the 1997 *Yankton Sioux Tribe v. South Dakota* case, which is an example of one of the most recent land thefts based on this reasoning, the U.S. Supreme Court further "diminished the Yankton Sioux Lands by 168 thousand acres," and gave these lands, possessed and occupied by the Yanktons for hundreds of years, over to the state of South Dakota in violation of the principle that treaty rights holds primacy over states' rights. The latest Yankton case was not just a jurisdictional case, the state said. It was historically based on the "diminishment" intention and results in "disestablishment." In this case, it is an astonishing fact that the state of South Dakota argued for the *total elimination* of the Yankton Sioux Reservation. Again, the courts have assigned no blame for these acts of genocide, they have simply accepted these actions as the way to progressive democracy, and have introduced the new phrase "disestablishment" into the legal language.

This is the argument presented in 1997 by the state of South Dakota: the taking of this Yankton treaty-protected land is legal because it is based on an 1894 Act of Congress which (thirty years after the treaty was signed and seven years after the Allotment Act was passed) prevailed in the nation's Supreme Court. That act, said the state, "opened unallotted lands to white settlement," and the Yanktons, therefore, "ceded" those lands. The state of South Dakota had been at the time of the cession five years old. The Yankton Sioux Tribe, hundreds of years old, perhaps thousands, still clung to the idea that this new democracy would deal with them fairly. It had a difficult time looking at the reality that new and ubiquitous democratic ideas were legislating them out of existence.

This 1894 Act of Congress, occurring *just four years* after more than 300 defenseless Lakotas were murdered by the U.S. Army at Wounded Knee, was not an act of cession as it was called then. The Wounded Knee Massacre was a bitter, traumatic event, a crime of humanity perpetrated for the purpose of theft of lands, a premeditated act of genocide and political crime witnessed by the Yanktons and others of the Sioux Nation. Does any thinking person either then or now believe the murder and the theft were anything but acts of genocide?

The murdered Lakotas were close relatives of the Yanktons as well as the other cultural groups of the Sioux Nation, which makes the idea that these native peoples willingly yielded or transferred lands to the murderers of their relatives a fiction and a lie. Instead, these land thefts promulgated by congressional action were and are the subject of a policy of "extermination" at the close of the nineteenth century. That policy is now carried over, by law, at the close of the twentieth century as the courts and the legislation further "diminish" the Yanktons. Congress and the courts of the land carry on this policy of "extermination"—or "disestablishment," in legal terms—toward the Yanktons without recourse. No one, least of all present-day government officials, should ignore the reality of this history. No one should see this latest land theft from the Yanktons as anything but the bigoted, greedy, anti-Indian policy that has characterized the Indian/white relationship since the beginning. The *Century of Dishonor* spoken of by Helen Hunt Jackson in 1881 is a century without end.

Nowadays, this policy, which thoughtful persons have recognized as a historical policy of genocide, is called by scholars the "diminishment" movement, an effort to "diminish" Indian lands and Indian rights, as has been the "intention" of treaty-making in the region. A few legal scholars are beginning to examine this movement, and their articles sometimes appear in the law journals of various universities. It will be interesting to see what future historians make of this. In the meantime the Yanktons struggle to go on, suffering poverty and humiliation, economic distress, and displacement.

A term that can be used to discover the intent of this legislation and these policies is Anti-Indianism. In the same way that Anti-Semitism was in the beginning an offspring of religious persecution against those of the Jewish faith, Anti-Indianism here in our region, in the West particularly, has been the child of religious intolerance. As the Nazis in Germany in 1920 and 1930 began to express this intolerance in their government, the United States has also expressed its intolerance in the political and legal institutions that govern Indian lives, and this intolerance is, now, four centuries in its making.

What history has shown is that even when the Jews gave up their religion and hid their identities, they were still unacceptable to German society. Likewise, even as Sioux Indians became Christians and signed peace treaties that protected their ancestral lands, they and their nation have remained unacceptable to American society, convenient targets for, if not the ovens, at least "dimishment-by-law" and "disestablishment" by law. There has been no avenue of escape from political oppression and massacre and discrimination for American Indians.

Anti-Indianism, like Anti-Semitism, lives.

It is one of the ironies of history that as Indian land is stolen in 1997, more and more white people who are descendants of early Puritans, Christians, Europeans, and Germans, in particular, want to come to the Lakota Sun Dance, to take part in religious and community festivals held on Indian reservations in South Dakota, to learn from Indians what it is they know about the land and the universe and the cosmos. A recent cartoon appearing in *The New Yorker* at Thanksgiving time shows a Puritan walking beside an Indian saying, "You must give me your yam recipe before you and your people are extinct." There seems to be no defense to this kind of communication between Indians and whites.

The problem is, Indians in America have no way to affect the body politic in general, and in the state of South Dakota in particular. When you have no way to affect the body politic and you are an Indian, you turn to the federal government, the "trustee" of Indian lands and rights, the "fiduciary" established through treaty at the beginning of our concomitant histories. When you can't affect the body politic and you find out that your "fiduciary" is corrupt or helpless or ineffectual in the face of American Anti-Indianism, you turn to the courts. It has taken Indians a long time to learn the lesson that they often cannot depend on the courts either. Indeed, today, in the face of the Montana Crow case in the 1980s, when the Crow lost significant water rights, in the face of Slade Gordon's effort to get the courts to declare sovereignty dead and the continuing Washington state effort in that regard, in the face of several 1990 Utah and New Mexico cases, and in the face of other outrageous attacks on Indians by the legal establishment of this country, courts are the last places Indians should turn to for justice.

The 1994 *Hagen v. Utah*, which is a central case in the recently identified "diminishment" movement, says that state power on Indian reservations holds primacy because past acts of Congress had the "intent" to diminish reservations. This is not unrelated, scholars say, to the Oliphant Case of 1974 in Washington state, which affected the sovereign status and jurisdictional status of all tribal nations, large and small. All of these state-inspired cases turn to nineteenth-century congressional acts to "diminish" Indian rights in this country. Slade Gordon of Washington state has in 1996 put forth legislation that requires of the tribes that they give up their sovereign immunity if they are to continue to receive federal funds, yet federal funds go to Israel, Afghanistan, and other obscure but sovereign nations throughout the globe with very little comment from him or other people sitting in the congressional seats of this country. The Indian cases, therefore, can be seen only as

Anti-Indian legislation useful for the same results that Anti-Semitism was useful fifty years ago in Europe. The year 2000 Republican Party Platform calls for doing away with what they see as "the Reservation system" entirely, a frightening example of political strategies driven by racial hatred.

In spite of all of this contradictory evidence, "ethnic renewal" is thought by some progessives to be a reasonable idea that might have bearing on the lives and histories of all Americas. Ethnic pride is on the move, we are told, yet there is little understanding of how it is that indigenous populations and treaty-protected lands and tribes fit in to this scheme. Americans should know that "ethnic" pride has nothing to do with Indians. Assimilation and Immigration as concepts have no meaning for Indians. Federal policies affecting Indian landholders are not based on ethnicity because the indigenes are not ethnic groups within an immigrant society. These discussions of ethnicity in America and the failure to defend Indian tribal systems can do little except confuse an already confused public. Those persons who come to the Sun Dances of the Lakotas must know that even as they pray, legislative acts of the U.S. Congress connive to do away with Indians as nations of people. It does no good to talk of "ethnic diversity" and hope that Indians will want "to be proud"; it does no good for whites to want to see us dance, to talk about how it is we are going to "save our indigenous languages" and give us foundation monies for those purposes.

The fact is that if we cannot save our homelands, our Indian reserved lands where ancient ideas about god and the universe reside, the places where we came from, and our families who often live in destitution because of federal diminishment policies, we can never save our cultures or our languages. If we cannot save the land we will become extinct, for there is no more important value to a native people than the lands of their ancestors. It is in the land that the native finds his morality, his life, his origins, and his survival. If he cannot save the land, he can save nothing.

10

SCIENCE, BELIEF, AND "STINKING FISH"

One reason often given in support of the work of scientists who sit in university and museum offices with untidy heaps of broken Indian bones including skulls on their oak tables, picking at them with dental picks and other sharp instruments and peering at them through magnifying glasses, is this: without this kind of scientific inquiry Indian history will be lost. "It will be like giving it all over to the Anti-Semites," one well-known historian told me recently, "who claim that the Nazi/Jewish Holocaust in Germany in the 1930s *never happened.*"

But a reader of Indian history and science might interject, "It is like a holocaust never happened here." "Tragedies" happened. "Unfortunate histories" happened. "Occupying lands" and "deaths" happened. But surely (they say) not a holocaust. Surely not a nightmare like the Jews in Germany. There are almost no admissions of a holocaust in mainstream scholarship or literature. The word is not used in American historical colonial narrative. Still, the argument goes, if we don't support the work that good and responsible scientists are doing, we will have no evidence of any rationale and theory concerning the history of indigenous peoples on this continent. Evidence of a holocaust or any other history will be washed away in the passage of time, they say. This rationale for science is strong, and it suggests that science is "truth," not a "belief" system; science is reason and logic, not religion. Today, Indians and many others are beginning to question much of this rationale.

The argument that without scientific inquiry Indian history will be lost may be a specious argument, that is, one that is seemingly fair and attractive but

actually deceptive, since it does not appear that any serious scientists anywhere on this continent are sitting at their oak tables or digging in the earth
for the express purpose of trying to prove the existence of an indigenous
holocaustic event, if by that term we mean the widespread destruction of a
native people by colonists. That is not their purpose. For the most part, many
do not themselves believe that a holocaust, like the massive destruction of
the Jews by Germans in this century, ever happened here in America. The
word *holocaust* is seldom if ever found in the vocabulary of the scientists who
dig and study Indian bones in America.

Rather, it seems to many observers that what scientists are trying to prove
and document for posterity is that Indians are migrants, like everyone else,
to this continent, that they came here like pioneers looking for a place to settle,
and they did that and now their time is gone and so are they. Most of the work
of these scientists is based upon the "empty continent" idea so dear to American and European colonists, and the Bering Strait Theory of migration so
acceptable to everyone except most Indians. Scientists who delve into the
Indian bone controversy are attempting to trace the various waves of human
migration to America, not to prove that a holocaust happened but to say that
this continent was once empty, and Indians, like everyone else, came here
from some other place. Some do their work by looking at teeth and bones,
others do it by looking at rocks and sedimentary material, and others by
countless other means. So-called humanists and multiculturalists are doing
it through their own methodologies, but no one seems to know if they are
on the right track either.

In a museum in Flagstaff in 1967, Arizona State University anthropologist
Christi Turner II discovered a collection of native bones excavated years previously from an arroyo situated below First Mesa on the Hopi Indian Reservation. This collection, long neglected and gathering dust on some laboratory shelves, has been labeled the *Polacca Wash bones.* Turner took the bones
to his office at his university to study for two years and carbonated them at
1580 A.D. Today, after decades of study and his first discovery of the long-
neglected Polacca Wash bones, Turner has concluded that these are the bones
of the Anasazi, a desert people who occupied Chaco Canyon in what is now
the state of Arizona and who abandoned their homelands before the American occupancy of the region. The reasons for this abandonment have been,
until Turner, unknown.

Turner's thesis is that the Anasazi became cannibals, ate each other and
their relatives, and caused such fear and revulsion that they simply vanished.
Thus, the long-anticipated answer to the question of "Whatever happened

to the vanished Anasazi?" has been given by Turner's science: they became cannibals and ate themselves. Turner claims that his research revealed several important discoveries, and he tells us how he came to these conclusions. First, he noticed that the bones from the museum in Flagstaff, the Polacca Wash bones, resembled the animal bones he had found in prehistoric Anasazi garbage mounds commonly called by scientists "food trash." Thinking that they were not "prehistoric," as had been previously supposed, Turner was reminded of some recent, modern-day bones he had examined in California in a police case in which the person had been "savagely beaten" to death. He concluded that the Polacca Wash bones exhibited the same traits as those California bones. His conclusion, after years of study, was that the Polacca Wash bones were those of the Anasazi and that they represented an internecine massacre that revealed that the thirty people to whom the bones belonged had been savagely beaten to death and consumed.

Since the bones looked to Turner like the "food trash" of his previous California examination, he wanted proof of his now-emerging theory of Cannibalism, i.e., that the thirty people whose bones made up the Polacca Wash had been savaged and eaten by their killers. This was and is an unpopular theory among scientists, and Turner, if nothing else, likes to take up unpopular themes. He has many detractors, among them the Hopi, who simply believe that the Anasazi were their precursors and represent a part of the prehistory of the People, that the Anasazi became the Hopi and did not "vanish" at all. A Hopi theory of "being and becoming" seems to be a concept most anthropologists who study them cannot fathom. Another detractor of Turner's theory is Anthropologist Kurt Dongoske, who as late as 1996 said that Anasazi cannibalism would not be proved until human remains were actually found in prehistoric human excrement. Thus, Turner accepted such a challenge and set about finding evidence of such human remains and excrement.

Human excrement is called coprolite in scientific vocabulary and is found, apparently, in "prehistoric" sites as well as in diggings of more modern sites. Several scientists such as Richard Marlar, an associate professor of pathology at the University of Colorado Health Sciences Center in Denver, and Brian Billman, an assistant professor at the University of North Carolina at Chapel Hill, and his two colleagues, Patricia Lambert and Banks Leonard, who were digging at a Soils Systems archaeological site in Colorado, were called in by Turner to provide man-made samples of coprolite. They had their findings tested at a University of Nebraska laboratory, and then looked around for a "control" stool sample with which they could compare their samples. They needed a way to identify the fact that human meat and human tissue had really passed through another human being's digestive system. The substance they were looking for, called human myoglobin, is a protein found only in skeletal and heart muscle and could only be evidenced in an intestinal tract if consumed by eating. They put together a chemically contrived sample that they used as the "control" sample and used that for comparison.

In order for these scientists to get to this point in their reasoning, they had to convince themselves that they had found what they considered chopped-up, "boiled" and "burned" and "roasted" human bones, the basis for a cannibalistic meal, at the sites that were available to them throughout this decades-long study. They went to the kivas on Indian sites to find bones that they could use as samples and that could be compared to the Polacca bones and others, and also to find excrement that could in no way be verified as having gone through an intestinal tract.

As they gathered their samples, they incorporated terms indicating culinary arts, sometimes making the distinction between bones that had been "boiled" and those that had been "roasted." They no longer confined their vocabulary to the term "burned" when they discussed their findings, because that would have indicated merely savage killing, not cannibalism. Their explanation for any variations in the samples was their supposition that variation was inherent in the activity itself, i.e., the eating and excreting of human flesh that they believed took place, though obviously there might have been any number of other explanations. Part and parcel of their evidence was that they also found axes, hammerstones, and two large flakes with sharp cutting edges, and they called these the "butchering" tools, not just killing tools, as a way to put the findings into the context of their theory of cannibalism. All in all, they gathered twenty-one samples of what they believed to be the tested coprolite or excrement that they said showed the presence of human myoglobin protein. When they devised maps showing various sites, they concluded that Chaco Canyon was the locus of this Anasazi cannibalism. They set the cannibalistic activity during the period between 900 and 1150 A.D., saying that the Polacca Wash bones were the exception to the time frame, occurring much later, in 1580 A.D. They gave no explanation for this exception except to say that these are, as scientists say, the "best guesses" of various disciplines.

Another likely example of scientific inquiry concerning the evidence for internecine violence in tribal society found in old bones occurred on the Crow Creek Sioux Reservation in central South Dakota, when the newly dammed-up Missouri River, in 1960, ate away at its banks and revealed a cache of what are believed to be Indian bones. The collection of bones from the site, called by scientists from the University of South Dakota the Wanagi Kte site, was examined by University of South Dakota anthropologist Neal Zimmerman. This dig actually started in 1951 and culminated ten years later. Often the conclusions were and are mere guesses.

Wanagi Kte is translated by the Sioux, Dr. Zimmerman says, as "the killing of the spirit" or "ghost killing." He offers no further discussion of the naming of this site, nor does he really convince everyone that these are Indian bones, much less bones of the Dakota/Lakota, from whom the site takes its name. Nonetheless, Professor Zimmerman has advanced this origin and has lectured on this find both in American universities and abroad, concluding that this find was an Indian massacre that could be said to be the first known example of internecine massacre, and dating it at about 1300 A.D., Zimmerman concludes that the Sioux were the perpetrators of the crime, and the Arikara (their relatives and neighbors) were the victims. When I attended a lecture at the School of Mines and Technology in the early 1990s at Rapid City, S.Dak., and expressed skepticism concerning Zimmerman's conclusion, he responded by saying that his conclusion was "the best guess of scientists from several disciplines." While this Wanagi Kte site is not said to be a cannibalistic site, it is used as an example of internecine massacre, a heretofore unexplored phenomenon. It is described here to indicate how it is that conclusions are reached, i.e., "the best guess from several disciplines." The question of whether this is good science, reliable science that says something real about the world, is rarely posed and never answered.

The problem of this kind of scholarship, which is based mostly on supposition and even on what they call the scientific principle of Occam's razor, i.e., the simplest explanation fitting the facts is probably the right one, is that it makes Indians and Indian scholars into firetruck and ambulance chasers when they resist accepting the results of this science. Indeed, Indians rarely get around to doing their own work, answering their own queries, because they have to put out the fires of those scholars whose work seems to defame and destroy them, or at the very least, goes against the grain of what they know from their traditions. Many scholars among the Sioux hold to the theory that there have never been endemic intertribal violence, cannibalism, massacre, torture, or mass killings among them, domestically. The complaint is that from the ubiquitous and pervasive work of scientists continually discovering bones and studying them and their ancient tribal environments, there is no method by which the Sioux theory about themselves and their past can be verified.

Challenges to ancient knowledge, i.e., the oral traditions of indigenous peoples, are nothing new; in fact, much of the archival material of the historical societies or the Christian religious orders in North and South America or the academic organizations around the world often suggest that native knowledge is mere fraud as it tries to answer its concerns about origins and spirituality. There is a long legacy of omission and distortion, and recent scholars in the sciences are beginning to admit to these distortions and omissions so there might be some reason for hope. Though there is an effort on the part of some scholars to understand and expose the biases of various disciplines driven to convert and assimilate the native populations of the world, these challenges of science and belief and religion remain powerful influences in academia. The challenge to the veracity of the native voice often gains authority by narrowing the canon and making it more and more exclusive. The argument concerning the veracity of scientific knowledge that emerges from European thought vis-à-vis native and/or multicultural interests in gathering knowlege is a battle of significance at the close of the twentieth century.

Examples of this battle arise from literary studies, ethnology, and anthropology, as well as from what is called hard science and even politics. A foremost example comes to mind: following the emergence of a powerful native voice in ethno-biography from Guatemala, that of Rigoberta Menchú, who won the Nobel Peace Prize in 1992, scientific researchers and writers and university professors began a campaign to challenge the work of such cultural and political and modern storytellers through scientific research.

In the mid-1990s, David Stoll, a Stanford-educated anthropologist now teaching at Middlebury College, went to Chajul, Guatemala, a village near Rigoberta's hometown, Chimel, the setting for her memoir *I, Rigoberta Menchú,* for the express purpose of looking into the facts of the Menchú memoir. He conducted 120 interviews in order to discredit her memoir, saying that not all Mayans agree with Menchú's assessment of the leftist political struggle in that country. After his on-site inquiry, Professor Stoll wrote that Menchú was not a "witness," was not "poor," was not "uneducated," was not "brutalized," and was not "oppressed" as she had said in her book; she was, instead, a peasant whose family farmed in a small village, a woman who became part of the leftist political factions attempting to overthrow the government, intimating that she probably was unreliable as a teller of history.

Menchú's publisher, Verso, has had to attest publicly to the "accuracy" and the "truth" of her story, saying that they think it is a very accurate and eloquent statement of how things appeared to Menchú, who was twenty-three years old at the time she fled her homeland. Menchú herself has said that she will defend her book "to the death." The reason to look at such "documentary" evidence is to indicate that it is not only the sciences that are involved in this contemporary distortion of the native voice, it is other forces as well.

The Stoll controversy follows closely the publication of a text called *The Real Thing*, edited by George M. Gugelberger and published by Duke University Press in 1996, a collection of articles on rhetoric and literary criticism. It claims to be a study of language. It is probably more accurately described as the study of language as an art used to discredit the voice you don't want to hear; thus, quite naturally, the emerging voice of the native storyteller has gotten caught up in this very scholarly and academic discourse concerning the canon. *The Real Thing* suggests that while the native voice of the latter part of this century arose on what it calls "the margins" of institutional power, it has been canonized by the "academic left," moving it from the margin to the center. In the process, this text suggests, the veracity of what native scholars say can be questioned on the basis of fraud and inauthenticity.

The work by Dr. Stoll and the Gugelberger collection both seem to represent a backlash to the emerging native voice rather than a critique of how native knowledge is expressed. The current struggle for primacy by science, by anthropologists, by the defenders of the advocates of western civilization and right-leaning politicos is not new. At the initiation of Native American Studies as an academic discipline in the early 1960s and 1970s, antagonists disguised as scholars often registered their objections and suggested that such intellectual "movements" were political rather than intellectual.

While the political agenda of this kind of controversy should not be ignored, the attempt to contextualize the politics of either side should be registered within a broader scholarly debate concerning who is authenticated to write colonial history. Many intellectuals today believe that the colonial elitists should make room for the voice of the colonized. Even Stoll, who spent a predoctoral decade writing about the positive work of Protestant missionaries in Latin America, admits that he wrote this critique of Menchú's autobiography because it ignores the "less militant" Mayans who did not side with the guerilla movement but simply wanted the fighting in their country to end. In that admission he suggests that all voices must be taken into account but does little to assist in determining how the strength of the colonizer's institutions overwhelm an ordinary native voice.

One is reminded of the nineteenth-century arguments between Sioux Chief Sitting Bull of the Northern Plains of America, who refused to give up land to white colonists, and his "less-militant" opponent or detractor, John Grass of the same tribe, who was interested in accommodating white settlement, eventually (some say) making it possible to lay the groundwork for Sitting Bull's assassination, blaming the victims, and giving up the lands. The ability of historians and scholars to assess and disclaim the influence of dissenters in any cultural controversy is well known. To put it in today's postcolonial language, Sitting Bull was the "leftist" and John Grass the "conservative," and quite naturally, then, Grass was to be believed by the mainstream and supported by political dialogue and Sitting Bull was not.

What Stoll and the Gugelberger scholars and all those examiners of ancient Indian bones fail to recognize is that there is a real history, not just an academic one, that underlies these kinds of controversies. Whether, as Dr. Stoll believes, leftist politics expressed in Rigoberta Menchú's work is damaging to Indian societies, this bias, which initiates the interest for white American scholars in her work, may be the poorest coin academics trade with, because it eventually proves to be damaging to the nature of an emerging dialogue. Whether Sitting Bull was a threat to his people and John Grass was not is an idea that inculcates bias in historical scholarship. In the final analysis of what it is that scientists do, accepting the measuring stick of "*the best guess* from several disciplines" to give advocacy to scholarly analysis may lead scholars down the wrong path. What we believe as writers and scholars invariably infects what we know.

Once a long time ago, I read a comment by some scholar whose name I have forgotten, and he said something like "beliefs are actually stinking fish that ought to be held at arm's length." He was attempting to make the distinction between "belief" and "reason" and "science," obviously coming down on the side of science and reason against "belief." In the case of what has happened to scientific inquiry concerning the indigenous populations of North and South America, this distinction in favor of science over belief smells to high heaven. The "best guesses" by scientists smell no better than out-and-out beliefs, and they probably ought to be held at arm's length too.

11

LIFE AND DEATH IN THE MAINSTREAM
OF AMERICAN INDIAN BIOGRAPHY

I've been an avid reader of Biography, ever since I took a course in it as an undergraduate—you know, Lincoln Steffens and the Victorians. Yet today, as I read the recent biographies of American Indians, I have become disillusioned with how the genre has developed in specific instances concerning Indian lives. It was the scholar Natalie Curtis who said decades ago that the white friend had come to be the pencil in the hand of the Indian, so I suppose I should have been prepared for the ongoing work of writers who think they are scholars who think they are literary artists who think they are social critics.

The three works discussed in this essay are: *Chief: The Life History of Eugene Delorme, Imprisoned Santee Sioux,* edited by Inez Cardozo-Freeman and published by the University of Nebraska Press in 1994; *An Indian in White America* by Mark Monroe, edited by Carolyn Reyer and published by Temple University Press in 1994; and *Black Elk: The Sacred Ways of a Lakota* by Wallace Black Elk and William S. Lyon, published by HarperCollins in 1991.

After reading these works and several others that are similar examples of improvisational works that constantly mine their own currency, I've come to the conclusion that if there is to be a significant debate about the intellectual and political concerns of Indian America in the twenty-first century, we should not expect that it will come from biographers. In fact, to read them leads us into all sorts of trivial analyses. Even the preeminent historian Patricia Limerick says in her *Legacy of Conquest:* "Most unsettling is the experience of reading an Indian autobiography and finding in the details of the individual's life no mention of the federal policies that were supposedly the key determinants of Indian life" (p. 195). Reading Indian biographies and taking them seriously has led this major history scholar to say that it is possible to "overplay the significance of federal policy," and besides, she suggests, to study federal Indian policy leaves us with a "persistent muddle" that is far from clear and "no one knows what to do."

From the looks of things in so-called modern native scholarship in this discipline and others, then, the historic Lincoln Steffens's suggestion of the nineteenth century, that the scholars in this genre would contribute to the understanding of their own times, is sadly off the mark. At least as far as Indians are concerned.

Today's anthropologists, folklorists, humanists, photographers, and historians who write most of the biographies of Indians indicate by the depressing stories they tell that the time of gods on earth is past (to quote a friendly anthropologist of my acquaintance), and the present is the time for disappointment, mediocrity, and irrelevance. Even as a new generation of native intellectuals is said to be emerging as novelists, artists, university professors, visionaries, and politicians, the biography (sometimes called the ethnographic biography) of the American Indian, largely written, named, and defined by non-native scholars, remains a staple commodity of university publishing houses in the United States, and an acclaimed category in the teaching of Native American Literatures. This has occurred without much comment until recent years. Now, however, literary critics are entering the field of definition, writing books trying to make sense of this flourishing narrative art, which was once the domain of those trained in ethnography, and an educated American Indian public is asking scholars who engage in the discussion of failed and resurrected individual lives to be specific about the function of this literary genre as it is absorbed into academic fields of inquiry.

The "as-told-to" stories under review here are classic examples both in form and style of why this discussion is called for at this time. The subjects and their biographers begin by issuing the expected lamentations about being Indian in America, the latest even copping the name. They've made redundant statements of how the white man took over the land and how the Indians themselves, alas, fell to drinking great quantities of booze, committing debaucheries of various kinds, and emerging from such a hapless condition, rhetorically at least, redeemed and at the edge of self-knowledge.

This form and style is not unconnected to the art of biography, which has a long history in Europe and a more than bicentennial life on this continent, and, at least as far as Indians are concerned, it might have been expected that it would be developed into a literary genre for the purpose of capturing the essence of the old tradition in hagiography: limited, epic-like tragedy followed by glorious expiation.

Hagiographies, for those of you who don't wish to consult your dictionaries, are the life stories of the saints of the Roman Catholic church, which Indian mission-school students read in various childlike versions, stories of the idealizing and worshipping of models of virtue. Maybe this accounts for the Indian subject's willingness to participate in this brand of awful storytelling. Biography, the account of a particular life written by an Other, and Autobiography, a life written by the subject him/herself, are, naturally, generic relatives of Hagiography. The Ethnographic Biography can be described as a life story written about an individual in his or her own cultural context by someone outside of that context, the ethnographic method suggesting objectivity.

The point is, quite naturally, that the telling of the lives of Indian Others as genre has existed for a variety of reasons in the past, but if the works discussed here are models, it exists largely for the purpose of pedestal-raising. Pedestals are those places where heroes and heroines are placed. Surely in America there has been a curious method of making heroes and heroines of native personages, the Pocahontas, Sacajawea, Squanto, and Black Elk ideals, with the hateful Magua and warlike Geronimo and Inkpaduta as antiheroes. Indians who liked white folks, dedicating themselves to being helpful in working toward white needs and anticipations, have provided the most important lives for examination. While these figures may not be entirely saintlike, they are certainly useful models for the discussion of virtue based on unambiguous values in an ambiguous society.

In the case of hagiographies about the American Indian, they are always written by white writers, as-told-to mouthpieces who offer their services because, one supposes, Indians whose lives need to be told and held up to acclaim are unable to acquire the necessary literary skills to do the writing themselves. These white writers have social commentary as their main intent, and this means that the subjects are almost always marginalized or on the edge of their own communities, families, art, or profession. Even in the face of some remarkable native memoirists (i.e., N. Scott Momaday, who wrote *Names;* Ray A. Young Bear, who wrote *Black Eagle Child;* Joseph Iron Eye Dudley, who wrote *Choteau Creek: A Sioux Reminiscence;* and Percy Bull Child, who wrote *When the Sun Came Down*), as-told-to hagiographies by white writers seem to flourish.

An exemplar of the "mouthpiece" model has been *Black Elk Speaks,* a manuscript penned by John Neihardt just a few years before the Indian Reorganization Act was passed, when an era of astonishing access to native peoples for the purpose of gathering such scholarship occurred on the Indian homelands. This book has been, in many important ways, the modern prototype of the more recent formula of the past decade.

Some of these formulaic strategies are quite obvious even in the most cursory readings in the genre. For example, in the telling by the now-deceased Nick Black Elk, a man named Neihardt came to his door and said he wanted to write about his life. If you are to believe this telling, Nick recognized immediately his premonition of the appearance of this man and claimed it to be a signal that such a collaboration was destiny. Mark Monroe, in *An Indian in White America,* edited by Carolyn Reyer, says that one day in 1969, during a period when (having been sober for six months) he was setting out to run for police magistrate in the little border town of Alliance, Neb., "Ken Lincoln came to our door and introduced himself to me"—a fortuitous event with lasting consequences. Lincoln, a Nebraska native of white Alliance, and a man who has tried hard to transcend what he calls the "redneck prejudices" of the region, was to become the manager of Monroe's brief campaign for public office. Monroe didn't win the election and Lincoln left town for graduate school, and eventually he became a full professor and expert on native affairs at UCLA.

While Monroe himself says at the conclusion of his story, "I'm just a common man, trying to make a living for his family," Lincoln, in the Afterword, tells us that such a homely assessment can't be all there is to it: "A man has the need to dream, to measure the distance from past to present, to recall his time and witness changes" (p. 229). Further, he claims historical development in Mark's recollections: "His story charts a powerful change in Western ethnic dialogue where Native Americans now speak for themselves as peacemakers," and he compares Monroe's "vision" to Ghandi, Kennedy, and Martin Luther King.

This seems at the very least puffered praise for a perfectly competent, decent Indian male who pulled his life together, "went to treatment," and later worked in various unremarkable and federally funded social service positions among the people. Do not misunderstand the point here. This is not to say arrogantly that a plain life is unworthy. On the contrary, this is a valued life. But Ghandi? King?

Editor Reyer did not come to the story until sometime after Lincoln's appearance, when she read an article Mark had written for a Christian church magazine in 1982. She initiated the meeting, corresponding first by letter, and later during a family visit. According to the Preface, it was not long before Reyer was adopted by Mark's daughters as their mother, and by 1986 Mark was talking into a tape recorder, telling his story, which had been meant to address social problems in his community. This "adoption" process has become an important characteristic of this genre, as is evidenced in many previously published papers, and Inez Cardozo-Freeman, the humanities scholar from Ohio State University who edited *Chief,* claims it as well.

Inez Cardozo-Freeman, in recording the life story of the Santee Sioux subject Eugene Delorme, has put a name and definition to this "adoption" phenomenon that is slightly different from the anthropological/folkloric model by saying in her Introduction: "My approach legitimizes and explains the very personal and revealing passages in this introduction which tell why Delorme and I became "like family" and why he trusted me despite the fact that I am a square john and not a part of his underworld culture. Within the scholarship of *reflexive ethnography,* talking about my reasons for caring for Delorme and others like him who are often regarded as pariahs in our society is extremely important" (pp. xviii–xix).

She goes on, then, to describe the source of her deep sympathy for Delorme's life, which lies, she says, in the fact that her only child suffers from schizophrenia and has led a life of desperation, victimization, and psychiatric institutionalization. Delorme, after years of struggle, was in the psychiatric unit of a state hospital in Washington state as the manuscript for *Chief* was finished in August 1993.

In spite of this dismal fact, and Cardozo-Freeman's final sentence, "He is unable to function successfully in the free world" (p. 214), there is something cathartic about the ending. Delorme seems to recognize that in order to live he must be "under lock and key." When the two of them drive around Tacoma on one of their last visits together, Cardozo-Freeman buys him a tape recorder, an art table, and art supplies, "hoping to encourage him to work again on his beautiful Northwest Indian paintings" and urges him to "keep in touch."

The narrative pattern of poverty, alcoholism, the sobering-up period, the repetition of all that, and the final transformation toward that which leads to insight into self is not what America needs to recognize as overwhelmingly important facets of Indian history. White racism toward Indians born of colonial fiscal and land policy, a notable feature of this region in which these stories take place, is entirely missing from the tellings, and thus the stories themselves seem exploitive.

Such biographers as Cardozo-Freeman and Reyer, half in love with their subjects, impressionistic rather than analytical, record as scholarship heartrending examinations of Indian male failure in the modern white world and attempt to say that these lives are the history not only of this individual subject, but somehow the history of Indian America as well. This, too, follows the pattern. We are told that Neihardt, when he talked of his work with the old churchman, was said to believe the people's hoop "broken," and insisted that Nick Black Elk told the story not only of himself, but of his people the Oglalas, and perhaps even of all the people of the Sioux Nation. Today, if you are to believe the "new-agers," he has told a story for all humanity.

The truth is, these as-told-to lives (even that of the primogenitor Nick Black Elk) are at the margins of Indian history, not the center of it. The reason for that is that they are based in sociology, not the literature of the people. After "a good read" in the Indian-based hagiography milieu, there is little real understanding of the political pathology at the heart of American Indian experience. The seeds of continuing crises in our Indian communities, while laid bare and exposed, are given little in-depth cause-and-effect analysis, and thus no problem-solving model will emerge from these fields of inquiry. The meticulous, heartrending examination of Indian failure by writers who may or may not know they are from the world of colonial masters is depressing and distasteful. These scholars are providing almanacs of Indian faux heroes and faux heroines (no pun intended), contrived celebrity registers, if you will, that serve to reinvent Indians in some cheapened mode. Native grandsons and granddaughters, the latter-day readers of these materials in the coming decades, may eventually come to believe in the message of this contrived heroic age: failure as prologue to human accomplishment for Indians, redemption or expiation as prize.

If the biographies of Indian males published by university presses are rendered remarkable only in terms of their victory over fractured lives, another generic mode may be found in the more popular life story characterized as "translation" by a man who claims victory over spiritual power. This is a kind of life story that is supposed to "translate" for mainstream readers the esoteric knowledge of native shamans. A white anthropologist, William S. Lyon, says of his biography of Wallace Howard, who has claimed the Black Elk name even though he bears no familial (i.e., blood) connection to the original Nick Black Elk (*Black Elk: The Sacred Ways of a Lakota*): "This book is an attempt at translation" (p. xvi), meaning that "our assumptions about the basic nature of reality are false," and Indian people like Wallace Howard are "advanced physicists" who have a few things to tell us about reality.

Lyon says, too, "I consider Wallace's words here to be more accurate with regard to his personal understandings of the sacred mystery powers than any of the material written in the name of Nick Black Elk." The reasons this anthropologist gives for such a testament is that he used a tape recorder and

Wallace talked in English. Wallace's claim to English is in itself remarkable, since he tells his collaborator he was the first in his family to learn English and remembers that between the ages of five and nine he was taught by the spirits "all the English terminologies used in the universities today." If white anthropologists believe that, they will believe anything.

The first part of *Black Elk: The Sacred Ways of a Lakota* is said to cover Wallace's early training as a shaman, and the second half centers on his "application" of his sacred powers, so in some ways this book may be seen as a how-to book rather than genuine biography. It is used here to illustrate how far the genre of the biography has come in the dissemination of Indian life history subjects.

To argue that Hagiography (precursor to Biography) is just an expansion of western idealization stories (which is, admittedly, a far cry from the murderous savage Indian story of the past), or to argue that how-to books on spirituality for the new-agers is offensive, or that stories about overcoming alcoholism are redundant is not the point. To say that collaborations are corrupt or modification of genre development in literature and ethnology is an abuse or that white anthropologists are gullible and therefore quite wrong limits the possibility of academic freedom so necessary to the growth of intellectual curiosity and speculation. That is not the purpose here.

The reason to assess the works that claim to be telling the life histories of Indians cannot be said to be just a war of words. It is, in fact, a war for the future of Indian intentions. Art and literature and storytelling are at the epicenter of all that an individual or a nation intends to be. And someone more profound than most said that a nation that does not tell its own stories cannot be said to be a nation at all. To think that the reverse of that comment is still true, that at the close of the twentieth century the ascendant power of Indian storytelling still emanates from long-held patterns of colonizing nations, is profoundly disturbing.

To examine and comment publicly upon the origins and the unchanging biographical directions of the Indian story written by whites in America with so-called Indian informants and collaborators is to find out that the consequences of this scholarly activity assume a status quo whose norms are not in the hands of the subject. To know that is to move beyond a mere war of words into a place where the renewal of native consciousness can address powerful threads of tribal nationhood for the sake of the people. Challenging the status quo of these works is what must be done in Native Studies if the histories of our peoples and nations are not to be dismissed as unreliable and ridiculous.

PART THREE

ON WRITING
AND KEEPING A DIARY

Ordinarily I make notes as I do research, but I have never kept a diary nor do I write in journals—I'd like to think for the reason that George Sand gives in her Preface to the *Piffoel Journal:* "Writing a Journal means that facing your ocean you are afraid to swim across it, so you attempt to drink it drop by drop." I'd like to think I am not afraid to swim my ocean, so I keep no diaries.

Ordinarily I am fearless. When I travel, though, it is a different matter. When I travel, I am afraid of everything. . . . So on my summer 1998 trip to Mexico, I kept a journal that became the fragments of a diary. Incomplete. Unorganized.

I've shared them with no one until now.

12

FOREIGN SCULPTORS AND TIME ZONES: DIARY ENTRIES KEPT DURING A THREE-WEEK VISIT TO MEXICO, A ONE-TIME-ONLY EFFORT AT JOURNAL-KEEPING

Because of the close proximity of the two Americas, a journey into Mexico is always a reminder of what history and art have wrought. Probably it is the same across every border, and reason enough to scribble notes in a notebook.

In the company of one of my daughters, my reluctant husband, and our youngest grandson I went to Mexico in June of 1998 and spent some time thinking about history and art and the land and what I have been calling (not entirely with tongue in cheek) "the last years of the Monroe Doctrine." Now, I know that people like George Bush and Ronald Reagan and the present U.S. Congress don't agree about the demise of that early American doctrine, but it seems to me that the United States must face some realities concerning our southern neighbors. And one of the realities is that few of us can any longer support a doctrine that denies the very democratic ideals it was meant to protect.

JUNE 2, 1998

Our flight leaves Texas.

Sitting back in air-conditioned comfort, we watch an old (1980s) film and hear Crocodile Dundee say: "The Aborigines don't own the land, they belong to it."

He says this in response to the political question posed by one of his girlfriends: "What do you think of the Australian Aborigines wanting their land back?"

"The Aborigines don't own the land, they belong to it."

This is an old movie by our standards but it still plays on Dallas–Fort Worth Air as we head for the mountainous section of northern Leon, flying into a university town in an indigenous country south of Sioux country. And the movie played on. Do I understand this Dundee dialogue as Ironic? I suppose so. Because this stereotype of the indigenes (they don't own the land, they belong to it) is prevalent throughout the Americas. And because the Mexican indigenous peoples (like the Sioux and all the other indigenous peoples of this continent as well as across the globe) have done nothing in the last 300 years but make revolution to get their land back from colonists who say they have never possessed it. The truth is, even if the indigenous peoples aren't burning buildings and carrying rifles, they continue to know and believe that, *au contraire,* Dundee, *the Aborigines do own the land.* Colonial foreign policy aside, Indians own the land and want land reform to take priority in international discourse. I look about the airplane and wonder who, besides myself, finds this "entertainment" troubling.

JUNE 3, 1998

The first night we are in Guanajuato we look forward to an Evening Festival at the Internacional Teatro Juarez el callejón, an alley, should have known! "Composición, ideas y tecnología" was the name of the theatrical presentation. I'm no theater critic but these people are really into themselves! Bad flauta music/clarinets squeaking.

A male dancer, in a neon-orange body suit lit with dozens of electric bulbs that change position and hue intermittently, displays a permanent blue bulb over his penis like a huge codpiece that would shame even the most flaming Shakespeareans. This must be the cutting edge of technology and art, I say to myself. When my daughter asked an Indian on the plaza who spoke Spanish and English, "Where can we go to see Indian dancing?" he held up his hands and, horrified at the question, said in English, "NO! NO! We have no Indians here."

Walking back to our apartment along the narrow cobbled streets, we see a woman who sits in a doorway and we listen to her sing a song about this place, Guanajuato: "La vida no vale nada, empieza siempre llorando," loosely translated as "Life is worth nothing, it begins always crying." We heard that song many, many times during the next days and we took it to be a truth expressed in Mexican street songs.

JUNE 4, 1998

"Guanajuato is to Mexico what Flanders is to Europe," says Carlos Fuentes (or, to put it into my Indian context, what Pine Ridge is to the Sioux? or Gallup to the Navajo?), "the very core of a distinct style of life and the preservation in all purity of tradition. Their ancestors," Fuentes goes on, "during the centuries of New Spain were the students and foot-soldiers of Voltaire and Rousseau. The citizen of Guanajuato, in other words, is a practical, talented, and certified hypocrite. What in an Indian context is a blatant hypocrisy, in a Guanajuatan, is talented insinuation."

JUNE 5, 1998

I went out to buy sandals today, as you cannot live in Mexico without sandals. Small shoes were everywhere just as small people were everywhere. I tried on several pairs that almost fit. Small. Too small. "Muy Grande, muy grande," I kept saying, signaling with broad gestures. "Sioux women have big feet . . . muy grande. How else would we have survived out on the north prairies?!!" Finally, I bought a pair of the smallest in men's sizes. "Cool . . . a-a-ah."

JUNE 6, 1998

The marriage of Professor Diego Rivera y Acosta and La Señorita Maria Barrientos y Rodriguez in 1886 produced twin boys. Carlos, unfortunately, did not survive his infancy, but the other grew up to be Diego Rivera, famous for revealing the feeling of the old Mesoamerican cultures in his modern paintings and drawings. His art is said to be the initiator of what can be called authentic cultural revolutionary art with nationalistic roots. Diego's ancestral home, now a museum, is not far from the spot where the revolutionary arsonist, El Pipila, burned out the royalist troops and saved this place, Guanajuato, the "place where the frogs come," for the people. As I looked at the many drawings and paintings done by Diego and those of Frieda Kahlo, his wretched but talented wife, I thought of an older sister of mine who has the same massive eyebrows, large eyes. The same strong mustache. My sister and I are on benign terms but rarely speak as we have little in common. What one looks for in art, says Victor Hernandez Cruz, is meditation *and* action and, in Diego's works, there is the search for a comfortable alliance between the two that is quite compelling.

JUNE 9, 1998

At the university there is a white American student who wrote a paper on native blood quantum, never having been out of Chicago, never having seen an Indian. He won a prize for that essay and went to Arizona and took up with a half-Navajo girl. He is becoming a legal voice, an Indian law expert even before he is out of law school. He will pass the bar exam and may become one of the folks who wants to be in charge of Indian law. The greater portion of the population of Indian reservations in the United States knows this would-be scholar well. They have seen him in court arguing for the right to be an American.

Tomcats raged last night and woke me from a sound sleep, and I stared at the starless sky until dawn. Fundamentalist Christian Mexicans (which I mistakenly thought was a contradiction in terms) came to the door to tell us of the word of God. We told them we didn't speak Spanish, that one colonial language, English, was enough for us . . . and they went away, smiling. Feeding the pigeons in the plaza later, I heard car alarms in the streets below for hours. The pigeons in the plaza are friendly. I was reminded of when I was a child feeding chickens in the yard, sometimes in competition with bull snakes, who, oddly, seem to like chicken eggs, fuzzy baby chicks, and the warm nests made of straw and molt. My parents would drive me home from school for the summer holiday and I would wonder about the future. What am I doing here? I would ask silently. A little green/white house, many horses, a few cattle, haying in August, time stretching on like the longest pause. I would go to the shed and "pick" eggs, using the same verb I would use when I went to "pick" plums and chokecherrries at the creek.

JUNE 9, 1998

The treaty-protected lands of the Sioux were lost before they were won because settlers were invited in before the Sioux had a chance. Thousands of acres in the last decade have been lost to tribal title. In spite of the sounds of fireworks and church bells resounding in the air here in this Mexican town, because another student has passed his or her exams and graduation is finished, I find myself thinking of that old Dakota song our male relatives sing about *tunkashina*'s long life and his connection to a specific geography: *heche ya ya ya wiconi ye ye.*

JUNE 13, 1998

The Pyramid of the Sun at Teotihuacán just north of Mexico City has 242 steps. And the Pyramid of the Moon has 121 steps. My twelve-year-old grandson informs me of these statistics as he descends, changed irrevocably, a year younger than when he ascended.

The Plaza de la Constitución is the formal name for El Zócalo, which means "plinth," according to a Spanish-language dictionary I have consulted. *Taku?* *Taku?* Plinth??? I consult an English-language dictionary, which says a plinth is a pedestal or a column. It is an architectural term. El Zócalo is the second largest plaza in the world, second only to Red Square in Moscow, they say, and all of these plazas, of course, signify military regimes, even the plazas here at these sacred pyramids, built and abandoned a few hundred years after Jesus Christ was born, to face the massive cathedrals as old as anything but the land.

In Mexico City, the largest city in the world other than Río, the streets are full of tiny green-and-white Volkswagen taxicabs. To get to a downtown tourist hotel you take your life in your hands. Our first driver was a skinny youth much preoccupied with his shingled hairdo who played Madonna on his radio, drove at warp speed, and glared at everyone in sight including us. Our next driver was a silent, calm, one-eyed old man who drove as though we all had nine lives and there was nothing, therefore, to worry about. He, too, glared at the other drivers and faked them out over and over again. His radio played Hoagie Carmichael in Spanish, and I resolved that would be my next CD purchase, an offering to the green-and-white gods for the miracle of our survival.

We see tiny children crouched in doorways playing tiny accordians. There is food, food everywhere, but not a crumb to eat! Not for this diarrhea case, anyway. The soccer game is BIG on the television in the restaurant where I carefully sip tea. A flautist is trying to sell his wares. An organ-grinder is adding to the decible level, which is already almost unbearable. They say he used to have a monkey who eventually left for the countryside for some peace and quiet. The roar of Volkswagens and taxis and delivery trucks goes on until two or three o'clock in the morning. Do these folks ever sleep?

There is flame and fire and spit on every corner. They must cook billions and billions of *pollos* in this country. Night and day. It's the one Spanish word one cannot help but learn. Warp-speed taxis aside, the traffic here is efficient, and we never missed a deadline as we hurried about trying to see everything. Blood-filled mosquitoes were everywhere in the bathroom of our hotel. Squishing them on the mirror became *Nieto*'s pastime. I brushed my teeth every morning looking at long streaks of the blood sacrifice.

JUNE 15, 1998

We returned to Guanajuato on an air-conditioned "luxury" tourist bus and knew that we had been on a wonderful trip to the land of Oz, one we would not soon forget. We watched from our windows the passing of the country-side, which is divided into small squares, small acreages with precise rows and huge aloe vera–looking cacti (agave) edging the fields. Corn and other crops flourish here among the huge and ever-present rural electric towers.

As a taxi deposited us at the plaza near our apartment, we noticed that the plaza was filled with people. Again. Wasn't it just the other day that there were bodies against bodies like this in the plaza in recognition of the celebration of Corpus Christi? The Body of Christ. The Body of Christ. The Body of Christ. The Body of Christ.

The answer is *si,* but now we have St. Antony to consider. Instead of a wonderful night's sleep we were subjected to an all-night pageant in the saint's honor, people walking behind statues and coffins, making "stations" and signs of the cross, people selling hot dogs wrapped in bacon, bags of very unevenly sorted peanuts fresh from the fields. And constant drums from five o'clock until midnight, at which time the dogs started barking and the fire-works began.

As I tossed in my bed I wondered redundantly: "Don't these people *ever* sleep? Do they know the meaning of *silencio*? Even I know that word in Span-ish, but I'm alone! Alone!

The rain didn't come tonight. Even the rain gods wouldn't dare intrude on this cacaphony of human panic! They are powerless, too, in the face of this outrage! The squeal of rockets filled the night. I wanted to think that it might have been the revolutionaries following Emilio Zapata into the city to defend the land, but no, it was only homemade hand grenades, made and thrown by students proclaiming their academic success and graduation, and hundreds and hundreds of sweaty bodies following a Christian statue brought here by the Spaniards centuries ago. No wonder this country with its massive productive economy—the thirteenth largest in the world, I'm told—can't feed its people.

They've got to get some sleep!

JUNE 16, 1998

In Mexico, the invaders built Christian cathedrals on top of ancient native temples and obliterated the physical traits of civilized Mayan, Olmec, Zapo-tec, Mixtec, Toltec, and even later Aztec civilizations. It was the attempted and many times successful obliteration of native peoples' ways, customs that had predated the invaders by many, many centuries. Surely that's what foreign sculptors like Ziolkowski and Borglum had in mind when they began blowing up mountains to create Mount Rushmore and Crazy Horse Mountain in the sacred Black Hills of what is now called South Dakota, that essential place of Lakota/Dakota civilization.

They do it because they can and they do it because they must. It is the way of colonizers.

Christianity, the religion of Spanish invaders, was not negotiable in the lands that are now called Mexico. The spiritual claim to the ownership of the physical, therefore, became law. The claim to the ownership of the physical traits of the Black Hills in South Dakota was not negotiable, either. And so the Christians and the democratizers and the capitalists have settled down in the Black Hills. The invaders will, one way or another, possess, exploit, and use the physical place that has always been essential to Sioux life. There is nothing to stop them, as there was nothing to stop the invaders of Mexico. Not even the courts. In Sioux country, the courts said in 1980 that the invaders were thieves, but they have been neither indicted nor removed. And sadly, my observation here in Mexico is that these people have been thoroughly overtaken. Even in Chiapas, the protracted Zapatista insurrection in southern Mexico is given no credence by the people in power, the press, the man in the street. The public is told that it is a rebellion whose leadership is dominated by "non-indigenous partisans," and is thereby seriously flawed as an indigenous movement.

JUNE 17, 1998

We still don't know what *milanesa* really means, but *Nieto* orders it at every restaurant and eats it with great relish.

I noticed that I did not have a back pain when I woke up to shower this morning.

My husband, dark-skinned with brown eyes, walks these streets slowly, slightly stooped, as though he might have belonged here once. A man from one of the tribes of the northwestern United States, he fits in here, his white shirt open at the neck, sleeves slightly rolled up. Like the Mexicans around him, he shops in the morning. Makes slices of fruit for the afternoon and then takes a nap. He is a patient, tolerant man.

Our daughter the law scholar is a woman of much stamina, good looks, and good health. She is smart, studies hard, and has as her highest priority the raising of her son into a decent human being. She is the kind of girl, like her sisters, who makes a mother proud.

JUNE 18, 1998

I am embarrassed to say that I learned the thrust and meaning of a new word today, one that everyone knows, of course, but seldom uses, one that I should have paid more attention to in my thinking: *telluric, tellurism.* (I am reading Octavio Paz's *Convergences.*) Several years ago I was invited to read poetry at a place called Telluride, Colorado, and I was curious, then, about the name of that place, though I did no reading nor did I inquire about its significance. I did not accept the invitation, so the place has remained in my mind just a place of possibility. What I have found out about the word from which that place takes its name in the last few days is that literary critics used the word *telluric* in the past as "a term of praise." Octavio Paz, the Mexican author who won the Nobel Prize for Literature in 1990, says this: "It was fashionable to emphasize that a writer had deep roots in the soil of the American Continent," and that is what *telluric* means. Paz pokes fun at those writers of yesterday, those critics of the Henry James and Walt Whitman era who used the term. He even mentions that one U.S. critic divided writers into two races: palefaces and redskins. And he finds all of this absurd.

Paz wants to believe that we all will "converge," that probably divisions based on culture, race, class don't exist, and Paz even doubts the existence of such a genre as Latin American Literatures. "Maybe," he says, "there is no such thing as 'English Poetry,' or 'French Poetry.'" "The truth is," he says, "Latin America is a historical, sociological or political concept; it designates a group of people, not a literature."

What, then, I want to ask, does designate a literature?

Paz says that even now "no one can explain satisfactorily the national differences between Argentinians and Uruguayans, Peruvians, Ecuadorians, Guatemalans, and Mexicans."

This, I think, is simply untrue!

It is said about Paz that he is a European, that his views concerning nativism are clouded because he is part of the royalist European influence so pervasive in most of Mexican life and art. It is said about him that he has long been subsidized by the Euro-Mexican government to be an official apologist, a combination Bill Moyers and Joseph Campbell in the United States, who create mythologies for public consumption. Whatever the case, it is obvious that he is among the major writers, he and Mario Vargas Llosa of Peru and others, who increasingly are taking neo-conservative positions. They have moved away from Pablo Neruda's *Alturas de Macchu Picchu,* which was published, can you believe it? in 1946.

One of the myths about Mexico is that it is a democracy, but anyone who has read even the slightest political news of this country knows that there has been a one-party rule here for decades and decades. A little like the Republican party in South Dakota. This makes for a very rich stratum of the population vis-à-vis the very poor, and this reality makes it possible for the second myth to flourish, i.e., that victimization is an important cultural characteristic of Mexicans, that the dark-skinned Mexican—indeed, the Indian—is a victim of his culture. Paz has written about this matter in a rather astute way, and even he recognizes that victimization probably has little to do with culture; if you are a student of governmental strategies of exploitation, it has, rather, to do with politics!

Perhaps a more informed Mexican writer whose works should be read on this subject is Carlos Fuentes. Even he, though, disappoints me as he talks of the inevitability of the "divine couple" of Mexico, founders of the mestizo world, Cortez and Malinche.

"Travel is the original movement of literature," says Fuentes in *A New Time for Mexico,* but he says very little about travel as the essential truth-seeking strategy of politics. I like his idea, though, that "voyage and narrative are twins" because "both signify a displacement." I'm informed of that every day here on these plazas and streets.

JUNE 20, 1998

The smells of this Mexican town are pervasive, persistent, omnipresent: natural gas leakage, sewer gas, greasy chickens on a public spit, offal from dogs and birds, bad meat at open markets, sewers, sewers, sewers, tunnel gasses, cooking odors at every open restaurant door as you walk down the street, exhaust gasses from fast-moving traffic.

Newsstands display photos of massacres in Chiapas. We walk by, slowly staring at the journalistic story of this ongoing outrage as we make our way down the cobbled stairs at six o'clock in the morning hoping to catch a cab for a ride to the airport in León. I cover my mouth in order not to vomit. Three days ago I went to a clinic and talked to an Indian doctor about my stomach problems and loss of appetite and he said, "Oh yes, I treat many North Americans here with this same thing." He didn't say what "this thing" was. But others have called it Montezuma's Revenge.

JUNE 21, 1998

We just landed at the Denver Airport at a quarter to three in the afternoon. What was memorable about this trip to the southern part of the hemisphere? For those of my generation, educated since the 1950s by the experience of our lives to believe that we would inevitably be witness to the last years of the Monroe Doctrine, there is something compelling about traveling in Mexico in spite of the oppressiveness of the religiosity there.

I've concluded that we indigenous peoples must look beyond today's headlines and we must learn each others' colonial languages. Everyone in North America must become fluent in Spanish and everyone in South America must become fluent in English. Were we to speak to one another in these politically charged colonial languages, it seems to me, dynamic and pluralistic and collaborative efforts might be possible for the indigenes on this continent. Instead of using language (English and Spanish) to prolong the political order of colonialism, as we have feared, we might through multilingualism achieve actual reform without revolution. Surely, without common bilingualism in the conqueror's languages (English and Spanish) we must admit that our political monolingual dialogues have created tremendous vacuums.

To think about the use of colonial language as a solution in this way helps, though beneath the sentences there is a feeling of dread. I tell my daughter I am writing "a bit" about Mexico, but she knows little will come of it. I stretch my arms into the wind from the Colorado Rockies and know that soon I will be home in the north country. Home again, a Dakota Sioux woman who has visited a country where democracy is a myth (lower case) and the Indian people are solely dependent upon the church and the government. I have a clear recognition of this reality all around me, a recognition of the problematic histories of all indigenous peoples everywhere. This woman knows that she can bury that awful knowledge in the folds of the north wind for the moment but she cannot disown it.

13

WRITING THROUGH OBSCURITY

With some rare and wondrous exceptions, like the novels of Louise Karen Erdrich, for example, or *The New Yorker* short stories of Sherman Alexie, the writings of native Indian writers in the Americas and Canada are seldom included in what may be called "the big picture" as it is defined in national or global terms. Peter Parker, editor, and Frank Kermode, consulting editor, in their 1995 text *A Reader's Guide to Twentieth-Century Writers,* include Erdrich with Bobbie Mason, V. S. Naipaul, Ferlinghetti, and Rushdie, but not Momaday, Ortiz, Silko, or Welch, or any of the other lesser luminaries so familiar to those of us who read and study Native American Literatures. All of this exception in spite of the fact that some Indian writers of my generation in the twentieth century have written astounding and unique and flawless stories that have received disappointing audience. While this problem of obscurity and audience is certainly evidenced for most of the writers one knows, this discussion addresses the situation of the Native American writer and his or her works in particular.

The ability to write, such critics as Parker and Kermode suggest, is the only criterion for entrance into the literati, the only skill necessary to join the ranks of writers throughout the country and to produce works that will constitute an addition to the so-called canon. The suggestion such critics make is that there is nothing that bars the entry into the ranks of writers except the ability to write. Nothing, that is, except *the ability to write what is pleasing.* What one needs to write in order to be included in *A Reader's Guide to Twentieth-Century Writers* is a bit more obscure, but we can be comforted by the fact that M.F.A.s in Creative Writing are, as we speak, hard at work researching the answers to that question.

My thoughts on this phenomenon of exception would have been at one time filled with thoughts of prejudice (which is by definition the trait of literary canons), or bias or even what schools you went to (or didn't), or the class into which you were born. Lately, though, I've taken a more sanguine view of this whole matter of who is included and who is not. Perhaps I've just got to accept the fact that Garrison Keillor (America's tallest radio humorist from Minnesota) is included in the American canon of twentieth-century writers, and my good novelist friend John Keeble, a Canadian who now lives in Washington state and writes stunning novels about the culture and geography of the Northwest in such works as *Yellow Fish* and *Broken Gound,* is not. Yet I will not accept these notions without comment. *To* write what is pleasing as criterion for inclusion, an obvious matter of taste, is apparently not all there is to it.

When *Circle of Dancers,* my second novella, eventually published as part of a trilogy, was read by fourteen editors in the mainstream of East Coast publishing houses and rejected by them, it was said to be "problematic," "almost as if there is a beautiful novel there trying to emerge, but hasn't quite succeeded." My then agent was sympathetic but unable to budge any one of them.

One reader/editor went on to say: "Any storytelling must use certain well-known techniques such as strong character development, built-in suspense and visual settings, to make the story accessible to the reader. Consequently, the story seems a little flat. I find this most unfortunate because, as *From the River's Edge* proves, Elizabeth Cook-Lynn is a very talented writer and I believe with a good rewrite, *The Circle of Dancers* might be as good as the other novel."

This was a particularly baffling reading of the piece, since almost the same criticism was made about *From the River's Edge,* before it was published and even in subsequent reviews, that it was "flat" and needed "plot rewrite." In spite of these assessments, Arcade, Inc., published *From the River's Edge* in 1990, and it was a successful novel and has become a valuable addition to the fictional works studied in university courses under the rubric of Native American Fiction. It is now included in the Crow Creek Trilogy published by the University Press of Colorado in 1999.

The above-mentioned reader/editor observation, like many others, about fiction methods concerning two areas of novel development, namely character and plot, as requirement toward "accessibility," are troubling. They seem, more than anything, to be the kind of evaluation that asks that novels search for some kind of global mission called "accessibility." This probably comes as no surprise to anyone in the literary profession, since the novel, more than any other genre, is nationalistic in intent, a supposed democratic art emerging in the eighteenth and nineteenth centuries from those nations whose governmental structures were said to be democracies. Thus, to be accepted by a wide readership is a necessary thing. There is no question, as the poet Eamon Boland has observed, prizes are never given to work that excludes the reader. This unfortunate truth doesn't mean that writers whose works are notorious for excluding the reader don't produce good and meaningful literature, though. We all know that Kafka received no prizes, nor did James Joyce for *Ulysses.* Those recognitions came much later, but for contemporary writers these facts offer little solace.

Dr. Ian Watt's *The Rise of the Novel* indicated the intent of the art of novel-writing some decades ago as rising from the democracies of the European world, which were throwing off the burdens of aristocracy. Watt's text was among the first modernist works in criticism to pose questions concerning the democraticization of the art. Modernity connected to nationhood was one of his interests. It is the nature of the discussion, then, that at the close of the century ideas about such a thing as a democratic canon rather than an elitist one are still ambiguous and uncertain, the subject of controversy.

How characters are made "accessible" has seemed pretty straightforward: what they say and what others say about them. As to the matter of character development in my fiction in the specific case of *Aurelia, a Crow Creek Trilogy,* of which *Circle of Dancers* is the second piece, the protagonist is a Dakota Sioux female character, a storyteller and a witness, and she plays these roles as a marginalized figure who is neither postcolonial nor postmodern, since she is still committed to the nationalism of her native life. She knows she is uncommunicative, as do many of the characters in the story, but she fails to move on from that knowledge. Her unintentional moves toward modernism, when she attempts to understand and undertake her obligations to her tribe as required by contemporary life, are slight. Aurelia is a very marginal character in the story, which has as its central focus native/colonial relations, the destruction of a tribal environment, and in that sense her participation is almost an existential one. She seems to be rejecting the monolithic mainstream yet she has not made a clear either/or choice between the white and Indian worlds. She lacks dialogue. Purpose. The use of minimalist dialogue (a technique of characterization) and terse style (a technique of narrative) suggests that she is simply less pragmatic and less emotional than one would expect if her real intent is to become one or the other. It is not her intent to make that choice. Almost like the nameless character in Camus's *The Stranger,* she simply is and does.

If it is my intention as a writer, like that favorite writer of mine, Albert Camus, to find my way back to a few simple truths, I cannot really articulate what they are in terms of today's values. There is much mingling of Dakota myth and ritual and culture in the entire trilogy that concerns Aurelia, and if she represents me in some obscure way, she knows much but tells little, and thus seems to be a flawed character as I am a flawed writer. This woman character, as she was in *From the River's Edge,* continues to be driven by what the river and the geography and how she is connected to all that has meant to her. It is not important to her that she make the decision to be white or to be Indian, or to "assimilate" or to "resist," or to do any of the other things that usually concern characters who are stereotypes in the "caught between two cultures" themes of most contemporary Indian stories. The ruination of the river in her lifetime continues to be her tragedy, and that is because she is kin to the landscape.

Aurelia has seemed to some readers to be paralyzed and mute but she is not. The one thing that is clear about her is that she is still very much a part of the living, on-going tribal story. She is still living on the land of her ancestors, among her people and her relatives. That should give the reader hope and should forever remove her from any "victim" role, at least in tribal terms. That, too, is what distinguishes her from her brother-in-law, Sheridan Big Pipe, who is found paralyzed and mute in Texas far away from the homelands in the concluding scene of *Circle of Dancers.* His is a penultimate ending (pp. 228–33), *hin han ke,* the end this way. Here is a truly tragic character who is, much like Bartleby, the "lost letter" in Herman Melville's novella *Bartleby, the Scrivener,* outside of the tribal story forever. Aurelia, on the other hand, representing women who after all carry the ideals of any culture, has not violated her identity. Women of her tribe are expected to know and teach the language to the young. They are expected to know the stories. They "witness."

The characterizaton of Aurelia is an attempt to present a unique modern Indian woman character (reservation-based) who represents what happens to people in a colonized, suppressed cultural environment. This would seem to be a rare Indian woman character in fiction or even in history, if Pocahontas and Sacajawea are the models. Though Aurelia may seem "flat" and "inaccessible" to some because she has no traits that brand her either heroine or victim, to others there is much rich, cultural longing that is represented in her minimalist language and posture and behavior. Few, however, are able to understand the cultural integrity that is presented in this characterization. Even critics who do not claim to be in the mainstream of American literatures have their doubts about the characterization of Aurelia. Feminist critics, for example, who have read the manuscript have not liked Aurelia any more than mainstream critics have, for many of the same reasons. When editors from a feminist press in Boston read *From the River's Edge*, they specifically said they didn't like the female character because she wasn't "pulling herself up by her bootstraps" and seemed too passive.

Aurelia's role, rising as it does from native tradition and from a repressed, colonized cultural experience, must be understood as a gift, even if it is not celebrated by the mainstream or feminist thinking on the subject of womanhood. There is an array of information about Indians from which twentieth-century critics and readers and publishers make observations. This information seldom gives credit to characters who fail to meet the emotional and descriptive needs or standards of the mainstream readership.

In the first novel, *From the River's Edge*, Aurelia is Tatekeya's "mistress," a role usually maligned in mainstream America. But she is really not that in the native Dakota perspective. She plays a modern female role in a culture that at one time not so long ago was polygamous. Thus, she may represent a "second-wife" figure, and there are some native professors who have taught her in that way. Dr. Laura Tohe, a Navajo Indian literary scholar at Arizona State University, has used the novel twice, once with undergraduates and again in a graduate seminar, to show cultural change in the roles that family members adopt in the face of relentless change. Aurelia has integrity in her role as the old man's lover only if she is taken out of the mainstream American thinking concerning sex roles and, rather, is understood within a changing native culture. Further strength that this second-wife role may be legitimate is evidenced in the reaction of Rose Tatekeya, John's "legitimate" wife, his "first wife," if you will, who had "the ability to distinguish between matters which are merely profoundly serious and those which are tragic." She seems more profoundly affected by what "the failure of reciprocity among the relatives" may signify as it concerns loss of land and trust and culture than whether or not her husband carries on a love affair of ten years with a younger woman. She knows that loss of land and trust among the relatives will ultimately affect the people adversely, and if looked at from a tribal perspective, her husband's second woman partner is not part of that threat.

In the second novella, *Circle of Dancers*, Aurelia is "becoming," and in the third novella, *In the Presence of River Gods*, she "becomes." Her witness role and her connection to the Corn Wife in Dakota mythology seems genuine and real, becoming more profound as the story progresses. *Circle of Dancers* becomes Aurelia's story, and she matures in the process of the historical events that have taken place on the Dakota Sioux Crow Creek Reservation homelands during two important decades, the 1950s and 1960s, and even into the subsequent decade, the 1970s.

Unwilling, to be sure, and still resisting, Aurelia performs the essential and traditional role of the Corn Wife, one of the many wives of the buffalo in Dakota mythology, if not by intent, surely by an accident of fate or carelessness. She bears a son, a tribal heir. *Circle of Dancers* ends in 1974 with the coming of the American Indian Movement, which, in the context of her characterization, is bound to fail since the woman's role in the contemporary movement was almost nonexistent. Because the nature of the woman's role (the Yellow Woman, the Corn Wife, the White Buffalo Calf Maiden, etc.) was so minimal in that politically charged Indian movement of the 1970s, it was bound to become a mere abstraction, less powerful than it might have been had it constituted all of the ideals of a Dakota mythic female spirit along with warriorism.

The second criticism by many mainstream editors and readers to such fictional works as the trilogy called *Aurelia* is the expectation of what is called "built-in suspense" in plot-making. In the first novel, *From the River's Edge*, a trial transcript is used as a plot device, but it is mere ruse, for it soon becomes clear that who wins and who loses in the trial is unimportant. Such suspense mechanisms are seen by the reader as charade, even as the protagonist Tatekeya sees the seeking of justice as charade.

Instead of such an obvious "suspense" mechanism in the second story, *Circle of Dancers,* the story is deliberately divided into Part I, Part II, and The End. This structure suggests that this novel should not be read as a modern American novel, rising out of a deeply domestic culture preoccupied with detail and emotion and the traditional plot line of rising and falling action. This is a deliberate attempt to write a fictional novel that is not dependent upon conflict and resolution, because in the nature of American Indian struggles, there are few resolutions so long as the Indian exists in a colonial structure. The function of plot is conflict in modern American novel-writing technique, a technique taught in creative writing classes to rise to an emotional or climactic pitch out of which resolution emerges. *Circle of Dancers* meets little of that expectation.

While the general public often likes to read novels of suspense and complicated plot structure, the point being made in this trilogy is that there are no real solutions for Indians as long as they remain a colonized people, as long as their rivers are destroyed by their colonists, as long as their treaty-protected lands like the Black Hills are not returned, and as long as justice systems are biased. Unfortunately, there is practically no dialogue in American Indian fiction concerning these dilemmas, so the reader who has not been trained to find these kinds of stories satisfying, or, in the words of critics, "pleasing," feels disappointed or let down. This is reason enough for exclusion, perhaps, or obscurity.

It seems to be a minority opinion in the novel-writing world that novelists, if they are thought to be the intellectuals of the culture in which they thrive and not just entertainers, must try to tell real things about people and history and politics. What *Aurelia* tries for is a true feeling of the period and the place, not just a Perry Mason success at trial or a triumph of good over evil or a complicated plot with many puzzles to be solved.

There is a difference between authors of Indian novels who merely tap into an American guilt or an American racism as they tell Indian stories, and those authors who really engage their audiences in serious issues of land restoration and reform, or survival issues of one kind or another. Because the function of plot is conflict and because the consequence of plot is resolution, the structure of the three novellas of *Aurelia*, which does not serve those ends, is significant and intentional and purposeful in determining fictional realism and must not be ignored or thought to be flawed.

Even though novelists become spokespersons for their ideas and their cultures, they are often left out of truly democratic reading places if their critics and publishers and readers believe they do not write *what is pleasing*. The struggle to have an audience, the struggle to become a part of the literati and contributors to the canon, does not overcome some artistic prejudices. It may be useless for writers to deplore this reality, they must simply do their own work.

The third novella, *In the Presence of River Gods*, asks what role mythology and geography play in literature and history, which some tribal scholars believe to be the essential focus of traditional narrative. In this story, the third and final novella of *Aurelia*, the Mni Sosa river spirits take a larger part in the story, but still give no answers to the betrayals that continue to haunt Aurelia, who is convinced that she is in their presence. The silence of the spirits pervades the subdued action and dialogue of this section, and is undramatic but profoundly felt in the last scene of the novella.

In this section Aurelia moves with her children and her dying grandmother to the Cheyenne River Sioux Reservation just about the time that the Supreme Court redefines the 1877 "taking of the Black Hills" by the federal government as a "theft." She is devastated when her grandmother dies, but is revitalized when she encounters a man whom she might grow to love. She is present in the community as a witness during the disappearance of a young Indian woman whose bones are found a year later in the river. No one knows for nearly twenty years that two young white men who have lived among them as neighbors are the murderers and rapists who have committed this crime againt the community. Aurelia "witnesses" the final trial of these young criminals in the same way that she has "witnessed" all of the crimes committed against the Sioux tribal people in the past sixty years—the land thefts, the destruction of the river, the injustices endured by colonized peoples.

As Aurelia's identity evolves in this trilogy, she emerges not as a heroine but as an uncertain survivor, in the same way that the possibility for the survival of the river and its spirits is uncertain in a modern world driven by technological exploitation of the natural. In the final scene Aurelia, now a gray-haired grandmother, is driving her car alongside the familiar river, looking at the lights of the white man's town from a distance and listening to the meaninglessness of a radio program, instead of a message from the mythological figures who reside in this land with her as her relatives. The tragedy is that there is no message from them.

Fiction is, perhaps, an art that is indistinctly heard. It is often imperfectly known or understood. Thus, "obscure" may be a most appropriate adjective to describe much of what is important about it and many of its practitioners. Yet like Isaiah (59:9), who said, "We wait for light but behold obscurity," we inevitably complain that we cannot know everything.

What I really have to admit about the trilogy *Aurelia* is that it is not mainstream fiction, and it excuses *A Reader's Guide to Twentieth-Century Writers* for excluding it. Still, I make that admission with regret. On the issues of Obscurity and Canon and Race and Colonialism (usually discussed as "Contact Zones") there are, perhaps, only three kinds of stories in the world: there's the zippity-doo-dah kind, then the kind that makes you angry, and, finally, there's the kind that breaks your heart.

In one sense, *Aurelia* is the kind of story that breaks your heart. But in order to understand the real function of this story in the context of colonial discourse, the reader must understand that this is a crime novel. Not a "true crime" novel, some would say, because in "true crime" literatures the crime is solved, and in *Aurelia* we not only are not certain what the crime is, but we don't know if it is solved or if it will ever be solved. But it is a crime novel nonetheless. It was written as a response to historical theft, tribal murder, terrorism, broken treaties, and government malfeasance, all of which are considered "crimes" in the general lexicon of legal thought if not literary thought. If it is true, as Joyce Carol Oates says as she reviews the several books on Jon Benet Ramsey for the *New York Review of Books*, "The commission of a crime demands a response," *Aurelia* is the response to crime.

Since 1965, the nonfiction novel *In Cold Blood* by Truman Capote has become the standard by which we judge "true crime," and it is notable because it is the effort to use fictional elements in the analysis of a crime that really happened, the murder of an entire farm family in Kansas by two drifters. *Aurelia* is a novel about crime, but the problem that plagues *it* as an example of the true-crime genre is that while it is a fictional analysis of the effect of American colonialism on Indian reservations, which is generally defined as "the conquest and control of other people's land and goods," neither the Conquest nor the subsequent colonialism is regarded in and by America as criminal behavior. Thus, the possibility of misunderstanding the point made by this novel as an important artistic discussion of the crimes of race and colonialism in America is substantial.

The profound irony with which this crime of colonialism is told in *Aurelia* is not clarified through the use of elements of fiction so much as it is in the absence throughout the text of any solution to illegal behavior confronted by characters and behaviors and events. Literary texts of imaginative art are crucial to the formation of colonial discourse, but only if they move out of the critical practices that link them to the sympathies of the colonial class, and *Aurelia* is an attempt toward that move. If there are no solutions to the unnamed and unidentified crimes in this trilogy of tribal stories, there are no excuses for them either. Aurelia looks them squarely in the face and so must the reluctant reader.

PART FOUR

SPEECHES

14

PTE—COMING BACK FROM OBLIVION

In keeping with the title of this conference, *Sacred Buffalo: Back from Oblivion,* I have prepared a little story concerning history and mythology. So I hope you'll settle back in your seats and listen to this story of mine.

First, though, in the early program draft distributed by mail, you might have noticed that my presentation was entitled "*Methodologies* of Origin and Historical Migration"; this was a typographical error.

The word *methodologies,* as you know, implies a system of rules and principles that underlie the organization of the various sciences and the conduct of scientific inquiry. I was never very good in science. So I must tell you I am not going to talk about methodologies.

The word *methodology* implies, also, I suppose, that it is possible to know the "truth" of something. This is, of course, the mantra of scientists, as our colleague Vine Deloria has pointed out to us in the body of his work and in his latest book, *Red Earth, White Lies.* Methodologies of Truth-Seeking. What is true? What is Truth? This is what scientists seek. So Methodology is a word that comes out of science and a word that also, we shouldn't be surprised to hear, comes out of American university education departments. Education and Truth. Much of this, as it has been explained by science, becomes what Professor Deloria has called contrived Scientific Mythology. Deloria, a major native scholar by anyone's standards, speaks of the theory of the Bering Strait and other such contrivances as Scientific Mythology. It comes about through methodology. So don't confuse the word *methodology* with the word *mythology.*

Mythology, of course, which is what my presentation today is really about, is a word that has many meanings. What Mythology really refers to, as we use it in Native Studies, is a body of knowledge created for the purpose of explaining origins and migrations. Mythologies rise up around other interests as well, other than science, other than origins, so we use the word very loosely. The other day I was talking about my trip to Mexico and I was saying, "There is the myth that Mexico is a democracy, which of course we know it is not, since there has been a one-party rule there for decades and decades. So the myth that Mexico is a democracy is what they want you to think about Mexico. . . ." Well, in that case I use the word to imply that mythology is something false. Many use the word with that connotation.

We should be more careful in our useage of the word because Mythology is not something that is false. It is often something that cannot be proven through scientific metholodogy, but it is not something that is false. Mythology, if it is not something that is false, neither is it something that is true. We must stop using those terms (true or false) to talk about what it is that people believe. Mythology is a body of knowledge possessed by a people and believed by the people, and it is based in experience and observation and geography and language, and because that is so, it is often considered Sacred Knowledge.

So I am going to talk a bit about Mythology today, and I have also been asked to say something about the role of women, which I will try to do. I don't know how much I will say about that because I don't know much about women. I know even less about men, frankly. I don't consider myself a scholar or a feminist (although I have been described that way), because I know too little about women and too little about men to be considered a feminist scholar. So I sort of reject that label and just say that I am a student of most of these subjects just like everyone else. I am learning.

What I would like to discuss with you today is the broad subject of Mythology, making specific reference to the mythologies of the tribal peoples called Lakota/Nakota/Dakota of the Northern Plains. These mythologies are vast bodies of knowledge possessed by the people. And they are very old. As old as the land and the mountains and the rivers. And the buffalo.

What the people know and have known about the buffalo or the bison, that essential indigenous figure of the northern hemisphere, must be said to be an *enormous* body of knowledge. We cannot begin to know everything there is to know about the buffalo and the origins of the people, but we can, through continued storytelling and the continued use of our languages, give meaning to the relationship the Sioux have always had with a specific geography called the Northern Plains, and perhaps the universe. And, of course, the buffalo.

Indians of the Northern Plains have always heard the stories of the buffalo and I am no exception. My relatives are Yanktons and Santees and Hunkpapas, and I was born and raised in the Big Bend, Fort Thompson, and Crow Creek areas along the Missouri River, where the Santees and the Hunkpapas and the Ihanktowan people (which is what they called themselves) had lived for many generations. This is a place, some 250,000 acres, that was designated through white/Indian treaty-making in 1863 as the Crow Creek Indian Reservation, after the Santee War in Minnesota that erupted and ended the previous year. This war is often called the Little Crow War. There is a lot of history about the "removal" and "incarceration" of the Santees in this area, and surely that history is very complex.

But Indians had always lived there, even before the U.S. government designated it a concentration camp for the Eastern Sioux. Indians have always known the Crow Creek: *kudwichacha*, my relatives would say. It was not an uninhabited place. Because of the nature of the mythologies known by these peoples and the stories that were told, it is now accepted that these "D" speakers of the Sioux language of the region knew and possessed a vast area along the Missouri River all the way, some say, from what is now Wisconsin to what is presently Wyoming. And they had complex relationships with their relatives, the Lakotas and the Nakotas, in addition to intertribal and political and cultural ties to their neighbors, the Winnebagoes and the Arapahoes and the Cheyennes, who also possessed this territory in their hearts and in their religions.

In the beginning, there are stories about when we were the Star People, the Wichakpi Oyate, when there were only the *wican pi* in the darkness. The stars. Nobody seems to know exactly how the stars were made (though, naturally, the scientists and their methodologies can tell you more than you want to know), but what they say about them is that they were made from water, and it is in water that the essential power of the universe is held. It is said that the *wican* could not give a shadow because the moon would do that, nor could they give any heat because that would be left up to the sun, and so their function was to witness, to look all around, and they could only help themselves to make it across the dark sky to the Dakota homelands in the Northern Plains.

The wind, then, at that time, was their only fellow traveler. It was their only essential relative. The Santees remember that. Even today. The wind, the only and essential relative. Anybody who has lived in the Northern Plains knows that you must make your peace with the wind if you are to camp anywhere in Sioux country. Many of the stories of this period are called *ohunkaka*.

And so the wind is the first relative, and then there is the buffalo, the first ancestor. There are the *keyapi* stories about when we became the Buffalo People, the Pte Oyate. These stories tell more of what is called the *ohunkaka* times, the times when the holy people developed more fully certain narrative themes that we began to call *keyapi*, the oral traditions. These are legends (no longer myths) about how we eventually became Santee, Oglala, Minneconjou, Sicangu, Ihanktowan, Hunkpapa, Sihasapa, and these are the stories of how we occupied the geography of the Minnesota River and the Missouri River and the Black Hills and all of the sacred places. These places, it is said by those who keep track of such things, are at least two or three billion years old. Probably much older. No one needs to tell the Sioux that we made our journey to our homelands from Asia. We know the sacred geography of our earliest times in a far different way.

The people kept these tribal accounts, largely unwritten and imbedded in our own language and the land, because they are the integrated and sacred mythologies of origin and historical migration that tell us who we are. These are the mythologies that are created not for public consumption, like the Bill Moyers stuff you see on television, or the Dances with Wolves you see in the movies, or the silly, contrived Ken Burns colonial documentaries about Lewis and Clark. These unwritten accounts are popularized among our own people for the purpose of cultural and physical survival. You hear them at Sisseton, at Pine Ridge, in the Big Bend area of the Missouri River, in Minneapolis and Denver and all throughout Indian Country. And you hear them in our songs and our prayers and at every communal gathering.

When we talk about the buffalo "coming back from oblivion," as we are doing at this conference, we must realize that we are talking about the creation, death, and recreation cycle that is everywhere in the old stories. The buffalo and his many wives have always had a difficult time surviving in this world, and there are many versions of his death and his coming back to life. The phenomenon of his birth and his death and his rebirth, all of which was witnessed and remembered by the people, is a mysterious life cycle that they have taken into their hearts and understood as sacred.

I remember my father telling me a story told to him by his father about the last buffalo that was seen on the Crow Creek. It came right up to the people and it was very old, its withers shrunken, its hide filled with mange. They shot it with an arrow and they took it to Fort Sully and the people danced there and it was a sacred communal act done for the sake of the land and the natural world.

The Dakotas, the Santees and the Yanktons, knew this Fort well. Fort Sully. It was named after Alfred Sully, who had helped General Henry Sibley lead the U.S. Army west of the Missouri to hunt them down in the summer of 1863, the year after the Little Crow War.

When Sibley went back to Minnesota, Sully built his outpost at Fort Pierre, a mere forty miles from the Crow Creek, and Sully allowed William S. Harney's troops to stay there. Harney's troops, as you know, marched through the heart of Sioux country, and now there is a mountain named in the sacred Black Hills for him. Harney Peak.

My father's story was that Inkpaduta, the Santee chieftain who has now been discredited in history as a savage killer, fought Sully there the summer of 1864 in defense of the land and in defense of the people. And many years later, my father told me, Inkpaduta was at the Little Big Horn. I remember the story because my father believed that the consecration of the old buffalo in the ceremony done that summer day was for the purpose of telling all of us that the death and the rebirth of the buffalo is essential to our lives.

After the coming of the white man and his planned indiscriminate slaughter of the buffalo during the nineteenth century for reasons unfathomable to the Sioux, the death of the buffalo seemed to signify the end. Even a large segment of Indian populations believed it was the end. There are many white-man accounts of the death of the buffalo and the predicted death to the Sioux people. *The Long Death: Last Days of the Sioux Nation*, by Ralph K. Andrist (1964), as just one example of the kinds of predictions that abound in American scholarship, was written by a preeminent white scholar, who recreated the long-held theory and the hoped-for idea of the "vanishing Indian," an idea predicated on the death of the buffalo: when the buffalo is gone, the Sioux are no more, says this scholar. This theory and this mythology is, as we all can attest to here today, indefensible. It is false. It is a self-serving lie.

Today, as you know, and has been said by many of the people who are here at this conference, the U.S. federal government is still killing the buffalo and, in many ways, by stealing land and perpetuating a failed federal fiscal policy, is still killing Indians.

As you know, there is a plan to slaughter buffalo in Yellowstone Park. We are told that two years ago, Yellowstone had about 3500 buffalo, and today that number is down to 2300, a decline that is directly related to the federal killing plan. Last year alone, 1100 buffalo were killed. This slaughter is a throwback to the nineteenth-century policy of killing buffalo and killing Indians. And who knows how to stop it? There is a lot of discussion about "management" plans, and the Park Service's Environmental Impact Statement, and tourism, and herd reduction. And so on and so on. But until people change their attitudes concerning the function of science and its relationship to the living earth, the killing will not stop. That's why the Buffalo Project and the Summer Institute at Cheyenne River Community College is so important. That's why the new book by Vine Deloria concerning the role of science is essential. These are the things that Indians are doing. What is being done by whites in these regions?

As the death of the buffalo is predicted and planned for by white communities all over the region, Indians still tell the stories of the rebirth of the buffalo and the rebirth of the people, which have also been predicted in the oral cultures of our ancestors—predictions that go back hundreds, perhaps thousands, of years. The buffalo represents an important power of the universe and he shares his power with his many wives, primary among them the Corn Wife.

On the Crow Creek Reservation, where I grew to adulthood, they have said that the Corn Wife told them to move there, to take up the Big Bend in the Missouri River country. They tell how the Corn Wife of the buffalo wanted him to spend his life with her people there, they tell how she gave her life to him and they say she withers and dies every season in order to come back to life again in the spring. They tell these stories in spite of the pervasiveness of the white man's story of establishing the Crow Creek Reservation for the purpose of incarceration of the Santees during and after the war with the whites. Most people believe that reservation was the concentration camp for the Eastern Sioux after the War of 1862, and it was. In native mythology it is also the home of the buffalo and his Corn Wife.

These narratives, of course, illustrate the essential conflict that points out the role of narrative in history. The narratives that have been told by whites differ considerably from the narratives told by Indians. And a different notion about the universe has been the result. If the Crow Creek Indians tell the stories of the buffalo and his Corn Wife as the essential origin stories that connect them to a specific geography, we can be assured that they will understand the sacredness of that place.

This sacred acknowledgment of life and death is essential to the recognition by the Sioux of the rules of the world. The Corn Wife, the essential fertility figure, disappears in the same way and for the same reasons that certain stars, certain constellations, disappear from the night sky at certain times of the year. These are signals of the cyclical nature of life. And the Old Ones, when they tell you about these things, say, "what is in the stars is on the earth and what is on the earth is in the stars." The Dakota Sioux have known of this reality since the beginning, when the *wican* helped them across the heavens to their homelands.

The buffalo represents the hunting life and the warrior life. Corn Wife, who also goes by a variety of other names, seems to provide the feminine part of the mythological explanation for the relationship between the agricultural life of the people and the warrior life of the people. These stories were particularly important to the Santees, and I heard various versions of them as a child when we planted gardens along the creeks and the river—huge gardens of corn and squash, mostly. I remember going along the rows and stepping in between the plants to pick out the weeds, carrying a pail and spilling a cup of water on the roots of each plant as I went.

The thing about native mythology is that it provides a reasonable account of what the people observed over hundreds and hundreds of years, and how they wanted to live their lives. The Indian people believed that there had to be a connection between planting and hunting, between humans and other creatures, between the land and its inhabitants, between the sky and the earth; thus, the stories of the buffalo's wives were told so that we would know about that relationship. The buffalo was and is a powerful force in the universe, and the killing of the buffalo as recorded in the white man's historical accounts amounted to a crime against humanity, a human act of deicide, a crime against the land. The horror felt by the people of that awful period of slaughter in the nineteenth century must have been unimaginable, for they had been taught from infancy that it was the eternal order of the world for the buffalo to go to live with his Corn Wife's people, and this reality would keep the balance of the earth's fertility. It was a sacred compact imbedded in language, in myth, in ceremony, and in their everyday lives. It is the saddest story on earth that the white man's interest in killing the buffalo is still the story that is told.

In closing, I want to say that when the Europeans who colonized the Americas came here they had very little knowledge about the central truths concerning man's place on this continent. They had little ethical perspective about how the vibrant cultures, the indigenous cultures of this planet that they tried so hard to destroy, had originated as relatives to everything in the universe. The stars and the wind and the buffalo and Mother Earth. Thus, because the Europeans who invaded these lands knew nothing of it, had no relationship to anything they saw here, they came to believe the universe was a hostile place and they had the right to conquer it.

Only now, at the close of the twentieth century, are the surviving, still-remaining Indian cultures throughout the world reaching out to share what they know, their knowledge, insight, morality, and their own version of technology. The work of the Bison Cooperative is essential to that reaching-out, for it will assist not only the buffalo in his survival, but it is essential to the nationhood of the people.

I thank you for inviting me to share with you in this discussion and I hope you will continue in this important work.

Lecture given at a meeting of the Intertribal Bison Cooperative, Denver, Colo., Nov. 20–23, 1998.

15

NATIVE STUDIES IS POLITICS:
THE RESPONSIBILITY OF NATIVE AMERICAN
STUDIES IN AN ACADEMIC SETTING

Nape ch e u za pi taku inicia pi he? I offer my hand to all of you. . . . What
are your names? How do they call you? *Who are you in relation to all the
rest of us.* . . . This is the essential tribal question. . . . It is, of course, the
essential question of all inquiries . . . scholarly, personal, historical. . . .

At the close of the twentieth century, which is seen by mainstream America
as the universalist moment, the responsibility of Native American Studies
remains a challenge to that universalism. In the 1990s a task force on Indian
education (yes, another one) set about its work in Washington, D.C., and it
was called the Nations at Risk Task Force. It seemed to some of us to be the
same old thing, and it was in many ways. How many of us over the years have
been involved in task forces and in commissions and in NIEA conferences
in our efforts to say something sensible about Indian education? I have, and
I am continually surprised at the ability of native scholars and communities
to withstand the dismal nature of them.

But there is sometimes some interesting stuff that comes out of such gath-
erings. In this case, this study, "A Nation at Risk," written by former Secretary of Education Lauro Cavazos, who later wrote "Indian Nations at Risk,"
rendered this fact: American society is engaged in a secret war against native peoples in the United States, and its major weapon in that war is Education. I want to talk today about that fact, and I want to connect it to the
effort we have made toward developing Native American Studies as an academic discipline.

The relentless misfortune of American Indians is that today, in the last decades of the twentieth century and the first of the twenty-first, American society continues to be engaged in its secret and sometimes not so secret war against native peoples and their autonomous nations. It perhaps comes as no surprise to Indians that the struggle continues. Yet the particular finding of this study must be said aloud. It must be published. It must be said again and again. We must act on its reality. And we must recognize that it is a po-litical reality.

Just a quick look at the past will tell us that this war has always been upon us. First, the Christianizing and civilizing era, which meant the rise of the boarding schools, the mission schools and the federal schools based on a military model designed to separate young people from their families. Many of these, as you well know, are still in existence in our part of the country. These were war weapons used to destroy our families and our cultures. Sec-ond, the mainstreaming era, which meant the rise of trade schools, the de-velopment of curricula that would get us and our children into the "main-stream" of American society. But what it did was make us tradesmen not scholars, welders not lawyers, barbers not teachers. We could become hair-dressers and carpenters. We could be educated to earn a "minimum wage" and move away from our homelands. And now the tertiary stage of educa-tion for Indians has become the age of "diversity." This is the most recent weapon used against us in education; it has meant the development of Eth-nic Studies, in which we are not citizens of Indian nations, but, absurdly, we are very simply made over as part of the flotsam and jetsam of American immigrant and colonial society. Postcolonial studies have been developed to hurry us along that path, the "after contact" nature of our relationship to the rest of the world being that in which we largely dismiss treaties and the au-tonomy of tribalism and our native languages. All of these so-called ideas are given various names. But the failed "melting pot" theory underlies it all. Assimilation is the name of the game, and no one is left in academia to de-fend our lands and our resources and our languages and our religions. As-similation as we have known it is the complete taking over of one society by another—the "war" in which no one wins.

Recently, in the last twenty or thirty years, we have been engaged in an Indian Studies Era in the universities of America. This Native American Stud-ies Era functions to bring Indians into the systems of education as leaders, directors of curricular development, professors, researchers, and writers. It was meant to develop not only the tribal intellectuals but also a system for the study of native societies from the inside, the study of language, culture, historical and legal relationships with the United States as nations-within-a-nation. It was meant to have as its constituencies the tribal nations of America, and it was meant to have as its major intent the defense of lands and resources and the sovereign autonomy of nationhood.

I am going to say that again. *Indian Studies as an academic discipline was meant to have as its constituencies the native tribal nations of America and its major purpose the defense of lands and resources and the sovereign right to nation-to-nation status.* That was its first ideal intention, and its scholarship in literature and law and science and economics was to reflect that intention. The second was that it was meant to counter the related disciplines that have been in the business of colonizing the natives. For 200 years education has been assisting in the exploitation of the land and resources of native nations with very little criticism. So an essential part of the function of NAS is the criticism of failed ideas and systems.

Now I know this is hard to think about on university campuses, where we are all presumed to be working together in the pursuit of knowledge—some kind of pure, ivory-tower search for the truth. But we have native scholars who know what the score it. What it's always been. Thirty years ago these scholars started the criticism of the university educational systems and disciplines. Anthropology in particular. It is these native scholars who pointed out what we all have known, that Anthroplogy was and is the handmaiden of colonialism not just here in the United States but all over the world—Africa, Asia. That Anthropology was never the non-political regime of study that it claimed to be. These native scholars pointed out to us that the discipline of history was a fraud, that it originated the "savage," the "primitive," the stereotypes confirming racial supremacy, the inferior/superior race theory.

Recently, in his new book *Red Earth, White Lies,* Professor Vine Deloria has said that Science itself is a self-serving white man's mythology, that the Bering Strait Theory of native origin on this continent is unbelievable and insupportable, that it is a methodology created by scholars who fear the natural world and are interested only in western expansionism. He calls the Bering Strait Theory a "scientific myth" and says it should be rejected by thinking people as it concerns the indigenous populations here in America. As you might expect, this book has not been welcomed by much of the scholarly community.

Well, all of this history is the reason for the rise of Native American Studies as an academic discipline, and some of us have been lucky enough to have worked for its development. I'm particularly concerned at the present time about our direction(s). Have we drifted away—no, have we been driven away from our original intent? I think so. We've been driven away by America's secret war against us, and we've been drifting away by our own apathy and failure. Do we still remember that our constituents are the native nations of America? Often, the answer is no. It is difficult to remember that, when we are stationed at universities in isolation from everyone who cares and everything that has meaning. We in these educational stations often get to thinking that we serve the institutions, we serve the university, we serve students, we serve our faculties, we serve other disciplines. We serve ourselves. We serve the American Dream.

No. We do not. Our responsibility is to the tribal nations that have survived terrible wars, that have signed solemn treaties with our enemies, that possess vast resources, the rivers people live by, the lands where our relatives are buried. This legacy is our constituency. We in Indian Studies have always known that we should acquire power not for ourselves or for the sake of power, but to engage in the strategies by which we can defend our lands and ourselves as nations of people who exist in one of the most greedy, exploitive capitalistic systems ever devised. America. We must acquire power, maintain it, and utilize it to develop ourselves and our homelands in ways appropriate to our cultures, beliefs, and histories. One of the ways to do that is through education, through the new concept of Native American Studies.

The central conflict between Indian nations and the United States resides in the assurance that the United States is the great democratizer, the great assimilator, all-knowing and all-powerful, organizer of the world. Co-existence, therefore, has been fraught with risk. The United States has always been opposed to the autonomy sought by Native nations as they have attempted to co-exist. As nations of people native populations are seen as undemocratic, as anomaly to America. Not too many years ago, this reality was brought home to me when the Indian Studies program right here on this campus sought federal funding for Lakota/Dakota/Nakota language study. We were told we could get some funding if our intent in the study was to make us more fluent in English. That's a good idea, we said, but the real intent here is that we want to become more fluent in Dakota, in Lakota; we want to study our own language because it is worthy of study as a repository of our culture. Well, we were told, that is not the intent of native language study, the only reason for bilingual language study was to assimilate. We had a hard time convincing America that we were not subversive just because we had a different view. It was only with the rise of the tribal homelands-based community colleges that our viewpoint has been able to thrive.

More than anything we have done in the last thirty years, we have defended the notion that education is a cultural process. More than anything we have done in the last thirty years, we have recognized that the "secret war" described in the 1990 task force is ongoing. One of the things we face in this state, in South Dakota, which is the direct result of education or lack of education in the real history of the Sioux Nation, is that the state of South Dakota since its inception has been an enemy to our development if not our very survival. For a hundred years the state has fostered an attitude of hostility and competition with tribal-nation development, both culturally and economically. Partial evidence of that is the fact that in this decade, the South Dakota state legislature passed an "English only" law that was probably meant as a message to Indians in the state, a line drawn in the sand, the white man's power structure saying what civil administrations mean to do in terms of limitations put on education and culture.

Right now there is an effort to write legislation that is called Water Resources Development, legislation that would "transfer" treaty lands along the Missouri River to the state. What this legislation represents is the state effort to force the doctrine of state authority and control on Indian tribes. Such legislation threatens to undermine the process of Sioux Nation self-government and control of our own resources. Educators in Indian Studies should be talking about these kinds of things in the classroom. We should be educating ourselves and our children and our non-Indian neighbors and politicians.

The historical fact is, none of the northern tier states (South Dakota, North Dakota, Washington, Montana, Wyoming, Idaho) that became states after the treaties were signed should believe themselves "equal" to Indian tribal nations or "superior" to them in the matter of water resources. Read the writings of an old water lawyer by the name of William Veeder, who has worked out of Washington, D.C., if you doubt this historical and legal fact. These upper states in the Midwest and the Far West did not exist as governmental entities until *after* the treaties were signed between the tribal nations and the federal government of the United States that furthered the government-to-government status inherent in tribal experience. This historical fact has brought about a *principle* in Indian law that gives tribal nations primacy in treaty matters of resource development, and water rights in particular. These are the kinds of principles that must be taught in our classes.

Whoever said tribes should be "equal" partners with the state in this long-standing dispute concerning the Missouri River resource? Bill Janklow, governor? Tom Daschle, senator? Neither of them has apparently ever read a treaty, and certainly they seem to be ignorant of the vast body of law that has derived from the treaty relationship of tribal nations and the United States.

They should take a course called Federal Indian Policy, one of the core courses of the discipline of Native Studies, wherein they could read the works of Felix Cohen, William Veeder, Vine Deloria, Robert Berkhofer, Don Fixico, Charles Wilkinson, and dozens more who have written sensibly on Federal Indian Policy in the last few decades. This is a course that is never taught in anthropology or literature, and rarely in history or law courses.

But because these politicians haven't taken this course and are unlikely to at this stage, that does not mean we can or should forgive them for their ignorance. I am very disappointed in the stance that the Cheyenne River Sioux Tribe and the Lower Brule Sioux Tribe have taken concerning this state-generated proposal on resource development. These tribal councils are wrong to defend this giveaway of our land and resources. These elected officials should be ousted. How about impeached? Or is that a punishment reserved only for people who are fooling around with interns? Frankly, who they fool around with is their own business. But when they are giving away treaty-protected assets that belong to the tribal community, it becomes our business.

The discussion of this kind of legislation, called the Water Resources Development Act, is central to what should be going on in the development of curricula in the discipline of Native American Studies. It is as essential as the study of the Constitution in history classes, and the study of the Puritans in Social Studies. This legislation is being promulgated by state and federal officials at the beginning of the new century for the continued purpose of exploiting resources that belong to our children and grandchildren. It should be vigorously opposed by all thinking people who know that Indians and whites must live together in this world. We are told in the political discourse, in the media, in our history classes that such legislation will "end" the Missouri River dispute and right the wrongs done by the building of hydro power dams that flooded 550 square miles of treaty-protected land three decades ago. It will do nothing of the kind. It will simply give free rein to the power-hungry groups who have never defended the rights of native peoples.

On campuses like this one, disciplines struggle for autonomy in the same way that Indian tribes struggle for the right to exist. It is time now, twenty or thirty years after the Institute here was developed and the Native American Studies programs began to emerge as disciplinary studies, to ask whether or not Native American Studies has been successful in two of its important and practical goals. First of all, what is our status on campuses around the country? Is Indian Studies a department? Are we emerging as a discipline? Just because we have put together a few courses does not mean that we have ventured very far into disciplinary development. What are our principles?

What is our methodology? Have we developed an appropriate academic structure so that we can go forward in producing scholars and intellectuals from our tribal constituencies?

The struggle for the autonomy of Native American Studies will be the struggle of the future. Often, we are pushed into Interdisciplinary Study, Postcolonial Study, Ethnic Studies, and we have discovered that this strategy is useless if what we want to do is defend tribal sovereignty. It is impossible in these paradigms to use our bodies of knowledge (the oral traditions, languages, treaties) as the bases for the development of defensive, regulatory, and transformative mechanisms. In most cases, thirty years after Deloria's attack, we still must fight off the mechanisms of anthropology useful to the study of moribund cultures but incompetent in teaching about the legal and historical bases for sovereignty, never making the connections between culture and vital nationalism. We must fight off activist English departments that simply want to study third-rate novels and poetry, yet omit any discussion concerning treaties and land reform. We must confront the social sciences that want to study what is wrong with us, as though pathology is inherent in Indianness.

We've had enough experience now to know that interdisciplinary programs are a weak entity. Interdisciplinary programs hooked to sociology or anthropology or history will always advantage the main discipline and well-established department. In the interdisciplinary programs, which often call themselves Cultural Studies, where Native American Studies is often located, the FTEs will advantage the department of long standing. You often get the "old wine in new bottles" approach to curricular development and you rarely get to hire native faculty. If Indian Studies is not a department, if it is not a discipline, it does not get the FTEs, the student ratio mechanism upon which academic budgets are built. Under these conditions Native Studies will soon wither on the vine, be absorbed into other more aggressive programs, continue to be what Colorado University Professor of History and Native Studies Vine Deloria calls "the orphan of academia." (Reference comes from a series of six articles appearing in the journal *Winds of Change* [Winter 1991].) FTEs are central to hiring, to promotion and tenure, to research, and they are the backbone of academic success.

The second important goal of Native American Studies is the development of professionals in the field who will teach and write research designs, conduct research, write, and publish. This means that we must promote the core curriculum of the discipline because it is from this body of knowledge that we can transcend our underdeveloped status. Our students must know the bibliographies promulgated through the research and writing of the last several decades, and we must concern ourselves with the development of internships for our native students in the areas we feel are significant.

We must promote research and writing in appropriate and meaningful ways, which means that we don't need too many more doctoral dissertations on "Who Am I?," "Who Is an Indian?," "What I Learned from My Cherokee Grandmother," and "Mother Earth Is My Friend." We don't need too many more doctoral dissertations on the life of N. Scott Momaday (interesting though that may be), unless the scholarship includes a critique of his outrageous defense of the Bering Strait Theory and the role of science in describing native origins, and what this essential conflict means to indigenousness (a major concept of the discipline) on this continent. This defense of science concerning native origins by Momaday appeared in the *New York Times,* and a rebuttal by Vine Deloria appeared in *Indian Country Today,* which gives us some notion of the places noted scholars publish their works. It is successful Indian novelists who get to publish in the *New York Times,* where they write on subjects they often know very little about.

We need dissertations on the Yankton Land Case that will reveal the anti-Indian legislation that comes out of Congress and is promoted by the state and federal court systems. We need to publish the facts of the Dann Case and the Utah Land Case revealing more of the illegal activity of lawmakers that reduces reservation life to a life of poverty. We need to study the water rights cases of the Missouri River tribes and we need to publish our studies.

Obviously, as a writer who has struggled to make sense of the political world, I believe we need to train our young people to do research and to write and publish. They must learn the fundamentals of research design and writing and publication. This may be the most important set of skills they can bring back to their tribes from university training.

It is our responsibility to continue the struggles toward a decent future for Indian people and the empowerment of Indian nations. In our twentieth century, the antagonists, the enemies of our nations, the thieves who want our land and water and other resources, they are still out there. I believe that the 1990s task force on Indian education, which says that our nations are at risk, is something we all should take very seriously.

Lecture given at the University of South Dakota at Vermillion, Oct. 10, 1998, to an audience of students and faculty and directors of NAS institutes and programs.

16

RECONCILIATION, DISHONEST IN ITS
INCEPTION, NOW A FAILED IDEA

Hau. . . . nape che u za pe. . . . This is a brief greeting used now by contemporary Sioux speakers to ingratiate themselves with their audiences, a greeting used to say that I, the speaker, am friendly and on good terms with you, the audience. I am not sure how appropriate that phrase is for me to use today, because when I look at the focus of our coming together at this university today, "Reconciliation" and "Tribal and State Relations," I realize that I have little to say that is friendly. Indeed, I will probably, on the contrary, have many unpleasant things to say.

I know that Mandela and Bishop Tutu talk of reconciliation in South Africa to those who have murdered and oppressed them for most of this century. I know that the Irish now talk of peace, and the Palestinians and Israelis talk of how to forgive one another. In the face of all that recognition, I want to talk seriously to you about why, in my view at least, the so-called Indian/ white reconciliation movement in South Dakota, apparently initiated by newspaperman Tim Giago, a member of the Oglala Sioux Tribe, and George Mickelson, a former governor of the state, is a dumb idea and should end up on the scrap heap of dumb ideas. Reconciliation, so far as I undertand the word, means "to cease hostility or opposition," or "to accept or be resigned to something not desired." It could mean "to compensate someone." That latter definition has been used as a tactic in the Black Hills Case, and it is unacceptable to those Indians from whom the state of South Dakota and the U.S. federal government stole the Black Hills. Since 1980, in a century-long litigation brought by the tribes, that "acceptance" or "resignation" or "opposition" or "compensation" has been unacceptable. It is important to recognize the unacceptability of these tried and failed solutions.

Before we can talk of "ceasing of hostility" we need land reform in the state of South Dakota, and that means that stolen lands must be returned to their rightful owners. This is not a church matter, after all, in which we can give in to the buying and selling of indulgences and various forms of penances. This, instead, concerns the very survival on this earth of a nation of people, the Sioux, who occupied the land for millennia before the white man's invasion. We need to have a state government that is based in ethics and history rather than greed, racism, and tourism, and a federal government that will stand up to pressure.

My talk today will attempt to convince you that the reconciliation movement of the 1990s is ill-advised and doomed to fail, and is in fact, at this moment, if not defunct, certainly moribund. I will tell you why.

I want to start by telling you a brief little story. It was, I think, in the summer of 1980 that I went to a tribal water meeting with my father, who was then very old and very ill and was no longer an elected official of the tribe as he had been. He was using a cane and could no longer drive his car and had to rest frequently. Another old man, a white man whose name was Bill Veeder, was there. He was an old water-rights lawyer from Washington, D.C., who had worked with the tribes for many years, and that's why we were there, so my father, a longtime rancher and politician from the Crow Creek Sioux Reservation, could visit with the old lawyer, whose business was the defense of tribal water rights along the Missouri River and its tributaries.

I remember the speech very well that Mr. Veeder gave that day. The old Washington, D.C., water-rights lawyer talked about land and water monopolists and states' rightists and racists. He talked about the courts and the Winters Doctrine, which most of you know was first enunciated in the upper Missouri River basin back in 1907, a very important piece of legislation that defended tribal rights to the use of the Missouri River and its tributaries. Implicit in the Winters Doctrine, the old lawyer said, is the fact that Native American tribes are sovereign nations. Explicit in the doctrine and many others, not the least of which are the treaties, is that our forefathers guaranteed to the tribes that their reserved rights are exempt from state control and jurisdiction. Our forefathers. That means white forefathers as well as Indian forefathers. All of the white people who live in South Dakota should understand that it was an agreement their forefathers made with Indians and Indians made with them.

As you know, the Secretary of the Interior and the Corps of Engineers totally ignored the Winters Doctrine rights of the Sioux tribes in the Pick-Sloan

Plan, which brought about the development of hydro power dams in the Missouri—Garrison, Fort Randall, Oahe, and the others. Up the river for hundreds of miles, lands were seized and inundated and the tribes were paid a pittance payoff and deprived of any participation in the economic development for years and years. Had we participated appropriately in that development we would today have a sound economic base on Indian reservations up and down the Missouri River. We did not. So we have Bingo palaces and casinos. And poverty. And substandard houses in which we raise our children and take care of our grandparents.

This kind of history is repeated throughout the West. Salt River rights of White Mountain Apache in Arizona. Ahtanum Creek rights of the Yakima Nation in Washington state. The Colvilles. The Spokanes. We could name tribe after tribe.

When the old water-rights lawyer Bill Veeder talked of these matters seventeen years ago, he said this: "The Missouri River is now *totally controlled and channelized* and Indians find themselves in irreconcilable conflict with politically powerful water users who are claiming rights under state law."

While some may argue that much of this dilemma has been attended to through recent legislation and state government action, "state/tribal compacts," various "agreements" reached, coalitions established, quite the opposite is true. Even the much-touted Mni Sosa Water Coalition is a strategy to *quantify* tribal water rights, not defend them.

At present, there is what is being called a "land transfer" bill in Congress promoted by thrice-elected (soon elected a fourth time) Bill Janklow and Senator Tom Daschle that is called "South Dakota Land Transfer and Wildlife Habitat Mitigation Act of 1997," which is designed to diminish tribal sovereign status in the state, to claim land for the state that is treaty-protected land, to broaden a tax base for the state, and to claim jurisdiction concerning hunting and fishing. Look at that bill carefully and you will see that it is another land grab by the state, that it will benefit no tribe along the Missouri River economically on a long-range basis. Yet it is touted as a measure to "put to rest" all jurisdictional questions over hunting and fishing.

The tribes do not need this legislation to reserve and protect native hunting and fishing rights along the Missouri River. These rights are, according to water-rights lawyer Bill Veeder, implicit in treaty and history. Tribal nations have the right to use, to administer, to control and exercise the property rights independent from state control and interference. And they should be developing the strategies to assert those rights. Moreover, the federal government in its fiduciary role must assert its defense of tribes through providing funding and assistance for tribal development along these waterways independent of the greedy and self-serving state and county governments.

The kind of legislation that prevails, unfortunately, brought to bear by pressure from state officials, the Secretary of the Interior, and officials of the federal government, should be recognized for what it is, a failure of the "fiduciary" responsibility of the federal government, and an effort to drastically limit the claims of Indians. In the kinds of "reconciliation" legislation offered here, something called "settlements" are undertaken. These "settlements" attempt to convince the tribes that their rights are being preserved and protected. But in actuality, their rights are being sacrificed over and over again in the furtherance of the needs of greedy water monopolists and states' rightists. Non-reservation-based farmers. Hog producers. Cattlemen. We should know that. And we do know that. The deception practiced by the Secretary of the Interior to seize the invaluable reserved rights to the use of water from the tribes was known when the great Sioux Nation lost its rights in the Pick-Sloan Plan. This is a superb example of the kind of manipulation that is ubiquitous in native/state relations. No one should feel that the future is secured by the now-agreed-upon Mni Sosa Water Coalition, because it denies the sovereign rights of native water holders and does nothing to ensure an economically sound future.

In a *Rapid City Journal* article last December, the offices of Janklow and Daschle put out some information to the public concerning a "settlement" idea about land "transfer" and "wildlife habitat mitigation" and it sounded good to the uninformed public. The headline read "Legislation Ends Missouri Dispute," and it referred to their self-centered, state-inspired legislation on "mitigation," a new word, perhaps, for the now-trite "reconciliation." The article quoted the officials as saying that the dispute would be ended because "the Federal Government is no longer the *middleman* [my emphasis] in deciding who owns land and who has jurisdiction."

What kind of history is this? What kind of law is this? Everyone knows that the federal government has *never* been a middleman between tribes and state governments. It has been a "trustee" of Indian lands and it holds a "fiduciary" responsibility to its treaty co-signatories, the United Sioux Tribes. What this kind of talk and this kind of legislation mean is that at the end of the day, the federal government, the fiduciary in the cases the Sioux Nation faces with the state, forgoes its legal responsibility and enriches itself and the state while draining the assets of the tribes to which it owes treaty obligations. It's like an estate lawyer selling off his client's assets to enrich himself. For such actions in the real world, lawyers go to jail!! Only in Indian cases is the fiduciary rewarded for such illegal behavior.

I find the public silence toward this strategy of white politicians in their dealings with Indians very interesting. Where is the free press? Where are the scholars? Where are the educators? Where is the native leadership? In the highly organized "misconduct" and "malfeasance" which have characterized the behavior of one government toward another, there is a consistent theft of not only the corporate assets of the tribe like land and water, but also the very sovereign status embedded in our concomitant histories. And there is no outcry from the public, by and large. The reason is that *the general public benefits from every one of these thefts* from Indians and always has. Indians don't need leveraged buyouts or insider trading or greenmail. Indians just need congressional legislation or executive order or an inert tribal governing body, along with a state attorney general at the local level who believes it is his *duty* to constantly harass and confront the tribes in court, appeal every decision, argue and thwart every move the tribes make. What I want to point out here is this: the success of these outlaw maneuvers is dependent upon the public silence that accompanies them.

Many times, the kinds of issues talked about here between governments and government officials are called "conflicts." I'm reminded of the Minnesota history that calls the theft of Santee country in 1862 the *Dakota Conflict*. That is what it is called in the history books that are written. The truth is, the Minnesota event of 1862 was not an "uprising," or "conflict"; rather, these histories can be described as acts of war, and Santee chieftain Little Crow was unambiguous about declaring war, leading his people in opposition to the U.S. military. This war ended with the hanging of members of the Dakota forces by the United States of America, the largest mass execution in U.S. history of the only people to be hanged by a colonial government for defending themselves. Certainly there was no mass hanging of Confederate military men during or after the Civil War during that same era. These modern acts of war against the Indians are generally perpetuated by the elected and appointed officials of one of the most powerful countries in the world against some of the poorest, colonized, and oppressed people in America not because the victims are poor, not because they are freemen or slaves, but because they are Indians, non-Christian indigenous peoples claiming to be landowners.

If you want another example of "reconciliation" efforts, look at the recently litigated case *Yankton Sioux Tribe v. South Dakota*, in which the state of South Dakota and the courts have "diminished the Yankton Sioux treaty-protect-

ed tribal lands by 168 thousand acres," and, in fact, the state of South Dakota in that case argued for the total elimination of the Yankton Sioux Reservation. This is astonishing behavior on the part of the courts of this democratic country now, at the turn of the century, a time when we are supposed
to have learned something from history, a time of supposed enlightenment
concerning race relations. It's not only wrong. It's genocide.

Your elected officials are responsible for this. Jim Abourezk, the former state
senator who now has a law firm of his own that does "business" with the
tribes, and who took this case to the courts in spite of hesitation on the part
of some local tribal leaders, has tried to put the best face on this enormous
loss by saying that tribal leaders have said "they can live with divided jurisdiction." If that is the case, tribal leaders are as complicit as anyone. But
whether or not that statement is accurate, that is hardly the point. What is
made clear here is that any "reconciliation" effort to litigate fairness has always meant to Indians that they be resigned to their fate—continued land
loss and rights and underdeveloped economic systems. The point is, Indians and the future of Indian nationhood have once again been sacrificed.

This recent Yankton court case, we are told, is based upon past federal legislative action. Thus, a racist history begets a modern racist legal interpretation. Explicitly, according to the legal argument, the court decision to give
the state 168,000 acres of Yankton Sioux land is based on an 1894 Act of Congress that "opened unalloted lands to white settlement," in which, it is said,
the Yanktons voluntarily "ceded" these lands. This argument is wrong morally, ethically, and probably legally. If you understand history, you understand
that this Act of Congress was undertaken just four years after hundreds of
Lakotas were murdered at Wounded Knee by the U.S. Army. The so-called
cession of Yankton lands occured just four years after that massacre by U.S.
government troops, which were, by that time, stationed on all Sioux homelands. Four years. Hardly enough time for the grass to grow over the grave.
And the U.S. military was stationed within the borders of the reservation, a
fearsome occupation army. Does anyone believe Indians were voluntarily
"ceding" lands during that period of time?

This 1894 Act of Congress, which is cited in 1997 as evidence for further
land theft, rose out of a policy of extermination and genocide. A policy that
was put in place because the Sioux could not be defeated on the battlefields
of the Northern Plains. They could not be coerced, in a hundred other ways
that were tried, into giving up their lives. The Sioux efforts to survive thirty
years of warfare in defense of their place on the Northern Plains was dealt
with by these illegal actions of Congress and the courts and other bureau-

cracies in which the Sioux had no status. This Act of Congress in 1894 was inspired by the officials who made up the government of South Dakota, which was then in its infancy. Its powerful land monopolists were everywhere. Today, these same powerful interests in South Dakota, sitting in high places and throughout the country, prevail upon their racist past to continue land theft. They do it through government and the courts. Make no mistake, this 1997 court decision to "remove" Indian lands from Indian title and "transfer" them to the state is a crime not only against the Yanktons but against all peoples who are powerless and colonized.

The state has not been, as anyone can tell you, an innocent bystander in the continued theft of lands and rights, and for us to suggest that a people's movement in this state toward "reconciliation" can have any meaning while these acts of war continue is foolish. The Santees, the Oglalas, Hunkpapas, Ihanktowan, Sicangu, Minneconjou, and Sihasapa, all of us have suffered from this kind of paper warfare that not only legalizes land theft but legalizes the death of the tribes. To have your courts legally declare the tribes nonexistent, in case you care to give a name to it, is called genocide. Isn't genocide a crime? In Bosnia? Iraq? But not in the United States? No wonder our Sioux leaders have gone to the international courts in the last few years to try to get a hearing on what is happening to us. In the international arena there may be more of a chance for an appropriate discussion of the consequences with those who perpetuate genocide as national policy.

The governor of our state considers the Yankton Reservation case resolved. He is "optimistic" about building relations with the Yankton Sioux and he now wants to talk about "tracking down" Indian parents who do not support their children. If this kind of inequality and hypocrisy is allowed to continue in our state and on our reservations, untold crimes will follow and we will be horrified by them. Child abandonment will be the least of them.

There is a term that needs to be used here. The term is Anti-Indianism. In the same way that Anti-Semitism was in the beginning the offspring of religious persecution, Anti-Indianism here in our region has been the child of legal and church institutions that govern our lives. What history has shown us is that even when the Jews gave up their religion and their identities, they were still unacceptable to German society, and Hitler began to move toward their complete extermination. Likewise, even as Sioux Indians became Christians, there has been no avenue of escape from political oppression and massacre and discrimination, and, finally, the theft of the homelands. If there is to be a peace process here, we must begin with the return of land for two important reasons: first, there is no more important value to colonized peo-

ple than the land; and second, it is in the land that the native finds his morality and religion, his life and his survival.

What Indians here in our region have understood is that we have had very
little power to affect the body politic in the state of South Dakota and this
has always been true. When we have no way to affect the body politic in our
state, we have tried to believe that we could depend on the federal government, with which we have signed solemn treaties. Unfortunately, the federal
government, our "trustee" that holds our lands in limbo, has proven to be
as corrupt and unreliable as any other self-serving institution in its dealings
with us. When you cannot affect the body politic and when your "trustee" is
corrupt, you turn to the courts. It has taken a long time to learn the lesson
that we cannot depend on the courts either to go all the way with us. Half-
way justice is no justice at all.

In the last decades, the courts have turned out to be the last places Indians
should turn to for justice. Indeed, a 1994 case called *Hagen v. Utah* has been
a central case in what is now called the "diminishment" movement, a movement led by key states in the West, among them Utah, Washington, New
Mexico, and South Dakota. I call this twentieth-century movement a movement of legalized genocide, which is traced to a denied history. The decision
in *Hagen v. Utah* holds that Utah state courts have jurisdiction over Indians
as to crime on land within original reservation boundaries. This is based on
a ruling that Congress in past acts had the intent to diminish the reservation.
A ruling which, if upheld, is evidence of a genocidal federal policy. Obviously,
this is an effort on the part of states to place land outside of Indian Country
as defined in 1902, and it clearly indicates the ambiguity concerning Indian
tribal survival. On the one hand, the courts say they try to be fair. On the
other, they express the historical view that America must be rid of tribal
nations once and for all.

You might be interested to hear Blackmun's and Souter's dissenting views
from the Supreme Court on the Utah case. They wrote:

> ... the state of Utah lacked jurisdiction because lands where the offense occured
> were Indian Country, since (1) there was no clear expression in either the face,
> surrounding circumstances, or legislative history of the 1902 statute that Con-
> gress INTENDED to diminish the reservation and (2) even if the 1902 statute's
> public domain language constituted express language of diminishment, such
> language did not remain operative in the 1905 statute, which actually opened
> reservation lands for settlement, but did not restore unalloted lands to the public
> domain.

Blackmun and Souter did not agree that jurisdictional issues in Indian Country could be decided on such flimsy evidence of historical intent. Dissenting views do not always carry the day, but they are often concerned with the larger issues and are often used in defense of further legal, political, and legislative dialogue. In the view of many, we have not heard the last of this discussion. The unfortunate fact about this kind of behavior on the part of the courts and certain ideologues who sit in high places is that sooner or later these decisions will have to be reexamined, and very likely overturned or rewritten in the name of justice and fairness. In the meantime, tribes have spent hundreds of thousands of dollars in defense of themselves, money that could have been used to develop tribal economies. In the meantime, tribes remain in poverty and dependent on the church or the Bureau of Indian Affairs or the tribal government, or gaming, for reservation jobs. And in the meantime people wonder why racial relations suffer in the very contested places where it is vital that the people learn to live together in harmony.

Under these circumstances, I do not talk to anyone about "reconciliation." I feel it is inappropriate and hypocritical to talk of reconciliation in the face of this kind of massive assault on tribal lands and rights. This current "diminishment" movement is a powerful one, and it is backed by states' rightists and several current governors, senators, and the courts, and if anyone cares about fairness between the races, he or she had better be informed about who these antagonists are and what their motives and strategies are. White folks in this state don't need to learn our tribal language, white people don't need to invade our sun dances and other religious rites of the people. European-inspired sculptors and politicians don't need to blow up mountains in the Sacred Black Hills and call it Crazy Horse Mountain, when his people live desperate lives not a hundred miles away. No one even needs to talk about Wounded Knee to come to some kind of rational thinking on these matters. What is needed is a critical examination of the institutions that surround all of us, Indians and whites, with racist strategies.

What is needed is political opposition to what is now the status quo in the legislative and political arena here, discourse concerning the Black Hills land-reform issue and a way to keep the governor off the Missouri River—real things that affect the real lives of real people.

Let us be honest and admit there are many antagonists to tribal sovereignty and the defense of tribal rights, land, and resources, not the least of which is the powerful state government and its agencies, which are the center of the current move to diminish Indian rights. This should come as no surprise to anyone, since state governments everywhere in the American states have always had contentious relationships with tribes. The history of the state of Georgia and the Cherokees a hundred years ago taught us about the risk to tribal nations in the aggressive rise of state power. The state of South Dakota has been constant in its desire to dispossess the Sioux. There is no ambiguity about where the state stands on matters of land and jurisdiction. Before we can talk about reconciliation, South Dakotans have to understand this history of dispossession and its connection to present life. White South Dakotans who have benefited from this dispossession and continue to benefit have to be willing to return stolen lands to tribal title and jurisdiction. They must honor and respect old agreements before new ones can be made.

Drastic measures are sometimes needed. Right now we hear that in New Mexico, the Pueblo Indians, who are just outside of Albuquerque and who have been in constant litigation over jurisdiction with the state, are talking of blockading main highways and freeways, I-25 for example, the main artery that crosses Pueblo lands. There is serious talk in some sections of Indian society in New Mexico of blockade and it is reported in the newspapers of the state; this shows how desperate Indians can get. In fact, this talk by the Pueblos is in response to the reality that the Pueblo casinos pay hundreds of thousands of dollars in taxes to the state of New Mexico. Some of these groups, among the poorest people on the face of the earth, pay as much as a quarter of a million dollars to the state every year and never see anything in return except racism and joblessness.

I want to return, as I close this talk, to a quote from that old water-rights man, Bill Veeder, who spoke with my father twenty years ago. He said this: "It is an ongoing practice in America to devastate Indian tribes. You tribal people must expose the deadly consequences of being subjected to state court jurisdiction. There must likewise be exposed the devastating consequence of federal and state officials practicing deceit upon the Native American tribes under the guise of 'settling' conflicts among the tribes and non-Indian claimants."

Not much has changed in twenty years. The old man, that day, was talking to tribal people. He did not say what well-meaning white people should do or could do. Today, "settlements" and "reconciliations" go forward, but there is no dialogue concerning land reform, the return of stolen lands, the sacred Black Hills, the return of the state-run Bear Butte Park, the illegal allotment act, which devastated tribal economies for the last hundred years with the result of "checker-boarded" Indian lands, the wrongs commited by Congress and the courts in diminishing the tribal land base. Indeed, since the old man spoke to my father and the general public that day, hundreds of thousands of acres of tribal lands all over this country have been removed from tribal title and tribal peoples are further impoverished.

The violation of the tribes' vested and reserved rights for the benefit of greedy developers of this country has to be stopped before tribes and tribal people can talk seriously about reconciliation. At universities like this one, we must not become irrelevant to the struggle for justice and the struggle for decency in Indian lives and on our homelands. We must inspire our children by doing the right thing; by understanding the crimes of the past and paying the price of punishment. We do that through self-examination, by looking critically at the institutions that govern our lives and reforming them.

No one would deny, and certainly not an old college professor like myself, that what we talk about and what we teach to one another about American history is critical to self-understanding. Surely we should include in our teaching the study of the Constitution, 1889 statehood, the Civil War, Thomas Jefferson, brave pioneers, explorers, and scientists. But what we have to say about all of that history is that it dispossessed the indigenous peoples of this country, among them the Sioux in South Dakota, through verifiable criminal behavior that has been legitimized in the courts. What we must say is that this criminal behavior still goes on in our present lives. What we must say about this so-called reconciliation movement is that it has provided a mechanism that has allowed us to excuse past crimes, to cover them up with avoidance and denial, and that there has been an intention to fool ourselves concerning equality and the right and the possibility of Indians to make a good life.

Most of all, we should teach our children that crimes, just like the rivers that have been exploited, stolen, and damaged, do carry footprints. Those footprints are what have kept the Sioux people from sharing in the abundance of their own lands, but they are also the footprints of our ancestors, who fought wars and signed treaties so that we could live.

In conclusion, I say that it is time for all of us to examine those footprints. They are the footprints of history. It remains to be seen whether the United States can reform its behavior toward its indigenous peoples and take its place among nations that live up to their treaty obligations. It remains next to inquire whether or not the state of South Dakota can live with its Indian co-residents or whether it will continue its relentless effort to extinguish us and our rights as tribal people entirely before it will be satisfied. At the close of the twentieth century these matters are crucial. It is time to look closely at the genocidal practices I've talked about here today and stop them.

As you know, it is not easy to do the right thing. I tell this often to my children and my grandchildren. It is not easy to do the right thing. But it is noticeable in all of the conversations that I have with people now how often this phrase, "Do the right thing," appears and reappears. That, in itself, is a hopeful thing.

Presented at the seventh annual history conference of South Dakota State University at Brookings, Feb. 25, 1998. The theme was "State/Tribal Relations."

17

AMERICAN INDIAN STUDIES:
AN OVERVIEW

Good Afternoon!

The title of this conference, "Translating American Indian Cultures: Representing, Aesthetics, and Translation" is a bit intimidating, especially to a tribal scholar like myself who has always thought of Indians in America in terms of *nationhood*. Culture, it seems, has been left to Anthropology, and there seems little sense in pursuing that line of scholarship if we are concerned with the struggle to survive as nations-within-a-nation political entities.

Nationalism, I think, is the major focus of Native American Studies as an academic discipline, in contradistinction to Anthropology. So the title of this conference is broad and, yes, intimidating, but of course quite useful to all of us who have gathered here at this moment to discuss the differences in disciplinary approaches to bodies of knowledge.

I'd like to begin by saying that there is a disturbing reality about the academic dialogue these days concerning the intent of NAS, and much of it is centered in the language we have used and the languages we have invented for whatever purposes have emerged. Much of the dialogue suggests that unless you are willing to talk about diversity or multiculturalism or postmodernism or postcolonialism, you are simply out of the loop, to use a George Bush phrase with which we have become familiar. In fact, there is even a native scholar of our acquaintance who is now promoting the use of the term *post-Indian* in his particular dialogues.

Post-Indian? What is this? Could it be an effort to conceptualize the annihilation of Indians or their nations or their histories? Well, maybe not. I can see the point that is on the board here: since natives did not call themselves Indians until Columbus came along and misnamed them, perhaps we should rid ourselves of the word. For 500 years Indians were the subjects of American History, but now we are the subjects of Postindian Studies. The truth is, language has a tendency to take on a life of its own. And for some of us this kind of language obfuscates and confuses. What does postindian mean? What does postcolonial mean? In the same way that the postcolonial desire is the desire for decolonized communities, is the postindian desire the desire for deindianizing communities? If so, what does that mean in terms of history and sovereignty, land, identity? More words that need examination and definition. Well, my only point here is that language matters—as all of us know. And we must treat it with great care.

What I really want to do this afternoon is to make a few observations about the condition of Native American Studies now in the process of three decades of development. First of all I think we must take seriously the very real presence of a very real backlash to our work; not a backlash to the stuff that kowtows to the mainstream stereotypes (and there is plenty of that), but a backlash to the research and writing that thoughtful Indian scholars are doing in defense of the land and geography and rights and obligations of the indigenous condition.

This means that those of us who want to do serious work must recognize differences between those authors who merely tap into an already legitimized scholarship, or the authors who tap into American guilt of some kind, and those authors who really engage their audiences in serious issues of land, sovereignty, survival. There is a difference between those Indian authors who are merely self-serving and those who are in the service of their tribal nations.

I don't mean that there isn't room for all kinds of authorship, and I'm not advocating some kind of censorship. But my point is that there is a real backlash to the serious tribal-nation work that serious scholars are doing. And our reaction to this backlash is critical. It is interesting to make this comment about backlash here at Yale, here in New Haven, since this is one of the places that was central to the academic revolution that took place in 1968 and 1970 and beyond and the revolution that is now so much reviled by conservatives and right-wingers.

No one here at Yale will forget (at least I hope they won't) the suspended classes, the Black Panthers' rallies, and the statement of Yale's patrician president Kingman Brewster, who said at that time: "I am skeptical of the ability of the black revolutionaries to achieve a fair trial anywhere in the United States." He could just as well have said this about Indians getting a fair trial.

I wonder how much has changed since that time. I wonder how much it is possible to challenge the public order as the revolutionaries of that era did, and still get a fair trial.

I wonder about it because in the decade of the 1990s it has seemed to me, nearly thirty years after President Kingman said those words, the idea that Indian Studies has gotten a fair trial in the institutions across the land is debatable. As a discipline it has had to fight off the scientific community, the oppression of anthropology, the opportunism of ethnic studies, postcolonial studies, literary studies, activist English departments, history, the conservative right. It seems that we must consider the possibility of an unfair trial and the consequences, i.e., a severe backlash, the deliberate trivialization, co-optation, marginalization of our work.

It is significant that we meet here at Yale University, thirty years after the origins spoken of here, for every Indian scholar knows that here, at this place, on this campus, the papers of Felix Cohen, the "Father of Indian Law," are housed. More than any other scholar Cohen assisted an academic culture in understanding the importance of defending the moral and legal rights of minority populations in America, and in defending the situation of American Indian populations, indigenous populations, in specific ways. His work made it possible, make no mistake, for us to understand that academic institutions have never been the "ivory towers" they've claimed to be, that they have always had a political agenda, one that has been in serious conflict with the interests of native populations and Native Studies. Cohen's work made it possible to admit that the law has rarely been moral in its treatment of Indians unless it has been taken up by ever-critical minds. And sometimes not even then.

The myths, the clichés, the caricatures that have passed for education and law and politics concerning the American Indian Experience are laid bare in Cohen's work, and his legacy here at Yale is an important one. He and the student and faculty radicals on this campus during the many crises of the sixties finally took the hidden politics of the privileged few out of the closet, and we have all understood our academic institutions in a very different way ever since. Of course there is still George Bush and all the CIA guys that come out of this place—speaking of the legacy of the privileged few at Yale—yet I think we will never return to the era of pretended scholarly disinterest in politics that we once knew.

One of the traits that distinguishes Native American Studies as an academic discipline (and it is a trait much maligned but finding its origins in those early times) is its demand that its intelligentsia expose the lies of the self-serving

colonial academic institutions of America; and to bolster the right and obligation to disobedience; and to resist the tyranny of U.S. fantasies concerning history and justice and morality. This trait has not made the development
of the discipline popular. Indeed, the backlash that we speak of rises out of
this ongoing trait.

Sometimes the backlash is savage, sometimes it is subtle. To illustrate just
how pervasive it is, I'll tell you a little humanities story. In October 1997, I
had the opportunity to hear Doris Kearns Goodwin, the biographer/histo-
rian who wrote about the Roosevelts and LBJ, give a talk to the Humanities
Councils and faculty and students at Black Hills State University in Spearfish,
S.Dak., a half-hour drive from where I live.

It was a wonderfully fluid talk as she told us about her work, her private
and friendly relations with the powerful in Washington, D.C., the presidents
and their families; and then the Q&A period followed. As Goodwin finished,
a young, blonde university undergraduate, born and raised in the state of
South Dakota, rose to ask the following question: "Why do we have to denigrate history? Denigrate western culture, tear down this wonderful history
of western culture and America? It's a shame that we have to push it aside . . .
to push aside what is here . . . to . . . to . . ."

She didn't finish her sentence. This is a young woman who lives in the
presence of eight Sioux Indian reservations that have suffered a cruel and
racist history known as Western History and Culture, where poverty and
colonial practices reign even today, more than a hundred years after the peace
treaties were signed. I wondered who she was, what her experience had been.
Obviously, I thought as this exchange went on, this is a young woman who
thinks Disney's movie about Pocahontas is the kind of history we should
know, that all was well in the colonies as it is now in this part of the world: a
young woman who possibly thinks Ken Burns's dreadful Lewis and Clark
documentary "The Journey of the Corps of Discovery," in the tradition of
all colonial narrative, is good history, when in truth it is a largely whitewashed
history that allows Burns to finalize his thoughts at the end of the piece in
this way: "The wonderful thing about this country, America, is that it *started at zero.*"

That is, I think, very nearly an exact quote. Burns's dismissal of thousands
of years of occupancy by indigenous peoples of this continent is an astonishing omission. I wondered if this young woman, lamenting about the "denigration" of history, a woman very likely from the Black Hills, could be cogni-
zant of such omissions. No. Of course she could not. She was, perhaps through
no fault of her own, unwilling to hear about the historical, legal theft of the

Black Hills from the Sioux Nation by the United States; resistant to the idea that a real history revealed that theft in 1980, as the Supreme Court of the land answered the Lakota/Dakota Sioux question Was our land taken illegally? The answer from the court was yes. Was this the history this young woman described as a "denigration"? Did this woman know this history? Did Goodwin?

Probably not. But what interested me most was not that the young woman's question was asked, but the way historian Goodwin answered it. She said to the young woman: "You are right to worry about the 'denigration' of history. There is so much beauty in the old, white, male culture. It is unfortunate that certain movements have had such a negative impact on us, the past . . . what is here . . . who we are."

She went on. "We need a balance. We do not have to denigrate what is here." The Goodwin response suggested to some who know a silent Indian history in different ways from those who know a public history (and there were a few Sioux Indians in the audience) that colonial countries can murder indigenous people and steal land and never pay the price for their crimes. When such murders and thefts are brought up as part of a real history they seem somehow too unnerving or rude, somehow unnecessary, that is to say, "denigrating."

This exchange reflects one aspect of the backlash to which I refer. It is expressed subtly, with poignancy and innocence. For some of us, there is no question that the guardians of the cleansed history longed for by this student and Ms. Goodwin must be overthrown. And there is no question that the newly crowned historians like Ken Burns must be challenged. I would suggest that you read the collection of essays called *The New Historicism*, edited by H. Aram Veeser, published by Routledge in 1989, to get a feel for what must be done.

As far as we here in this room are concerned, those of us engaged in the development of Native Studies, there is no ambiguity about the "movements" that Goodwin laments: Black Studies, Native American Studies, the Feminist Movement, La Raza. There is no ambiguity, either, in her position of calling our attempt at rewriting history "negative." When Indian scholars call attention to the errors of a vicious colonial history and demand that such histories be acknowledged, our work is "negative." In my understanding of the word *denigration*, it means to belittle, to defame the character or reputation, to attack the good name by libel or slander. What we may conclude, therefore, is that it becomes a crime to revise a well-loved, scrupulously cleansed, and largely mindless history while the attempt to do better, to correct, to investigate is seen as inappropriate scholarship.

Much of what I've wanted to talk about lately has had to do with the "good name" or the "character" or the "reputation" of what we have called the American Experience. Why else would I have published an essay called "Why I Can't Read Wallace Stegner," which became the title of a collection. Because it is important to Indian Studies to critically analyze the western image of which Wallace Stegner's work is exemplar, many of us would like it to become important to all historians to find answers to the thorny questions that plague native populations across the land.

My recent collection of essays, because it focuses on the darker aspects of a whitewashed western history, has not been universally well received, as you might expect. Students in midwestern colleges don't like it, I'm told by the professors who try to bring it to their classes, because they say it is too mean-spirited—yes, denigrating. A few historians who have reviewed it in their academic journals say it is merely a "polemic," and I am oppressive in my views. But I'm not complaining. This collection will go into its third printing soon, and some believe it to be an "important" work. In 1997 it was awarded the Myers Center Award for the Study of Human Rights in North America as "the outstanding work on intolerance in North America." Just the other day, though, my editor at the press sent me the review of one Dr. Forrest G. Robinson of the University of California history department, Santa Cruz, who says this collection is clearly an absurd, one-sided polemic. "Most readers," he says, "will not be comfortable with Cook-Lynn's hopelessly one-sided account of American History."

What writers must do in the face of such conflicting historical narratives can, perhaps, be summed up in two ways: First, writers have to decide what it is that they are going to look *hard* at. Certainly Stegner did that. I try to do that. If we come to two different conclusions, it is the function of historical narrative to be explicit. I would never say, for example, as Stegner has said, "The Plains Indians are done." Or "Western history sort of stopped in 1890" (the year of the Wounded Knee Massacre in South Dakota). Why is it left up to me to call attention to Stegner's one-sidedness and then be condemned for it? That is a rhetorical question, as most of you know, and also, as most of you know, all rhetorical questions are accusations. So I am accusing the scholarly community of a failure to act responsibly as intellectuals in fairly examining these kinds of different conclusions. It is a harsh accusation but I do not apologize.

The second thing that writers and scholars must do is engender significant audience participation. Stegner did that. His audience was and is huge as he shares the experiences and values of mainstream America. He is preaching to the choir. On the other hand, it seems obvious that many brilliant, authentic Native American scholars have not been all that successful in getting audience participation. By audience participation I don't mean just a rejoinder or conversation: first you say this, then I say that. What I mean by audience participation is the willingness to engage in real discussions of what concerns American Indians—land restoration, sovereignty, treaty and survival issues that will affect our children and grandchildren, the citizens of what my grandfather used to call "the Great Sioux Nation." What are we to tell young people about the future? What advice can we give them as they face their lives? Much of the work we do does not reach what I would call a mainstream audience. Only Pocahontas and Dances with Wolves and the Indian in the Cupboard reach the mainstream. If Doris Kearns Goodwin's remarks tell us anything they tell us that we have not engendered audience participation, as our dialogues are still missing or denied or dismissed.

Part of what we must do in Native American Studies as we go about engendering audience participation is recognize that it will get even more difficult, not easier, as technology takes over. In addition, we have at the present time very little political support for what we do. In the 1960–70 era, when NAS began its modern development into disciplinary strategies, there was a movement across the land, a political movement, several of them, as you remember. Black Power. The American Indian Red Power movement. Feminism. Movements that we will not be witness to again in our lifetimes: all manner of organizations, efforts, programs, even legislative efforts on the part of activists in the U.S. Congress, economic and social upheavals led by people desperate for change.

So far as we here have been concerned, the American Indian Movement comes to mind, a time brilliantly chronicled in Dr. Robert Warrior's *Like a Hurricane*. NAS centers, research centers, curricular designs, course development, media work, reservation-based community colleges, the training of people for intellectual and political life, scholarship support, mentoring programs, all sorts of important mechanisms and strategies came out of all the activism of that period. A great deal of publishing by scholars concerning the American Indian Experience was pushed along in the momentum, and textbooks became available for course development.

The challenge today as we see this century come to a close is to keep the focus of the early ideas of nationalism and our connections to specific geographies *in the absence of those political movements*. And, unfortunately, in the presence of a significant backlash. To keep the focus as we manage change and transformation, and as we move away from the political radicalism of the past.

Some say that to retain one's radical credentials is to remain marginal and desperate. Some say that remaining marginal is to remain ineffectual. Every intellectual must make his or her way in the context of such ambiguity.

The challenge today is to remember that our constituents are the Indian nations of America, who are in great jeopardy. Continued land thefts, now called "land transfers" in the part of the country where I come from, go on relentlessly, and we all know that without our homelands we will cease to exist. "Diminishment" and even "disestablishment" are the thrust of the court systems. The challenge today is to remember that our constituents are not now and have never been just students, many of whom can fend for themselves, not just faculties, many of whom compromise for personal gain, not just universities, notoriously self-serving and Euro-centered. The challenge today is to remember that the focus of Native American Studies was in the beginning an attempt to create a mechanism in defense of the indigenous principles of tribal sovereignty and nationhood in a democracy like the United States, with whom the tribal nations signed solemn treaties.

Sovereignty. Nationalism. These are political principles, make no mistake. In today's global thinking, these are considered pejorative terms except for great powers. Yet for a colonized people the most essential value in the defense of self is in the land, for it is in land that the native finds morality, and it is only in land that rights and nationhood reside. We must do the work in exposing land "transfer" legislation as theft. We must examine the work of the Senate Select Committee on Indian Affairs, a white male entity in Washington, D.C., that often works against tribes in spite of its auspicious name. We must find out who is behind the "diminishment" movement that has been developing in the Supreme Court in the last ten years. And we must encourage them to work for change. We must use the concept of sovereignty as history has given it to us, continue to understand how it functions in a democracy such as ours, develop it as a unique concept in the democratic fields of endeavor. We must not be afraid. And most of all, as intellectuals in the modern world, Indian scholars must not let themselves become irrelevant to all that by ignoring the risks therein.

Speaking of irrelevance, one could go on and on about how much of what is done in Native American Studies is irrelevant to the real lives that real people are living. In the description of a recent conference on Native American Studies, their work was described in this way: *Native Americans have found an audience by the blending of a tribal world with the Euro-American worldview. The result is a Native American Renaissance that seeks to combine the best of American Indian cultures with the American mainstream. Such a combina-*

*tion may help to address two pressing concerns: (1) healing our damaged envi-
ronment, and (2) slowing the disintegration of our nation's social fabric.*

Is this what we have come to? Blending in? Saving the Ozone layer? Well,
there's nothing wrong with all that surely, and someone should attend to it.
But one must ask, is this what the development of Native American Studies
as an academic discipline has had in mind since the 1960s when we fought
off the U.S. congressional legislation called Termination and Relocation?
When we looked hard at federal Indian policy as a policy of continuing genocide? When our rivers were assaulted and stolen and our rights and territories diminished? When we came close to the end as nations and America said
we no longer existed? I think not.

Though I was not in attendance, I was told that there were several presen-
tations at the conference that illustrated the rise of irrelevance in native schol-
arship. One presentation was entitled "My Multicultural Identity: Where I'm
From and Where I'm Going." Reminds me of that country and western song,
"Here's a quarter . . . call someone who cares. . . ." Another presentation was
"Audible Vanishing American from a Crossblood Elder." And another was
"Looking for Buffalo Bill's Wild West." Do we really need more Buffalo Bill
stories?

What I've been complaining about recently and especially in the decade
of the nineties is this kind of tokenism, marginalization, domination, co-
optation, and irrelevance in Indian Studies, because what it amounts to is the
effort to honor irrelevance, and in the process ignore or discredit genuinely
significant work. I'm thinking particularly of the response to the work of
Professor Vine Deloria by the scientific community concerning his latest
book, *Red Earth, White Lies.* Much of Professor Deloria's work and much of
our work, as many of you don't need to be told, is the work of decoloniza-
tion. This is often a violent enterprise causing great upheaval, but in the
United States and as far as Indians are concerned in this period, it is a passive violence that is easily ignored. There are no guns or knives, no murders,
no police coming in the night. The violence is hidden, often undiscovered
or whitewashed.

What we have to contend with is a colonialist infrastructure, university
faculties, writers and novelists who are determined to evaluate our work as
regressive or irrelevant or denigrating to western civilization, and therefore
radical or unscholarly. Unfortunately, many Indian scholars who might be
called "colonial laureates" by readers of Camus or Franz Fanon agree with
the negative and regressive description of what we are trying to do. Today,
self-centered colonized intellectuals who are in charge of the discourse see

the Indian world only in terms of deficiency or assimilation or self-centered egoism or exploitation. Indeed, many of the new native novelists and writers are rewarded for describing what I call the "deficit" model of Indian life. They are rewarded for many reasons, but for no reason more dangerous than America's need to see us as non-players in developing the human dialogue so necessary to the making of a just and civilized world.

Many native scholars who, because they have been largely missionized by the academic elite (most of the time through no fault of their own), are removed from the ongoing political struggle for freedom on the homelands, removed from the notion that the defense of the land is a legitimate reason, perhaps the only legitimate reason, for our existence as scholars in the universities of the country. Native American Studies in 1990 is littered with colonial laureates, those promising native scholars (or those who claim to be natives) who have been developed through university missionizing, those persons who carry on the dialogues created for them by a Euro-American scholarship, publishing houses, and graduate schools.

The question of what we are to do in the face of this dilemma is a critical one. The question of how and what one teaches is essential. Therefore, in conclusion, I would like to make a few remarks about pedagogy, for it is in pedagogy that scholars reproduce themselves, where knowledge becomes empirical, and where the future of any discipline lies.

For one thing, in our course development both in history and literature we must pay more attention to Third World scholarship and politics than we have in the past. We must get out of the mind-numbing education departments and the savagely aggressive related disciplines only that which will help us to understand the future of Indian nationhood. We must not be afraid to say that it is only through defending our tribes as nations of people rather than sociological phenomena or personal agonies, and our specific geographies as essential to social order, that we will take our place in world affairs and the future. It is only through national liberation and tribal autonomy that we will be able to tell our children who they are. As indigenous peoples these matters are absolute.

What this means in terms of pedagogy in Native American Studies is that this principle of nationalism is a style of thought upon which epistemological distinctions must rest. Unfortunately, today we have writers, scholars and teachers, poets and novelists whose work is being published as Native American literature or history or scholarship that is entirely devoid of this style of thought. Some may argue that this style of thought rose out of the militancy of the era of the sixties and (1) borrows too much from Euro-American history, i.e., "You tribes were not nations until America came along and signed treaties with you and designated you as semi-dependent," or (2) limits the possibility for transformation, i.e., "Do you want to go back to living in tipis and wearing hides?" But these arguments should be recognized as the strategies of co-optation and trivialization.

Co-optation criticism is usually based on the failure of America and its own "two-world" theory of the Other, the theory that expresses the notion that only in western civilization is there universality; in other civilizations, there is only the problem of "two worlds." Nothing could be more false and misleading. Most of the time what scholars take for universality in western literature or history or scholarship is merely narrow-minded, self-serving justification of western precedence. So to co-opt Third World theories as Other serves to change the subject.

In terms of how and what we must teach, the first thing to understand is that Native American Studies is not interested in censorship or in delegitimizing the idea of academic freedom. It is interested only in its own search for an academic structure through which its knowledge base may become useful to its own constituencies.

The claim to having devised new ways of teaching and studying history must be looked at very critically. In that context, it is now being written by native scholars here as well as in Canada that "ethnic" studies, which has made this self-serving claim, is an inappropriate paradigm through which American Indian experience can truly be articulated. This is an important criticism since indigenous peoples are native to a specific geography with specific histories, treaties, rights, and responsibilities, and their participation in American society as "ethnics" negates their very histories of origin and marginalizes them in dangerous ways. Indigenousness as a concept in the American Experience is rarely taken seriously in "ethnic" studies, but Immigration as a concept is given priority.

We must understand, also, that designation of knowledge as postcolonial will probably not assist in legislation or political solutions to make colonizing a crime, as slavery was made a crime against black people and outlawed as criminal behavior. As you all know, postcolonial studies refers to the period after the colonies become independent, and such independence has not occured for Indian tribal people. For the most part, as everyone knows, too, the lands of American Indian tribal nations are still held in colonial "trust" status by the U.S. government, and this contributes to economic dysfunction. Until that condition is understood, the term *postcolonial* is simplistic and incongruous. Failure to acknowledge this brings about and promotes, in case anyone cares, a situation of economic imperialism that has kept Indians in poverty for over a hundred years.

While it is important that Indian Studies consider the histories that from the moment of colonization to the present day have affected populations, we must move on from that position into the development of new epistemologies and strategies that will eventually lead to solutions in the real world. Let me remind you that our disciplinary strategies can be said to be threefold: (1) defensive, (2) regulatory, and (3) transformative. In the same way, studies in multiculturalism or diversity, while not bad things, are limited in their ability to clarify the political status of Indian nations. None of the strategies used in multiculturalism defend or transform the indigenous nations of America as possessors of specific tribal and political rights, land, and culture. And their regulatory strategies bind Indians into an awful historical context as non-participants.

In conclusion I want to say this: at the center of every debate concerning the nature and intent of Native American Studies as an academic discipline is the role of intellectuals as either dissidents or assimilationists or postmoderns or postcolonials or even, now, postindians. Dissidents are attacked or ignored but remain a powerful presence. Assimilationists are honored, revered, often carefully nurtured and rewarded. Many others simply become irrelevant. Are we satisfied with what all of this means? I'm not. Native indigenous nationalists is what I want us to consider ourselves.

There is an awesome range of intelligence and good intentions in the field of academic inquiry that we have chosen. I always keep in mind what some of the great Sioux leaders of the past have told us. Crazy Horse, Sitting Bull. Even the parents who raised us and taught us our languages and ways. They have all said: "Remember, the people depend on you."

Please keep in mind as you go about your work that the people depend on you.

I look forward to the rest of the conference and hope that we'll have a chance to go on with this preliminary discussion. Thank you.

Keynote Address, presented at an NAS conference entitled "Translating American Indian Cultures: Representing, Aesthetics, and Translation," Yale University, New Haven, Conn., Feb. 5, 1998.

PART FIVE

GENOCIDE

18

ANTI-INDIANISM AND GENOCIDE: THE DISAVOWED CRIME LURKING AT THE HEART OF AMERICA

Just before my latest non-fiction book, *The Politics of Hallowed Ground,* a book about the politicization of Indian histories and the Massacre at Wounded Knee was going into its second printing, I picked up a local newspaper and read in a column written by the conservative Republican television "talking head" George Will that the "Serbian atrocities in Kosovo [taking place in the last decade of the twentieth century] are *not* genocide, but they are war crimes." In the same newspaper Zbigniew Brezinski, National Security Advisor to President Jimmy Carter, wrote that "the Serbs are engaging in what may be called *mini-*genocide."

This confusion about the violent and oftentimes criminal actions of western governments is nothing new, yet there is something terribly disturbing about this confusion as we move into the new century. Often such crimes have been placed into the historical dialogue to describe what is a "just" war and what is an "unjust" war, but rarely have they been admissions of campaigns to exterminate an entire people. For example, when Theodore Roosevelt said that the American war with the "savage Indians" over this land was the most "just" war in all of history, he made the stealing of native lands and the murder of its possessors a most admired history, and he deliberately confused the killings done by the United States of America with what we may call justifiable homicide. It was a brilliant tactic of historical manipulation by a powerful man in the most powerful of nations, and it was a mark of his influence that continues today.

Teddy Roosevelt and countless other leaders of colonizing nations have no doubt believed and acted upon what Pericles in ancient Athens was supposed to have said: "Before I praise the dead, I should like to point to the institutions and by what *principles* of action we rose to power and under what *institutions* and through what *manner* of life our empire became great" (Thucydides, *History of the Peloponnesian War*). Pericles went on to enumerate the virtues of Greek civilization, i.e., "We are called a democracy," "The law secures equal justice to all alike," "Our style of life is refined," "The fruits of the whole earth flow in upon us," "We contend for a higher prize," and so on and so on. Under this kind of persuasion, it is easy to think colonization is a virtuous thing, and even easier to enlist the national population to destroy whatever stands in its way. The war of the Athenians with Sparta lasted twenty-seven years; they made slaves of women and children and killed all male children of military age of many surrounding nations. They put Socrates to death for the crime of speaking his mind.

In light of the atrocities of the past perpetuated in the struggle for power by democratic and non-democratic entities alike, the desire of western and non-western-style civilizations to achieve status in the twentieth century seems to predict continuing violence. Though they are thought by some to be rare throughout the world, look at some of the more obvious events: the Pinochet rule in Chile, Serb massacres of Muslims in the 1990s, the bloodbaths of African countries like Rwanda, and the murders by Pol Pot of his own people, as well as the over 100 million people who have died in the "just" and "unjust" wars of the last decades. We are living, then, in the bloodiest century in human history.

By contrast, the 1890 Wounded Knee Creek killings and violations of civilized human rights in the Northern Plains, the subjects of my latest book, seem a pittance. A mere 300 or 400 Indians. Primitives, after all. Savages in the wilderness. Yet to understand the unrelenting atrocities by the powerful against the weak that continue into present time, we must first expose those who claim to be innocent, and then we must try to understand the nature, the origin, the cause(s) of state-sponsored genocide.

The first thing to acknowledge is that on a cold December afternoon four days after the newcomers to western Dakota Territory finished celebrating the holy rebirth of their savior, Jesus Christ, their armed forces slaughtered over 300 hunted, starving, tyrannized, and unarmed Lakotas traveling through their own country under a white flag, threw them into a mass trench, and covered them up. The first thing to acknowledge is that this was not just an "accident." It did not "just happen." It was not some kind of tragedy of war. This deliberate, premeditated slaughter of a non-Christian people who could not be defeated on the battlefields of their own territory took place along a frozen tributary called Wounded Knee Creek, in the hills of a prairie ridge covered with pines, and it was a planned, inevitable crime committed by the U.S. military, an occupational force, and its legislature and its courts.

This crime, though still unacknowledged by many U.S. historians, the military, as well as scholarly and popular writers of history, has come to represent the federal policy of Genocide, which characterized relations with the indigenous occupants of the American continent and the West. Since the violent worldwide events of the last several decades, and particularly since the Vietnam era, this event at Wounded Knee has undergone some revision and is now described by some as it never was for a hundred years: a criminal act. It has come to represent the thousands of such killings of indigenous peoples across the land as the unexamined crimes at the core of a great nation developed since 1776 on the provocative principles of capitalistic democracy, principles based on the exploitation of resources and land.

Genocide, the systematic killing of a people, is always denied by powerful, tyrannizing, colonizing nations, and when they have talked of it, they have struggled to declare their innocence through careful defining of the word. To add to the problems of holding criminals responsible, those bent upon invading other nations and colonizing or destroying its people, which is seen as a major cause for the crime, rarely have left compelling evidence or written documentation of their policy and criminal behavior. America and its treatment of the indigenous peoples of this continent is no exception to this historical reality.

Throughout American history, the agonizing discourse concerning Indian/white relations is spoken of as "conflict," or "assimilation," or "postcolonial" in nature, but never as "genocide." As the twentieth century closes, it seems obvious that Genocide, in the matter of Indian/white relations in America, has not been just a matter of physical extermination. It has been broadened to include the concept of Ecocide, the intentional destruction of the physical environment needed to sustain human health and life in a given geographical region.

In the international arena there is dialogue concerning the deliberate destruction by the government of the United States of the buffalo in the Northern Plains and the salmon in the Northwest and the rivers throughout the land as a tactic to force submission of tribal peoples during the treaty era and since, and these acts are now debated as a function of genocide. This destruction, called ecocide (the killing of the earth) and deicide (the killing of god), is well documented. In the present light of nationalistic crimes across the

globe, this destruction has become a persuasive feature in the classical definition of historical genocide.

The repression of American native peoples during the last century is one
of the least known genocidal stories of our time. Few pay any attention to the
fact that native people in the Americas are among the most economically deprived and the least well educated of any of the peoples of the world, that they
live as domestic nations in one of the most repressive governmental systems
ever devised in a democracy. Hardly anyone says out loud or writes in the
public media that the neglect of Native American health issues is the shame
of the modern world. No one understands the brutal impact on a people of
the loss of two-thirds of their national/tribal land base in the last eighty years.
There is little discussion of the flooding of 550 square miles of treaty-protected
lands along the Missouri River for hydro power, one of the most ecologically
destructive acts of "progress" in the world, as representative of the actions of
an ecocidal policy toward all the rivers on the continent. Few admit that these
are the fruits of the national denial of historic genocide in the United States
toward indigenous peoples, and that they characterize the codified behavior
of the United States toward countries throughout the globe.

In contrast to those omissions in domestic public discourse, the capitalistic democracy called the United States believes itself to be benign toward
Native Americans, known as an unfortunate and pathetic race of inferior
people; believes it pours money down a bottomless pit called the "Indian
reservation" system, and often expresses its contempt for native peoples who
have tenaciously survived 500 years of Genocide. They often express these
thoughts much in the same manner that the eminent (and retiring) senator
from New York, Patrick Moynihan, expressed them in his 1993 book *Pandaemonium and Ethnicity in International Politics* when he said: "Reservations.
Our worst mistake or worst dilemma as you wish." Except for reservations,
he says, "the U.S. has been spared autonomous regions, bantustans, enclaves."

He should have said that except for reservations, the indigenous peoples
of the North American continent have been dispossessed and murdered.
Nothing is said in all of Moynihan's work, as far as I know, about the crime
of genocide perpetrated by the United States against the natives of this land.
And little is said publicly about the virtue that would be implicit if the modern development of Indian reservation lands were to be promoted as *treaty-
protected homelands* for the indigenous peoples of democratic America. The
native peoples who have survived the ongoing, persistent holocaust of the
nineteenth century in America would be pleased to hear of such public dis-

course, for they know their reserved lands to be areas rich in resources, histories, and wonder, which have nurtured them for generations.

"The systematic killing of a people" was said in the old days to exist legally in three contexts: religious, racial, and ethnic. Whatever the label, the United States has failed to accept its history as a genocidal country in any of these contexts, or in the related spheres of ecocide and deicide. The United States continues to claim its historical innocence and benign intention. In the future, however, with the world as witness to modern nationalistic and human events in Europe and Africa and Asia, colonial America might have to broaden its perspectives on this subject if for no other reason than to refrain from looking foolish.

It is in these recent human behaviors that the United States may more appropriately understand its own tragic role. Whatever context is given, and whatever hopes we as members of modern civilizations may assess, it should be obvious that all forms of genocide are interrelated, pervasive, and criminal in every society known to mankind. Genocide, the world must admit as it views its own history and present condition, is *always* premeditated, forethought, purposeful, designed. Genocide does not, contrary to public notions, *just happen,* the fateful events known only to uncaring gods. Its motives are sometimes obvious, sometimes not, and they often seem fathomable to those who examine them.

Religious genocide is mistakenly thought to be a feature of ancient history, as exemplified by, for example, the Middle Ages, when the Crusades or the Spanish Inquisition or other like atrocities went relentlessly on, even if and when the killing of an entire people ran counter to a specific theology held by the society. In spite of a theology that may have argued against the mass killing of "others," genocide persisted in religious praxis, with religious zeal more than reason or theology supplying the fuel. And it was not just an "ancient" phenomenon, as students of recent history in Africa and Europe and elsewhere around the globe can attest.

Racial and *ethnic* genocide, a feature of the more modern histories exemplified by the German killing of the Jews in Europe in the twentieth-century Nazi Holocaust, is still thought to be a function of ancient history, old irrational hatreds against "others," and kept alive through a religious intolerance in the mainstream, coupled by zeal in the military. There seems to be little historical sense of the present-day so-called ethnocide in the former Yugoslavia, except that it is a function of the historical persistent and pervasive cleavages between the sections that have made up the country for many generations. Racial and ethnic genocide is premeditated in every instance known to history, whether or not it is admitted to by the perpetrators.

Political or *economic* genocide usually arises out of colonization; thus, it is a feature of pluralistic societies created through the activities of migrating and settling. The plural society brought about by invasion and colonization provides a structural base for genocide as pressures for domination, exploitation, and subjugation arise. America's history finds firm ground in this definition.

All of these types of genocide have several traits in common. First, the societies that are the perpetrators of genocide often *pass laws* designed to bring about or prohibit certain behaviors, and these laws are thought to appropriately give license for the complete destruction of a people in their midst. These laws give veracity to deliberate acts committed with the intent to destroy the language, religion, or culture of a national, racial, or religious group within the larger colony. Often laws are passed to prohibit the use of certain languages in daily intercourse or schools, and they destroy the libraries or repositories or objects or otherwise criminalize their use. In the case of indigenous peoples of the United States, laws against the practice of traditional religions and cultural customs were swiftly enacted and rigourously enforced. The Sun Dance was outlawed on the Northern Plains while at the same time Christian ministers prevented traditional marriage patterns and child-rearing practices by instituting compulsory educational institutions. There can be no doubt, despite the defensive rejoinder concerning intent, that these are genocidal laws put in place by a powerful and brutal colonizer intent upon extermination.

Second, societies that are the perpetrators of genocide *construct "badges"* or distinguishing characteristics to be exhibited by the victims as well as the perpetrators suggesting origin and praxis, and this often is intended to subjugate or dominate a people and deny to them their basic human rights. The Jews in modern Germany wore a yellow star. Others must carry cards that identify them with their out-group. Natives in America had to be given "permissions" of various kinds by their oppressors to hunt or gather domestic or religious materials from the countryside. Today they carry cards to identify themselves as tribal persons in order to sustain their treaty rights, which would otherwise be denied.

Third, societies that are the perpetrators of genocide *concoct theories of conspiracy* meant to assist the general populus in understanding the need to destroy or exploit their victims. These theories are upheld through educational institutions and assemblies of various kinds, and provide the structural bases for longstanding and blatant aggression. *The stories of the Ghost Dance cere-monial, as the frenzied acts of a crazed Indian population* that preceded the Wounded Knee Massacre *has been concocted by apologist historians as the ra-tionale for the mass killing.* This conspiracy theory is perpetuated even by present-day historians. The idea that Indians of that era by participating in an essentially religious ceremonial were agreeing to perform together an ille-gal, treacherous act that endangered their white neighbors has become a com-pelling rationale for genocide. By and large, western and European histori-ans have accepted and promoted this explanation, rarely refuting it as a concoction of excuses. Even today, the governor of the state of South Dakota is quoted in the newspapers as fearing that Indian political action concern-ing land-reform issues in the state must be seen as an effort by Indians "to get the whole of western South Dakota returned to them." This kind of con-spiracy theory has been a mainstay in the political power of white politicians.

Finally, societies that are the perpetrators of genocide often build or *arrange appropriate centers for destruction,* annihilation, or subservience. The most bla-tant example in modern history for the annihilation of the Jews all over Eu-rope was the construction of incinerators and concentration camps. It has been suggested that in the United States the development of "plantations" in the southern states for the subjugation and exploitation of African Americans for slave labor would be another example of genocidal centers for destruction.

Some suggest that "reservations" for American Indians in the West were and are extermination centers, and it may have been the intent of the pred-atory democracy called the United States of America to kindle in this way an end either by death and starvation or economic destruction for the na-tive peoples with whom they had fought wars of annihilation for many de-cades for possession of the land.

However, the leaders of the hundreds of Indian nations who signed trea-ties with the U.S. government after the war period, in order to "set aside" reserved homelands for the protection of the people, take an entirely differ-ent view of reserved land bases, and have probably taken that different view from the very beginning of the treaty-signing process in the seventeenth and eighteenth centuries. The citizens of Indian nations now believe "reserva-tions" to be their homelands, and they defend them legally and economically on a daily basis. They do not deny the political possibility that at least some segments of American power structures at one time in the historical past set aside these lands and meant them as concentration camps and extermina-tion centers for peoples they considered unassimilable. There is much writ-ten evidence that people sitting in high places in the governments of the

United States believed that such lands would serve to do away with an un-
wanted and unassimilable population.

How these "reserved land bases," now called Indian reservations or re-
serves, are viewed and described by modern America is critical not only to
the survival of the native peoples of this continent, but to the promotion of
world peace and cooperation. These treaty-protected enclaves, now called
domestic "nations-within-a-nation," inhabited by the original peoples of
North and South America, internal now to a democratic society called the
United States of America, can become, in the future, an example of how a
hated minority resulting from generations of war and land theft and exploitation can rise above the domination and subjugation and exploitation ordinarily accompanying European colonization and invasion. In general, today's American Indians from First Nation enclaves view the accompanying
assimilation techniques of a colonial power on their homelands in government and school structures to be the continuation of genocidal practices, and
they therefore seek and assert domestic sovereignty.

The extermination of an entire people, which can occur at any juncture
in the relationship between various segments of a national society, are dependent upon certain elements and specific developments. The elements
usually have to do with Law, and the developments usually have to do with
Economics. Until World War II there was no competent tribunal, no global
general assembly, no criminal court to investigate the issues of genocide
throughout the world. Thus, the thousands of massacres of American Indians in North and South America were rarely investigated at all, and even more
rarely investigated as criminal acts. No criminal perpetrators sitting in high
places were indicted, and little real punishment was ever meted out. Much
of that genocidal activity was simply charted as reasonable and inevitable
colonial conflict, and it continues to be described in that way in most written histories.

After World War II, however, in 1948, a United Nations convention was held
in order to try to understand the nature of the deliberate and systematic killing of a people in terms of the international crime of Genocide, the description of legal parameters of the crime, and the appropriate punishment of
those who commit the crime. The interesting result of those U.S.-led conventions has been the persistent evasion of the issue of genocide in terms of
its own history toward native peoples. The United States is willing to indict
Adolf Hitler of Nazi Germany, Idi Amin of Uganda, and Pol Pot of Khmer
Rouge fame, but not the hated Zionist leader Menachem Begin, or the U.S.
frontier defender Philip N. Sheridan, or the Methodist minister-turned-colo-

nel John Chivington, or the relentless Manifest Destiny president and per-petrator of murderous policies toward Indians Theodore Roosevelt. This unwillingness is inherent in colonial origins.

From the beginning of the settlement of this country by the French, English, and Spanish colonizing nations, the systematic killing of the indigenous peoples of the continent was a fact of life and death. It was relentless and premeditated. Demographers say that by 1650 about 95 percent of the population of Latin America was wiped out, and by the middle of the 1800s there were said to be 200,000 Indians left in continental America. These survivors have now, at the close of the twentieth century, come back from oblivion. They have defended what is left of their meager land bases, and they continue toward the future as dual citizens—of Indian nations and of the United States. It is said that they are one of the fastest-growing "minority" groups in the country.

The deliberate and premeditated genocide of the early years of invasion and theft, however, has moved on from religious fervor and ethnic and racial hatred to economic genocide and ethnocide. These genocidal tactics are ongoing not only through denial practices but also through outright aggressive governmental tactics. The story of the national denial of this reality is evidenced in national parks all over this country, where there exist plaques and gravestones suggesting that Indian families and tribes "gave of themselves and their land so that this great nation might be born and grow." The fur trade is romanticized in history books and in movies as just a capitalistic or economic event, not a genocidal one. Land laws were passed that removed over half of the treaty-protected lands from Indian title. And, outrageously, in the 1950s, termination and relocation laws were promulgated by the U.S. Congress in order to remove Indians from what remained of the homelands and force them to assimilate into the "mainstream" of American culture. Because of these laws, two-thirds of the indigenous population of America now reside in cities, landless and poor, rather than on their own reservation homelands, which remain, for the most part, underdeveloped enclaves of poverty. With appropriate care and legal remedies, these reservations could become communities well organized to meet the needs of their citizens.

Genocide is not now nor has it ever been just a matter of the physical extermination of a people through mass killings, enslavement or torture, or enforced segregation or colonial apartheid. *It is the denial of basic human rights through the development of a nationalistic legal and social and intellectual system that makes it impossible for a domestic people or domestic nation to express itself collectively and historically in terms of continued self-determination.*

In spite of the reasonableness of any critique of history, nations that have developed genocidal practices toward others within their own nation or society, or even outside of their province, protest their innocence by bringing up the matter of "intent." The United States as well as countless other colonizers have used the rejoinder of "intent" to any critical analysis of their history: "We never *intended* to destroy the natives," they claim. Therefore, if there is and was no "intent," there was and is no "genocide." Even as genocidal legislation and land and resource theft is passed by the modern U.S. Congress without the consent of the tribes, the people who benefit from the colonial practices of the past will excuse themselves as it concerns "intent" by saying, "But I haven't done these things. Maybe these things happened in history, but I am not personally responsible for what happened way back then." They generally excuse and rationalize a history so ugly it cannot be acknowledged.

Even today advocates of an innocent U.S. history say to protesting Indians, "You still exist, don't you? You still have land, don't you?" The suggestion is that if there were crimes committed, they were just the unfortunate incidents of economic development of a country. Indeed, when Brazil was charged with genocide against the Indians in the Amazon region in the mid-1960s, representatives of the Brazilian government said to the world human rights organizations that there was no "malice" toward the Indians, and there was no "intent" to destroy them. And therefore there was no genocide. They even claimed ignorance, saying that they didn't know it was against any law to kill Indians. These are arguments accepted by many of the countries that make up the world investigative bodies.

In Vietnam and Cambodia, there has been the attempt by critics of the wars there to say that the United States committed genocide in those countries for political power in the region and the world, but the colonial answer is always the same: we didn't intend to extinguish an entire people. The defenders of the U.S. policy there attempt, often, to distinguish between the acts themselves, such as the massive bombings that destroyed entire ethnic communities, and the intentions of the United States, which was there to protect other groups in the region. If the intentions were noble, then genocide did not occur, and there is often a massive but bogus paper trail constructed for the benefit of apologetic historians. Quite possibly, in the modern context, the Nazis who frenetically documented their crimes in Germany, have offered a model of what *not* to do if you want to get away with your criminal acts.

In spite of many ambiguities, the Vietnam argument is especially significant to the indigenous peoples of North and South America because the con-

cept of *ecocide,* the intentional destruction of the physical environment needed
to sustain human health and life in a given geographical region, has now been
accepted in the international arena as part of the analysis of the term *genocide.* Its continuation into the present era is in need of further analysis.

This policy of deliberate destruction of the environment and resources and
the continuing theft of Indian lands, which is, unlike the physical destruction endured by the people, well documented and available to researchers,
could well become a persuasive feature in the definition of historical genocide as it concerns native peoples.

Indeed, contemporary federal policy, current court litigations brought by
the tribes in the last forty years since the tribes have acquired access to the
federal court system, must have as their main focus the examination of history in the context of U.S. nationalistic movements. The Wounded Knee
genocide must be restored to the memory of the United States, studies must
be conducted and human rights commissions must be instructed to reject
the neutral stand always taken with regard to the sufferings of the indigenous
populations in the Americas. An exhaustive and complete list of atrocities
must be compiled and a civilized international community must lead a
movement toward land reform and economic and cultural restoration. The
humane treatment of oppressed and indigenous populations everywhere can
no longer be discarded or avoided.

19

POSTCOLONIAL SCHOLARSHIP DEFAMES
THE NATIVE VOICE: ACADEMIC GENOCIDE?

The examination of Indian/white relations in America by academics in the disciplines has always been a contentious matter but for a few brief decades of this century, from 1960 to 1990, when there seemed to be an empathetic and mutually supporting relationship between publishers and scholars and Indians who had begun to provoke reassessments in the emerging postcolonial debates.

In the mid-1960s, as an early example of mutual interest and respect, *Black Elk Speaks,* the story of an Oglala holy man told by a University of Nebraska poet, John Niehardt, became an international bestseller. In the early 1980s *I, Rigoberta Menchú,* a life story translated by Ann Wright and edited by Elisabeth Burgos-Debray, an anthropologist in Paris and the wife of Regis Debray, the French philosopher who popularized Cuban theories of guerrilla warfare, also became a bestseller. This story was a major factor in winning for its Guatemalan Indian subject a Nobel Peace Prize. In these years also, a young Kiowa professor of literatures from Oklahoma, N. Scott Momaday, won a Pulitzer Prize for his novel about the twentieth-century "relocation" period of contemporary American Indian history, *House Made of Dawn,* and has been acclaimed ever since as the preeminent literary voice of Native America. These are just a few of the examples of postcolonial work by Indian scholars, who began during those years to wage a battle against what they alleged was a practice in academia to disbelieve or to blame or to damage their efforts to become a part of the American intellectual voice, i.e., the effort to combat a pervasive genocide of enforced silence.

In the last decade of this century, however, to the dismay of Indian scholars everywhere, the Black Elk ethno-autobiography has become a "how-to" book for new-agers seeking visions in America and Europe, and *I, Rigoberta Menchú* is said by Stanford-trained anthropologist David Stoll, now of Middlebury College in Vermont, to be a willful fraud. Momaday has been caught defending the Bering Strait Theory as an origin story of Native America, and scientists as the truth-tellers, even though this so-called scientific theory is notable only by its absence in the oral traditions of tribal America and refuted by many native spokespersons, most recently by Professor Vine Deloria, Jr., in his book *Red Earth, White Lies.*

The above-mentioned literary events, along with other lesser events, provide a backdrop for the discussion of what can only be described as the attempt to discredit a newly emerged Native Voice flourishing throughout academia in recent decades and as evidence of a major culture war.

As part of the democratizing focus of late twentieth-century academia, the popular emergence of the Native Voice has been called the Native American Literary Renaissance, and its acceptance, though not without its detractors, was thought to be one of the remarkable success stories for those who sought to broaden the American literary and scholarly canons. The stories told to the largest audiences have been the stories told by novelists and filmmakers, but the scholarly output of native scholars in the last twenty years has been an astonishing achievement.

Presently, it seems, the detractors have begun a serious campaign to defame and corrupt these newly emerged indigenous voices. At the close of the century, the effort that indigenous peoples have made to speak for themselves and their people, either through their own works or through the interpretative works of the translator, is being subjected to abuse and scholarly/political attack that goes far beyond the normal critical analysis of academic work.

The emergence of the indigenous voice in academia in the last several decades has been recognized as a huge breakthrough for the right to speak for oneself and one's people. It is thought by some to be as fundamental to the human condition as food and decent housing, an acknowledgment that men and women do not live by bread alone; they live by the creative arts, by storytelling and the intellect, all of which give vibrancy to culture and politics. Thus, the increasing presence of the Native Voice in the Americas provided much outstanding scholarship rising out of the analysis of oral histories and textual authority of native peoples. Suddenly, and to the surprise of those who scrutinized and supported new epistemologies in the recent decades, the adversarial scholarship seems now to be gaining in momentum. This adversarial scholarship, ever at the fringes of Native American Studies, is able to place ignorance, stereotype, reformist movement interests, the will to suppress, and, most significantly, conservative politics at the service of what may be called anti-intellectual debate.

The present dilemma began in the recognition that the placement of the indigenous voice in the national canon not only resulted in confusion concerning disciplinary protocol, but also added to the fear that since U.S. nationalistic perceptions of history and culture differed so greatly from the tribal-nation view given by Indians themselves, deformation and transformation might be the result. In 1996 John Beverley, an American scholar at the University of Pittsburgh, wrote about the contemporary native voice in an essay called "The Margin at the Center," in which he noted that the already established genres in the literary studies of the western canon have given rise to new forms of literature intended to include the self-told stories and experiences of the indigenous peoples of North and South America. He thought that such works, mostly thought of as liberation literatures, might be moving to the center of a postcolonial focus. It is significant that very little was said in that essay about the residue of imperialism influencing this directive.

This essay was included in an anthology edited by George M. Gugelberger entitled *The Real Thing*, which functioned as an attempt to sort out what was textually authentic and what was not. This collection perhaps began as an acknowledgment by many scholars that anthropology, journalism, studies in rhetoric, fiction, and history have been attracted to what is called a postliterary genre of self-told stories that must be taken into account but was in no way an attempt at advocacy. In fact, this collection by scholars may have contributed to anthropological criticism of the native text, *I, Rigoberta Menchú*.

The question of the meaning of these early stages of nationality, nationalism, identity, and veracity as voiced in native literatures did not emerge just since Rigoberta Menchú published her memoir. Indeed, a previous text called *The Voice in the Margin: Native American Literature and the Canon* by Arnold Krupat, a literary theorist at Sarah Lawrence, was widely used as a text in the study of Native American Literatures. This critical study had placed whatever new forms were emerging from native voices "at the margin" of the generally accepted canon of American literature. It is, perhaps, the placement of these literatures by scholars in the field, either "at the margin" or "at the center of the margin," that gives rise to further negation of what it is that natives have had to say.

Questions of "veracity," "authority," "representational" stories, questions of liberation theology, politics, and mediation have immediately emerged as

the various disciplinary methodologies used to interpret and analyze the singular native voice. In the process much of what is written and published as
the American Indian Literary Voice of the Twentieth Century is subject to
analysis as either inauthentic or too obviously transgressive and counterhe-
gemonic, and often is discredited as literature that can even be described as
aesthetically pleasing.

Tough-minded critics of the emerging native voice have appeared in anthropological studies, and certainly that discipline (always the handmaiden to colonialism while promoting a certain kind of advocacy to its indigenous "informants") has produced the current attack upon what some think is the most
important self-told native text of our time, *I, Rigoberta Menchú: An Indian
Woman in Guatemala,* published in 1984. In the last year, this memoir or autobiography has become the central focus in American Studies and Anthropological Studies and has been described as a fraud by anthropologist David
Stoll, whose book *Rigoberta Menchú and the Story of All Poor Guatemalans* was
published by Westview after having been turned down by several university
presses. Professor Stoll and many of those who embraced Menchú's work are
now embroiled in a dialogue concerning the veracity of such works, and how
the single native voice has or has not become "representational."

Rigoberta Menchú as a young native woman saw unbelievable torture, mass
starvation, and countless murders of innocent people by the armies of Guatemala. She had two brothers who died of malnutrition at an early age. Her
mother and brother were kidnapped and killed by the army. Her father was
burned alive. She retold her remembrances of these events in the book, and
these are the indisputable facts of her story. It was a story of the people, a story of how in 1980 the government of Guatemala killed tens of thousands of
Mayan Indians, displaced hundreds of thousands more, and entirely destroyed
several hundred Mayan villages in the highlands, including Rigoberta's.

Insightful critics and scholars in Native American Literatures probably
could have predicted that it would only have been a matter of time before
non-native anthropologists or other scholars trained in "scientific" methodology would "debunk" the long-silenced voices of such indigenous peoples
as Rigoberta Menchú for several reasons. Most important, the political regimes of South America have a long history of bitter prejudice toward native enclaves, and the United States has been overbearingly complicit in the
colonial strategies used to exploit them and their resourses. It is Rigoberta's
position that the worsening economic conditions and state oppression left
the Maya no choice but to take up arms against a clearly colonial and violent regime. Stoll, on the other hand, says that Menchú is not just a Guate-

malan Indian telling her story, she is very probably a Marxist who does not represent her people, but instead represents violence. In light of the history Menchú tells, it was only a matter of time before such native voices, nurtured by liberal scholars in academia and publishing enclaves since the late 1960s as multicultural voices of the Americas, would have to be discredited in order for the status quo of colonialism in such countries with huge indigenous populations to be successful.

A cornerstone in the multicultural canon, *I, Rigoberta Menchú* has become the focus for such a "debunking" written by Stoll, who points out that the Menchú autobiography "cannot be the *eyewitness* account that it purports to be," because during his trip to Menchú's home village some ten years after its publication he was able to compile some 120 interviews with informants and "elderly villagers" and others to refute some of the facts in her book.

Stoll's critical analysis of what he calls Menchú's "leftist" memoir appears to be a model critique done in the mode of the scientific methodology so well known to anthropologists. It will probably become this white male scholar's major contribution to his discipline, in the same way that feminist scholars have made singleminded contributions to the debunking of the work of Freud on sexuality in the last decade or so, attempting to become major spokespersons in their own scholarly fields.

Some of the white American scholars (trained in anthropology and related sciences) who claim expertise in the politics of Guatemala believe Stoll's book to be groundbreaking and bold, in that it may be one of the first to challenge the veracity of the native political *testimonio* in academia as reliable textual evidence. They suggest that this kind of display of political agenda in the memoir or testimony has no place in academia. Stoll chastizes the "liberal" scholars who were so quick to take up and reward this scholarship.

Stoll charges that Menchú *did not tell the truth* about her own personal remembrances in her *testimonio,* a work that purports to air the political problems of colonized and oppressed Indians in Latin America accurately and reliably. He calls her an "icon" for human rights advocates who blindly accept her story without analysis. He says she was not "uneducated" as she had claimed, since she had received the equivalent of an eighth-grade education when she was a domestic worker at a missionary school. Stoll says she did not work at the plantations as she intimates because she was away at school while her family worked there. He says her younger brother, Petrocinio, could not have been killed and burned in a plaza at Chimel and she could not have been an eyewitness to that torture and burning because such an atrocity never took place there. And he has the interviews to prove it. Menchú's claims to these eyewitness events, says Stoll, after ten years of what some have called a "Kenneth Starr type of investigation" of her background, are, very simply, untruths, and he wonders at the acceptance in academic circles of this work, which he believes is clearly a memoir with an ideological, "leftist" agenda.

Prior to his work in anthropology, Stoll spent almost ten years in Latin America writing pieces about the Protestant missionaries among the Indians there, and in the process of that work, he seems to have developed his own critical ideological stance toward the guerrilla movement(s) and the land struggle(s) in Guatemala that Menchú's work examines. Indeed, the central argument Stoll makes is that the guerrilla movement was unnecessary because the Maya were "making modest gains" before the violence hit their region. That's like saying that the Black Power Movement or the American Indian Movement of the 1960s in the United States were both unnecessary, because black Americans were now allowed to sit freely on the buses, and American Indians could get free commodities at food centers.

It is obvious Stoll's analysis is no more free of a political agenda than Menchú's, but of course his work is not a *testimonio*, and therefore free to be what it wants to be. Much of his research and writing has been funded through the Rockefeller Foundation, the Woodrow Wilson International Center for Scholars, the Harry Frank Guggenheim Foundation, and the Fundamentalism Project of the American Academy of Arts and Sciences. His journalistic writings have appeared in the *Christian Century, Hemisphere,* and the *Miami Herald.*

After a decade as a so-called independent journalist and writer in Guatemala, Stoll pursued his Ph.D. in Anthropology at Stanford University, where he may have read with some insight the criticism of the right-wing scholar Dinesh D'Souza, who derided a humanities program there for adopting the Menchú book in its pursuit of multicultural texts and wrote the now-famous essay "Illiberal Education" for a mainstream journal. D'Souza, later a researcher at the conservative American Enterprise Institute in Washington, D.C., has never been an advocate of multiculturalism nor does he know much about Native American affairs, but he has developed a following in conservative think tanks as a critic of affirmative action and a right-wing analyst of race relations in America. D'Souza's latest book, *The End of Racism,* a handbook on how to make racism respectable, is a work funded by the American Enterprise Institute. It fits in nicely with the Richard Hernstein and Charles Murray book *The Bell Curve,* and the work done by such right-wing writers as Irving Kristol and Rowland Evans and Robert Novak, all of whom are regular contributors to the conservative *Wall Street Journal.*

Memoirs of the sort published by Rigoberta Menchú have become a main-stay in the canon of multicultural materials and Native American Literary Studies. While many of these memoirs do not claim "factual" authenticity and are said to be narratives of the experiences the writer has lived through, there is considerable ambiguity in the genre development of the memoir. The word itself derives from the word *memory* (the mental faculty of retaining and recalling) and from the Latin word *memorabilis,* to remember.

In Latin American literary studies such works are often called *testimonio,* literally translated as "testimony," as in the act of testifying or bearing witness in a legal or religious sense. Labeling Menchú's book as either memoir or *testimonio,* which has been done by the scholars and publishers who assisted her in this work, is crucial. If it is *testimonio* and is said to be a nonfictional, popular/democratic form of epic narrative, Stoll does not have a leg to stand on in his frenzy to label the story a lie, because epic narratives are always exaggerations. If, on the other hand, it is an ethno-biography, his pedagogical complaints may have some merit, because translators and recorders have supposedly taken it upon themselves to seek "truth." To suggest that Menchú, with her eighth-grade equivalancy education, understood these generic distinctions of scholarship when she wrote her story and published it with the help of scholars is at the very least a dubious assumption.

The important thing to say here is that in neither case can we suggest, as Stoll does, that Menchú and her story are not representative of her social class, group, or people, because she clearly describes events that have taken place in the villages of Guatemala. No one, not even Dr. Stoll, denies the murders, the torture, the deaths suffered by the Indians there. Menchú's report on the crimes committed against the people in that nation's thirty-four-year fratricidal war was long overdue, and the scale and savagery of death to the majority indigenous Mayan population there was horrifying, and it needed to be published in whatever generic form was available. Today, the CIA still bars the public from full disclosure of these matters both in Guatemala and the United States. Menchú's personal truth commission, in the form of her "memoir," may be all the outside world will ever know, and Stoll's so-called scholarly accusations, if taken to their logical conclusions, might be seen as blaming the victims themselves for their plight, or, worse, a defense for governmental malfeasance. What this particular attack by Stoll means is that while genocide in Europe and Africa will be described and defined in this century and legislation will be undertaken in the Neuremberg tradition to prevent recurrence, such crimes committed by colonists against the indigenes of North and South America will continue to be mired in scholarly ambiguity and uncertainty.

Those anthropologists and ethnographers who "seek truth" through scientific methodology demand that "memoirs" be factual and truthful, while others who understand the act of remembering in a variety of different ways find the works useful as a way of "knowing," rather than a way of "truth." This controversy may be nothing more or less than a recognition of the different function of genre in different disciplines. Cynics, however, those scholars intent upon finding conspiracy in every disagreement, or the many disbelievers of another sort who simply know a political agenda when they see one, may want to discuss the ideology which underlies the confrontation between Stoll and the Menchú autobiography and the charges of fraud that he makes. This makes it possible for the Books and Arts Section of *The Nation* (Feb. 8, 1999) to write: "Stoll is interested in more than exposing Menchú: *He challenges the claim that the Guatemalan revolution had popular support.*" This challenge is what suggests that the "discrediting of the native voice in the twenty-first century" is, more often than not, a political challenge rather than a scholarly one.

The Menchú book came out during the Reagan administration, when U.S. conservatives and right-wingers were attempting to discredit human rights organizations around the world. Some in the Republican administration even claimed that the so-called militants in Nicaragua (which some readers claim Menchú's story seems to favor) were part of a "worldwide Communist conspiracy." Moreover, politically activist journalists (now turned anthropologists) like Stoll have contributed for almost two decades to the idea that guerrilla movements such as those in South America are themselves responsible for bringing about the repression experienced by the masses (a kind of "blaming the victim" approach), that they prevent reform practices that might be brought about by peaceful means, and that these movements are often led by "outsiders" and are therefore inauthentic. It is the essential colonial response to native uprisings. They also suggest that South American Indians are by nature passive, and if left untutored by the leftist elite, their political naiveté renders them unable to create liberation movements, and thus such events are not inspired from within.

The struggle of the colonized indigenous peoples of the continent to tell their own stories in the twentieth century either through politics or literature or revolutionary movements has been the struggle to reveal to the public the hope for a new and remodeled world. The denial of this basic human right through the development of nationalistic, legal, social, and intellectual systems that make it impossible for a domestic people, or a domestic nation of Indians, to express itself collectively and historically in terms of continued self-determination is a kind of genocide that is perhaps even more immoral than the physical genocide of war and torture.

Nineteenth-century anthropologists trained in methodologies that are essentially ideologically motivated have always had colonialism as their focus, and the sad truth is that many twentieth-century anthropologists have not cast off the colonialist model. Stoll's efforts to discredit a text like Rigoberta's book, which moves on from the oral traditions of the Quiché Indians to the new methods of storytelling, is not very much different from the 1955 state-sponsored arrests of Algerian storytellers who began, as an intellectual revolutionary exercise, the awakening of their people through written nationalistic epics. Countless other examples come to mind. Stoll's defenders say the public has the right to "the truth," but what has been more true than the unnoticed and unacknowledged slaughter of Indians in Guatemala in front of our very eyes?

Civil rights movements, indigenous movements, black consciousness movements, nationalistic movements around the world have been on the stage of history during this century. Writers like Rigoberta Menchú who have accompanied these movements attempt both in intellect and politics to escape the grasp of colonialism, which has brought about death and torture, poverty and disease. The culture that is affirmed in Menchú's work is native culture, not western European culture. That is reason enough for non-native scholars, particularly those trained in anthropological methods as sympathizers for colonial interests, to attempt to discredit her.

All of this has become serious business for conservative think tanks. The Center for the Study of Popular Culture, based in Los Angeles, paid a total of about $5,000 to advertise in student newspapers at Brandeis, Columbia, Harvard, and Yale, as a warning to students, an ad calling Ms. Menchú a "Marxist terrorist" and "an intellectual fraud." The president of the popular-culture center, David Horowitz, said the ad's purpose was to alert those in academic circles to the danger that "you have an academic left so powerful that it can make her [Menchú's] drivel canonical."

From the Internet, Horowitz ran a column in "Front Page Magazine" calling the Menchú story "one of the greatest intellectual and academic hoaxes of the twentieth century." He goes so far as to say that as a result of Stoll's research and the work of other like-minded scholars, "Menchú has been exposed as a Communist agent working for terrorists who were ultimately responsible for the death of her own family." He further states that "the fictional life of Rigoberta Menchú is a piece of Communist propaganda designed to incite hatred of Europeans and Westerners and the societies they have built and to organize support for Communist and terrorist organizations at war with the democracies of the West." The Center for the Study of Popular Culture and its advocates have the opinion that the Menchú book now stands, along with the Hitler Diaries, as "the great literary hoax of our age." Horowitz, who is the beneficiary of millions of dollars from conservative think tanks like Olin and Bradley-Heritage, has been on the front line for years portraying liberals and liberalism itself as illegitimate and dangerous to America.

There is no question that the existence of academic and literary hoaxes is a real thing, and that students and faculties and universities should engage in analytical discussions concerning these accounts. But the struggle between powerless Indians and brutal colonists in North and South America is also a real thing, and has been a real thing for over 400 years, largely unnoticed by the mainstream until people like Menchú, twenty-three years old when she began her public life, suddenly became the spokesperson for all the victims of colonialism.

What has happened to the native literary voice in academia as the scholars take sides and pretend to be unbiased and agenda-less is an unmitigated tragedy for America, a little like the *National Review,* in the same year that Stoll went to Guatemala, calling the ex-Nazi, ex-Klansman David Duke a conservative Republican and a "candidate of substance" in the name of unbiased journalism. Stoll's treatise, which calls the native voice a "fraud," is a treatise "of substance" in anthropology for the defenders of colonialism against the possibility that an oppressed people might devise a way to speak for themselves. At the turn of the decade, the rhetoric for a color-blind society and the skepticism about affirmative action and the effort to take advantage of racial and ethnic polarization in the country has so solidified that those of us in Indian communities see the values and ideas of native America sinking, along with any hope for justice, land reform, and economic stability in the communities from which such literature as the Menchú memoir emerges.

The interest in tribal stories in the United States burgeoned at the same time the Menchú memoir appeared on the scene, and some university presses, like the University of Nebraska Press in Lincoln, have so far published some forty or fifty titles in the genre. Today these are generally harmless boarding-school stories, or stories of overcoming alcoholism, redemptive stories of a life of poverty and tough times, a far cry from their progenitor, *Black Elk Speaks,* which had as its focus the mythic vision of a "traditional" religious figure, or from the political memoir written by Menchú, or from the activist challenge presented by writer/scholar Vine Deloria, Jr. Many of these new tribal stories are, by and large, sob stories by Indians encouraged to feel sorry for themselves because America does not love them.

Even western historian Patricia Limerick dismisses these texts of biography and autobiography as ineffectual political or historical documents by saying in her *Legacy of Conquest* study: "Most unsettling is the experience of reading an Indian autobiography and finding in the details of the individual's life no mention of the federal policies that were supposedly the key determinants of Indian life" (p. 195). This leads Limerick to the mistaken conclusion that there is a temptation to "overplay the significance of federal policy." Rigoberta Menchú, on the contrary, lets us know that governmental policy, at least in South America, cannot be "overplayed" or rationalized and that's what makes her work so significant as a modern Indian text.

Meanwhile in the states, if the Indian memoir of North America, or *testimonio*, or biography does not talk about federal policy or politics, neither does it talk about hot wars on North American soil. This is because the U.S. government ordinarily does not deploy its military into villages inhabited by brown people. Nor are the villagers armed. Not since 1974, anyway, when they took up rifles and shotguns against the U.S. and South Dakota National Guard, which had invaded the tiny village of Wounded Knee in what is now the state of South Dakota. This story, with the potential to become the inflamatory story of our time, has become, instead, a story of failure told mostly by white writers who want to take up the whitewashed Plains Indian history of "how the West was won" and discuss the divisions on Indian reservations between half-breeds and "traditionals."

One exception to the white writer–based work by an Indian writer, attempted by a foremost participant in the movement, is the book by Russell Means, *Where White Men Fear to Tread* (1995). This book is still on bookstore shelves, but one of the curiosities about it as a text is that it is seldom used in academic settings. At the close of the 1990s, Means, the American Indian Movement leader turned movie actor, published, with the help of a friendly journalist, his autobiography, which claimed to be a truthful *testimonio* of the people, and he claimed himself as witness to an unprecedented seventy-one-day takeover of Wounded Knee in 1973 and 1974. No one yet has called it a pack of lies, but it may be important to ask why this testimony was not taken up by scholars in American universities as the Menchú work was embraced, for there is no ambiguity in *Where White Men Fear to Tread* concerning the role of the U.S. government as oppressor of native communities and tormenter of native peoples. If scholars are interested in "resistance" literatures, this critical and historical document should not be ignored. It can be argued that pretending the work does not exist or pretending ignorance of it is one of the methods of discrediting the work itself.

It can be argued, also, that its journalistic tone, its stridency, and its lack of creative ambiguity, which is said to be one of the controversial traits of literary artfulness, may be one of the many reasons that accounts for the failure of *Where White Men Fear to Tread* to catch fire in the academic controversies concerning politics and literary studies. Means is, admittedly, like President Bill Clinton, discredited very often by his own less than stellar personal behavior, but he is a man who insisted for two decades that his people defend themselves against grinding poverty and racism in this century. His book, even if one admits it has flaws, is a political document that deserves study if one is to understand the violence done to Indian peoples by the federal government and the powers that be. Means was an inspiration to thousands of Indians during the decades of upheaval in this century, and was accepted then and now as a symbol for native resistance.

In the last decade of this century, Means's personal behavior has fallen into further disrepute, not from outside attack as with Menchú, but, rather, from what some Indians see as a flawed personal morality. He was charged with assaulting his aging father-in-law on the Navajo Nation Reservation in Arizona, the unthinkable and indefensible act of a wretched in-law relative in any tribal culture. As a result of that act and in a pathetic attempt to defend himself, he filed a legal action that had the potential to undo him as a spokesperson for the native rights and sovereignty issues that were his foci as a leader of the American Indian Movement for most of his adult life. This matter remains unresolved, and political analysts will no doubt have more to say on this subject later.

One of the most important threads of discreditation as it concerns the voice of Native America has been the effort on the part of university systems to deny departmental status to Native American Studies as an academic discipline, and to deny tenure status to professors who have worked for years in the disciplines as native scholars, teachers, and researchers. It is in faculties that the power of ideas resides, of course, reason enough to rid the academy of unacceptable ideas and their dangerous faculty repositories. In some cases, these professors were hired during the hopeful Affirmative Action years, groomed as innovators of curricular diversity but in the last decade of this century denied the fruits of their labors because of the rise of right-wing and conservative politics.

Several such examples come to mind, but the most blatant example is the 1999 denial of tenure status to Osage scholar and native intellectual Dr. Robert

Warrior at Stanford University. Warrior possesses a Ph.D., taught for seven years in the English department at that university, wrote two significant books in the discipline(s) of Native Studies and Literary Studies, *Tribal Secrets* (University of Minnesota Press, 1994) and *Like a Hurricane* (New Press, 1996), and is one of the most engaging young native scholars on the academic scene. He was an associate editor of the *Wicazo Sa Review*, a nationally known Indian studies journal, for several years.

Yet his struggle to produce important work related to the issues that affect indigenous communities is given little credibility if he is denied status in a top-ten university that finds itself embroiled in the same "cultural wars" of academia that have, as has been demonstrated here, attempted to discredit Menchú's work and ignored the political remembrances of AIM leader Russell Means. This racist drama of tenure politics is played out on countless college campuses and needs to be analyzed more carefully in the same way that the defense of multicultural texts must be taken up by thoughtful people.

Drawing on the consequences of what started it all, *Black Elk Speaks*, an ethnographic biography, and Momaday's *House Made of Dawn*, a novel, it is clear that the larger culture, both academic and popular, has been quite adept at replacing with its own pleasing fanasties whatever politial realities those works might have engendered in academic studies. The activities sponsored by the vast numbers of readers of those works have discredited whatever authenticity they might have had, and the really fearful thing is that there is no way of measuring the effect of these fantasies on Indian communities themselves.

A major example of that particular kind of discrediting stems from the unstoppable, ubiquitous new-ager abuse of native texts for the purpose of founding spiritual retreat centers and shaman shows and summer tours and bed-and-breakfast institutes that teach their participants how to "travel on the Sacred Path" and "deepen our self-healing, understanding, and connection with spirit through ceremony around and with the Medicine Wheel," how to find peace through "the purification lodge, vision, and ceremonial symbols." They do it for whatever price the traffic will bear. Unfortunately for the many Indian nations now at risk and the thousands of Indians who live in poverty, they never discuss land reform and the protection of the sovereign rights of the native peoples of America. They hold Takoja (grandchild) retreats in the hills of Arizona at $1,000 a week but fail to inform themselves about the devastating poverty and health issues on the native homelands 200 miles away, the direct result of colonial federal policies.

There is little in this vast manipulation of the native voice that acknowledges the complicated origins of the people on this continent, and the grisly nature of the survival of indigenous peoples confronted by 400 years of colonial violence. There are few models for rejuvenation of economic systems on treaty-reserved lands, the exception being, one supposes, the establishment of gambling casinos. Read the local papers and find out that many of the small pueblos in New Mexico, whose people are among the most hardworking and poorest in the state, pay hundreds of thousands of dollars in taxes to the state of New Mexico and get nothing in return except isolation and racism.

The discreditation of the native voice is even more dangerous when we engage in it ourselves. Sometimes, for reasons still largely unexplored, native scholars find themselves on different paths. A fundamental argument between two of the major scholars in Native American–related disciplines, Vine Deloria, Jr., and N. Scott Momaday, flared briefly in the past decade, then fell unaccountably into silence. It is an argument well known in Indian country, its importance vital to all tribal histories and cultures. It is the essential argument of our times, that is, the role of science as either fraud or truth.

Whether the role of practitioners of science and their findings has been used to undermine the native voice seems, to anyone who has read the history of natives on this continent, without question. Yet the latest public dialogue on this became an occasion for internecine argument when Professor Deloria published in 1995 a seminal work, *Red Earth, White Lies: Native Americans and the Myth of Scientific Fact,* in which he called the Bering Strait Theory of the origin of native peoples in the Americas a "scientific myth." He said that this theory had little or no evidence to support it, that it was a myth perpetuated through the biases and narrow foci of white American scientists and was used to discredit the native perspective of origins and cultures on this continent.

It was expected that scholars in mainstream America would appear in droves to refute this native contention, and as expected, they did appear in droves. The *New York Times* told its readers that the Bering Strait Theory is "embraced by virtually all archaeologists, that America's native peoples came from Asia across the Bering Strait 10,000 or more years ago." Deloria's book, which said that such an idea was absurd, received few glowing reviews, if it was reviewed at all. But no one expected that Professor N. Scott Momaday, the literary expert on the oral traditions of Native America and most eminent writer of important novels and poems, would immediately publish a *New York Times* op-ed piece that would say, among other things, that Deloria was wrong and that Indian fundamentalists who did not believe in the Bering Strait Theory were a little like Jerry Falwell, who believes that the world was made by God in seven days, and "Reason, naturally, is on the side of science."

The important thing that came out of this short-lived controversy is that many scholars who have taken a second look at things, with some exceptions, of course, have begun to welcome Deloria's plea, which is simply that *Science should drop the pretense of absolute authority with regard to human origins and begin looking for some other kind of explanation that would include the traditions and memories of non-western peoples.* It doesn't seem to many of us to be too much to ask as we enter the twenty-first century. It is expected that this essential disagreement brought about by the recent writings of two eminent scholars in Native Studies will finally be taken up as the challenge to America's scholars concerning 500 years of Anti-Indian history and falsified scholarship.

Before the rising voice of the native is again silenced or goes underground or simply self-destructs in some awful way, or before government-sponsored death squads have succeeded in destroying the entire native population on this continent, scholars (even scientists and/or anthropologists) must be willing to invent whatever concepts are possible within their ken to acknowledge that Indians know what has happened to them and that knowledge is in the language, culture, custom, and literature of the tribe. And, most important, that Indians are entitled to tell their own stories, that Indian scholars generally are not liars or frauds, that the 1492 arrival of Columbus in the New World was the beginning of a massive reign of terror and genocide that has not abated, and that Indians in a land trying desperately to be based on democracy can no longer be scorned and persecuted as inferior to the white race of intellectuals who for too long have been in charge of describing them and their conditions.

If we believe that America embodies the best in the contemporary efforts to create a rational world for its people, we are obliged to expose the practice in its many forms of colonial genocide toward Indians. The writers and scholars who acknowledge diversity also acknowledge that most public Indian voices are rare and precious, especially those voices, like the ones mentioned today, that understand the politics of colonialism. Without the critical analysis of reasonable scholars in every discipline, the politics of colonialism, strengthened in this century as it always has been by economic and global interests, will again deny the right of indigenous peoples to speak for themselves.

It is a right no peoples should be denied.

This paper was presented at the fifty-third annual Rocky Mountain Modern Language Association convention, held in Santa Fe, N.Mex., Oct. 14–16, 1999.

20

CONTEMPORARY GENOCIDE:
KILLING ALONG THE MISSOURI

Hate crimes are the special coin of the realm called Genocide. And they are the ultimate expression of Anti-Indianism in South Dakota. There is little record of this activity, by design. But Indians know it to be pervasive.

A hate crime to be called a hate crime must be motivated by all or any one of the definitions of the word *hatred:* loathing, detestation, enmity, disgust, irritation, resentment, malevolence, odium, rancor, repugnance, revulsion, scorn, animus, prejudice, envy, acrimony, malice, and on and on. Also the descriptors of Anti-Indianism, these are only a few of the words available in the English language that describe the emotion called hate. There are others. It is amazing how many words in the English language can be substituted for the word *hate,* thought of as a much-reviled subemotion and considered a sin in the common Christian thought that pervades America.

The classic hate crime in the lexicon of American justice is considered a crime directed not at who a person is, but rather the *category* to which the victim belongs. When forty-nine-year-old James Bird, Jr., was chained to a pickup in Texas, dragged for three miles, and then decapitated on June 8, 1998, he was the victim of a hate crime not because the three white men who tortured and killed him knew who he was, i.e., a brother, and a loved member of a large and caring family of people who worked hard and went to church but because they knew his skin was black and they hated him for being a black man. Hatred toward the category to which Bird belonged motivated the acts by white men against him. To understand the nature of this particular criminal activity, this white-on-black crime, it must be acknowledged that James

Bird, Jr., was killed not only because he was black but because the men who killed him were white.

Therefore, the cause or causes of this hate crime, like others, must be analyzed from the point of view of the hateful perpetrators, not the hated victim. What must be dealt with here on an analytical level is that white people in America hate black people. There is no place in this discussion, of the James Bird killing at least, for the fact that black people may also hate white people, but to avoid the rejoinder that is inevitable in this discussion, let us admit that such black-against-white hatred also exists.

In the state of South Dakota and perhaps in the Midwest in general, neither the courts nor the law nor the society itself has ever come to analyze in any significant way the tacit reality that there is racial hatred that exists between white people and Indian people in the state. In the West and in South Dakota, where Indians live, unlike in the regions where there are large black poulations, there is little or no analysis of the racial hatreds that beset the region, where, overall, more than 10 percent of the population is native and nine Indian enclaves possess hundreds of thousands of acres of land exempt from state taxation. Because of the silence toward these matters there is no such description in the annals of law in the region of a "hate crime."

This in itself is an astonishing realization, since there is evidence in the courts and at every level of society that Indian populations in South Dakota have been subjugated by white populations, placed on reservations that have been systematically diminished so that whites could avoid contact with Indians. In the beginning the South Dakota legal code prohibited intermarriage between Indians and whites, but that code was largely ignored and there resulted some intermarriage between the races. Indian land in South Dakota thought to be protected by treaty was taken by whites unlawfully, the most infamous example being the Black Hills Case, and there is the charge that such "theft" is ongoing. Because Indians were hated for who they were historically and culturally, the enforced assimilation policies of the federal government in boarding- and church-school education during the last two centuries was initiated. This and other such actions caused great human misery among the tribes.

While some of this history has been documented, the cause(s) for the actions have rarely been the subject of legal prosecutorial discretion. A couple of cases in this final decade of the century, however, may make it necessary for a long-overdue analysis of Indian/white societal hatred in the state of South Dakota to take place in open court, so that remedies may be sought and a new criminal code put in place.

This is one such case: in the summer of 1999 "Boo" Many Horses, a Standing Rock Sioux Indian, was severely beaten by four white youths in Mobridge, S.Dak., stuffed in a garbage can, and left to die. At least that is what the evidence as the public knows it indicates. Weeks of silence from the courts, the lawyers, the coronor, the press, and others have clouded this event. As the leaves fell from the trees and the winter months loomed, stories emerged. The killing was called a "prank" by the media and the law and the white people of the community. Indians in the community, however, contended that Boo was killed because he was an Indian, and several tribally sanctioned protests were organized. The four white youths were taken to jail.

It was emphasized by most whites in the area that "alcohol played a part" in this tragedy and was, they said, the sole cause of Many Horses's death. Even the coronor, after the autopsy report was made available, indicated the cause of death was alcohol poisoning, content 0.44, four times the legal limit to drive a car. The families of the four youths charged in the death hired lawyers who immediately obtained their release from jail.

Many Indians from the town of Mobridge and the nearby Cheyenne River Sioux Reservation and Standing Rock Sioux Reservation suspected that this was a killing that would not have happened had the victim, a small, disabled, retarded native man just turning twenty-one been a white man, yet many suspected that those in charge of the law and legal services of this white community would never allow this death to be called a killing or a murder, let alone a hate crime. They were right. It was not a hate crime, according to those who investigated the event. It was not even a murder.

Today, even in the face of such controversy, there has been little attempt by legal authorities or anyone else to understand the phenomenon of racially motivated violence in these communities. Few have asked what role race played in this event or in any other. The killing of Indians in Mobridge, S.Dak., where this crime took place, a mostly white "border" town that has existed at the edge of this large Indian reservation for over a hundred years, is an unexplained phenomenon largely shrouded in silence and ambiguity. Yet if you ask members of Indian families in the region, you are told that unexplained deaths and unexplained disappearances of Indians is a reasonably common thing.

Since 1980, after the occurrence of a major political uprising on Indian reservations called the American Indian Movement Takeover of Wounded Knee, the violence in the communities where white and Indian youths converge has seemed to be on the rise. As a matter of history, in 1980 a major case of racial hatred, the torture and killing and rape of Candace Rough Surface, a member of the Standing Rock Sioux Tribe, went unsolved for nearly twenty years.

No one brought to the attention of white and Indian citizens of this state that this was a racially motivated case, though it most certainly was.

There are hundreds of unexplained deaths that, if investigated, could lead to the conclusion that hate crimes against Indians is a huge societal problem in the state of South Dakota. The Rough Surface case was solved nearly twenty years after the killing only because one of the killers was forced to admit it during his contentious divorce case. Rough Surface was raped, shot, and dragged with a chain behind a pickup truck and thrown into the Missouri River. It was a crime not very different from the James Bird killing in Texas, a hate crime, though since white populations in South Dakota refuse to admit to such a phenomenon, it was never labeled as such by anyone except Indians. Certainly, white prosecutors and lawyers in such cases (even when they claim to have "some" Indian blood, as in the case of one of the court officers in the Mobridge case) are loath to bring up the issue at all.

In the 1999 Boo Many Horses case, Magistrate Tony Portra of Aberdeen, S.Dak., dismissed the charges against the four all-white teenagers who were accused in the alcohol-poisoning death of the Indian victim. Layne Gisi, age nineteen, of Mobridge, was charged with first- and second-degree manslaughter, aggravated assault, and abuse or neglect of a disabled adult who was known to suffer from Fetal Alcohol Syndrome. Ryan Goehring, age sixteen, of Mobridge, Joy Lynn Hahne, age eighteen, of Trail City, and Jody Larson, age nineteen, of Mobridge, were charged with aiding and abetting and with being an accessory to a crime and not reporting it.

Many Horses, found dead in a trash can in this small city of some 5,000 persons on June 30, was dead not only because he was Indian but because the teenagers who were originally charged with killing him, and who spent his last hours with him, were white. Many in this area believe that this is a hate crime very much like the killing of James Bird, Jr., of Texas, dead because he was black and because his killers were white, and very much like the killing of Candace Rough Surface on the same Indian reservation where the Boo Many Horses event took place.

The defense attorneys for the four white teens argued that Many Horses was intoxicated before he joined them and continued drinking the night of his death. They argued that the autopsy showed no trauma to support the assault charge (though he had bruises and abrasions) and even that he was not a disabled adult as defined by state statute. At issue, the news reporters said, was whether the teens contributed to his death by placing him in the garbage can or whether he would have died anyway because of the alcohol consumption.

Authorities say that Many Horses had been drinking beer before meeting the four teens at a Mobridge convenience store and went with them to a field northeast of Mobridge and drank more alcohol. Therefore, no charges should ever have been filed, it was argued, and furthermore, the placing of the victim in a garbage can was merely "a stupid action." Their arguments convinced the Aberdeen magistrate, who refused to bind them over to trial. For this death, like many other deaths or killings of Indians in this state, there is no recourse. The victim or victims, this thinking illustrates, simply deserve what they get.

The FBI has been called in, again belatedly. One of the questions that must be asked is, What is a hate crime? What is white hate toward Indians in this region? It is necessary that these *essential questions* be asked and answered in the same way that the Nuremburg crimes of Nazi Germany had to be investigated in open, public, and international trials. The Nuremburg Trials of fifty years ago were necessary because the crimes committed were hate crimes against a category of human beings, the Jews, and the international countries needed legislation for that particular body of crimes if the modern world were to sustain its values. The trials at Nuremburg had an educational effect. They were a good and necessary thing for the societies participating in World War II as the way to find common ground and common justice. Likewise, at the close of the twentieth century, the state of South Dakota (and all of America) needs to form a hate-crime commission to investigate Indian deaths, because there are many crimes being committed that are directed not at who a person is but what category he or she belongs to, and these crimes are dealt with in a climate of either frenzy or silence depending on where they take place. A public forum is needed for the purpose of taking a stand and proclaiming belief and theory so that appropriate legislation can be passed.

This forum can operate either at the national level or at the regional level. Certainly, in areas where there are large concentrations of Indians like the state of South Dakota, the regional approach would work best. Even though there are few statistics available for analysis, a cursory reading of newspapers and the analysis of the work of law-enforcement bodies suggest that the state of South Dakota has largely ignored white hatred *as a cause* that results in the indiscriminate killing of Sioux Indians not for who they are individually but for the racial category to which they belong.

Anyone who has studied the legal issues confronting the seven tribes of the Sioux Nation in this state knows that these killings are not unrelated to the land-theft cases (Black Hills, Yankton, and others), to the continued discrimination in legislation, employment, education, economics, and jurisdictional

issues of all kinds, not the least of which is the ongoing Missouri River water resource conflict.

It's all about prosecutorial discretion in this part of the country, it seems,
and if the regional legal systems can refuse to acknowledge the theft of the
Black Hills as they have done throughout history, they can certainly refuse
to acknowledge the murder of a lone, obscure Indian by white teenagers in
the fateful year 1999.

Yet reasonable people believe that *it is not too late* for people of good will
to work toward the development of mechanisms of law against hate crimes,
in Indian Country and elsewhere in the world. The first step is to acknowledge that anti-Indian hatred is America's essential cancer and that it is a
mortal illness, as devastating as anti-Semitism has been to other parts of the
world. The second step is to investigate anti-Indian criminal bahavior on the
basis of hate as a cause. It will not be easy. But *it is not too late.*

Notes

Chapter 1: Anti-Indianism in Art and Literature Is Not Just a Trope

Reference to *The Confidence Man* by Herman Melville, published in 1857, can be found in *The Confidence Man: His Masquerade,* ed. Elizabeth S. Foster (New York: Hendricks House, 1954). Karl Marx, letter, *New English Weekly,* May 30, 1940, p. 76; Theodore Roosevelt, *The Winning of the West,* in *The Works of Theodore Roosevelt,* 4 vols., ed. Hermann Hagedorn (New York: Charles Scribner's Sons, 1925). Walt Whitman's "A Death Sonnet for Custer" (1876) can be found in manuscript form in the Berg Collection of English and American Literature, New York Public Library; Adrian C. Louis, *Ceremonies of the Damned* (Las Vegas: University of Nevada Press, 1997); Louis, *Among the Dog Eaters* (Albuquerque, N.Mex.: West End, 1992). Praise from Chase Twichell and Martin Espada comes from the jacket of the latter book. Jean-Paul Sartre's "What Is Literature" is in *Existentialism and Humanism* (London: Methuen, 1946). "Announcing a Change in the Menu at Neah Bay, Washington," *The Temple: A Postnational Journal to Create and Maintain a State,* Qiutian (Walla Walla, Wash.) 3:4 (1993); Louis L'Amour, *The Sacketts* (1965; rpt., New York: Bantam Books, 1982); L'Amour, *Ride the Dark Trail* (1972; rpt., New York: Bantam Books, 1981); Ian Frazier, *Great Plains* (New York: Farrar, Straus, 1989); Frazier, *On the Rez* (New York: Farrar, Straus, 2000).

Chapter 2: Is the Crazy Horse Monument Art? or Politics?

A good reference volume, *Pocahontas* was published by Oklahoma University Press in 1969 by Grace Steele Woodward in the Civilization of the American Indian series, vol. 93. *Dances with Wolves,* the Kevin Costner movie, was based on Michael Blake's novel (New York: Fawcett, 1988). *Journals of the Lewis and Clark Expedition,* ed. Gary E. Moulton (Lincoln: University of Nebraska Press, 1987); Vine Deloria, Jr., *Red Earth, White Lies: Native Americans and the Myth of Scientific Fact* (New York: Scribner, 1995). Two collections of essays are particularly interesting: Joseph Marshall III, *On Behalf of the Wolf and the First Peoples* (Santa Fe, N.Mex.: Red Crane Books, 1995); Leslie Marmon Silko, *Yellow Woman and a Beauty of the Spirit* (New York: Simon and Schuster, 1997). Cynthia Ozick, "The Essay," *Harper's,* Sept. 1998; Elizabeth Cook-Lynn, "Seek the House of Relatives," *Blue Cloud Quarterly* (Marvin, S.Dak.), 1983; Cook-Lynn, *Why I Can't Read Wallace Stegner* (Madison: University of Wisconsin Press, 1987); Zora Neale Hurston, "How It Feels to Be Colored Me," *World Tomorrow,* May 1928. A handwritten letter from Standing Bear hangs in the vestibule of the tourist center at the monument site outside Custer, S.Dak. William Manchester, *The Arms of Krupp* (New York: Bantam Books, 1968). For further reading on the subject of the Black Hills Case, see the Spring 1988 issue of *Wicazo Sa Review,* 4:1; Elizabeth Cook-Lynn and Mario Gonzalez, *The Politics of Hallowed Ground* (Urbana: University of Illinois Press, 1999). Excellent stellar theology concerning the importance of the Black Hills to the Sioux is available in Stanley Red Bird and Ron Goodman, *Lakota Star Knowledge* (Rosebud, S.Dak.: Sinte Gleska College, 1990).

Chapter 3: Literary and Political Questions of Transformation

Rigoberta Menchú, *I, Rigoberta Menchú* (New York: Verso, 1984); Charles R. Larson, *American Indian Fiction* (Albuquerque: University of New Mexico Press, 1978); Louis Owens, *Other Destinies* (Norman: University of Oklahoma Press, 1992); Michael Castro, *Interpreting the Indian* (Albuquerque: University of New Mexico Press, 1983); David Seals, *Powwow Highway* (Rapid City, S.Dak.: Sky and Sage, 1983); Hertha Dawn Wong, *Sending My Heart Back across the Years* (New York: Oxford University Press, 1992); Ray A. Young Bear, *Black Eagle Child: The Facepaint Narratives* (New York: Grove Press, 1992); Robert Warrior, *Tribal Secrets* (Minneapolis: University of Minnesota Press, 1994). The work of Ron Karenga can be accessed in *Black Intellectuals,* ed. William Banks (New York: Norton, 1996).

Chapter 4: The Idea of Conscience and a Journey into Sacred Myth

Wole Soyinka, *Art, Dialogue, and Outrage* (New York: Pantheon, 1998), 20; Elizabeth Cook-Lynn, "A Visit from Reverend Tileston," *The Power of Horses and Other Stories* (New York: Arcade, 1990), 13–23; Cook-Lynn, *From the River's Edge* (New York: Arcade, 1991); Kenneth Rosen, ed., *The Man to Send Rain Clouds* (New York: Viking, 1974); Simon Ortiz, *Fightin': New and Collected Stories* (New York: Thunder's Mouth, 1983).

Chapter 5: Tender Mercies and Moral Dilemmas

These land cases can be examined in collections published by the Native American Rights Fund and also through library loan at the NARF Law Library, 1506 Broadway, Boulder, CO 80302. *The Handbook of Federal Law* by Felix Cohen is available in all federal repositories. Further reading see A. J. Liebling, "A Reporter at Large," *New Yorker,* Jan. 8, 1955. The South Dakota Historical Society has copies of David Miller's books, some of them by now out of print. See "A Historian's View of S.705, the Sioux Indian Black Hills Bill," *Wicazo Sa Review* 4:1 (Spring 1988): 55; Helen Hunt Jackson, *A Century of Dishonor* (1881), ed. Andrew F. Rolle (New York: Harper and Row, 1965). The case *South Dakota v. U.S. Department of Interior* is available in the Federal Register. About the time the Sioux took the Black Hills Case to the courts, two 1821 land-ownership cases of the Cherokee Nation (*Holden v. Joy,* 84 U.S.211, 244-1872, accord: 1 Op. A.G. 464-1821; and *The Seneca Lands,* 1 Op. A.G. 465-1821) shed some light on the court's thinking. An excellent reference volume is David E. Wilkins's *American Indian Sovereignty and the U.S. Supreme Court: The Masking of Justice* (Austin: University of Texas Press, 1997).

Chapter 6: Letter to Michael Dorris

Part 2 begins with a letter to Michael Dorris from the official editorial files of Elizabeth Cook-Lynn, editor of the *Wicazo Sa Review,* and a paraphrased response.

Chapter 7: A Mixed-Blood, Tribeless Voice in American Indian Literatures

Elizabeth Cook-Lynn, review of *The Broken Cord* by Michael Dorris, *Wicazo Sa Review* 5:2 (Fall 1989): 42–45; Cook-Lynn, "Who Stole Native American Studies?," *Wicazo Sa Review* 12:1 (Spring 1997): 9–28; Eric Konigsberg, "The Suicide of a Literary Star," *New Yorker,* June 16, 1997; Allan Chavkin and Nancy Feyl Chavkin, eds., *Conversations with Louise Erdrich and Michael Dorris,* (Jackson: University Press of Mississippi, 1994), ix; George M. Gugelberger, ed., *The Real Thing: Testimonial Discourse and Latin America,* (Durham, N.C.: Duke University Press, 1996).

Chapter 8: Innocence, Sin, and Penance

Some parts of this essay were published in the summer of 2000 in a tribal magazine, *Ikce Wicasta,* ed. Florestine Renville German. U.S. Misc. Doc. #1 can be found in the National Archives in Washington, D.C. Fritz Fanon, *The Wretched of the Earth* (New York: Grove Press, 1963); Keith Richburg, *Out of America: A Black Man Confronts Africa* (New York: Basic Books, 1997); Wallace Stegner and Richard W. Etulain, *Conversations with Wallace Stegner on Western History and Literature* (Salt Lake City: University of Utah Press, 1983).

Chapter 9: News of the Day and the Yankton Case

Yankton Sioux Tribe v. South Dakota, 1997; the state argument included the 1894 Act of Congress; *Hagen v. Utah,* 1944, 127 L.Ed. 2d 252, argued Nov. 2, 1993, decided Feb. 23, 1994, no. 92-6281.

Chapter 10: Science, Belief, and "Stinking Fish"

Much of the information about the Polacca Wash bones comes from two *New Yorker* articles, "The Last Men" (June 16, 1997) and "Cannibals of the Canyon" (Nov. 30, 1998) and can be attributed to the reporter-at-large Douglas Preston. Occam's razor has reference to the maxim rendered by English philosopher William Occam (d. 1349) that assumptions introduced to explain a thing must not be multiplied beyond necessity. On the Stoll controversy, see the following articles: Hal Cohen, "The Unmasking of Rigoberta Menchú, *Lingua Franca* 9:5 (July–Aug. 1999); Gregory Granden and F. Goldman, "Bitter Fruit for Rigoberta," *The Nation,* Feb. 8, 1999; Robin Wilson, "A Challenge to the Veracity of a Multicultural Icon," *Chronicle of Higher Education,* Jan. 15 and Mar. 12, 1999.

Chapter 11: Life and Death in the Mainstream of American Indian Biography

This essay first appeared in the *Wicazo Sa Review* 11:2 (Fall 1995). Patricia Limerick, *The Legacy of Conquest* (New York: Norton, 1988); N. Scott Momaday, *Names* (Tucson: University of Arizona Press, 1986); Ray A. Young Bear, *Black Eagle Child: The Facepaint Narratives* (New York: Grove Press, 1992); Joseph Iron Eye Dudley, *Choteau Creek: A Sioux Reminiscence* (Chapel Hill: University of North Carolina Press, 1992); Percy Bull Child, *When the Sun Came Down: The History of the World as My Blackfeet Elders Told It* (New York: Harper and Row, 1985); John G. Neihardt, *Black Elk Speaks* (New York: Morrow, 1932).

Chapter 12: Foreign Sculptors and Time Zones

Carlos Fuentes, *The Good Conscience* (New York: Farrar, Straus, 1961); Octavio Paz, *Convergences: Essays on Art and Literature,* trans. Helen Lane (New York: Harcourt, Brace, 1987); Carlos Fuentes, *A New Time for Mexico* (New York: Farrar, Straus, 1996).

Chapter 13: Writing through Obscurity

Peter Parker, ed., *A Reader's Guide to Twentieth-Century Writers* (New York: Oxford University Press, 1995); John Keeble, *Yellow Fish* (New York: Harper and Row, 1987); Keeble, *Broken Ground* (New York: Harper and Row, 1989); Ian Watt, *The Rise of the*

Novel (London: Chatto and Windus, 1957); Elizabeth Cook-Lynn, *Aurelia: A Crow Creek Trilogy* (Boulder: University Press of Colorado, 2000).

Obscure literatures that concern themselves with history and myth and the past are probably the most misunderstood and misinterpreted of all literary kinds. It was the Irish poetess Eavon Boland, who gave a television interview in the year 2000 on one of the book programs, who said that for the Irish there is a huge gap between *history* and the *past.* I think this is in some ways true for indigenous peoples everywhere, but is the subject of great debates. This distance between *history* and the *past,* she says, is because Ireland is a defeated country, defeated by the English, defeated by poverty, defeated by oppressive religiosity, and so it has had to construct its own heroes. And what they construct is Irish *history.* The *past,* on the other hand, is for Ireland, Boland says, not heroic; it is failure and humiliation and silence and degredation. Therefore, the huge gap she speaks of really does exist not only in literature but in history and personal experience as well.

This is an interesting perspective, but one that separates the Irish from American Indians, a consensually undefeated people except in the eyes of their oppressors, who have never really bothered with heroes and heroines in the European sense. No one, as an example, publicized Geronimo (though all knew of him) until the whites started making movies about him, and no one put Red Cloud up on a pedestal until mainstream American newspapers started calling him the "most powerful Indian on the Plains." For the tribal nations, these men were simply doing the work of the people, and thus *indigenous history* and *the past* mean the same thing. The telling of histories (which were rarely distanced as individualized achievements) did not require the distance that is required by the telling of other colonized stories, which were dependent upon total personalization. In American Indian life there was a contract with the people that made it unseemly for a personalized history to take precedence over tribal-nation achievements. Native tribal histories, therefore, are not filled with personalized heroes, in spite of the effort of non-native historians to make them so, but are, rather, seen as communal achievements. All the stories and songs say, "We are a great people," not "I am a great man." This point is important because we are, after all, the stories we tell and the songs we sing to one another.

Boland also contends that all heroes move to myth. If that is the case, we should be curious about why it is that the American Indian Movement leaders of the 1970s have not moved to myth in the tribal consciousness, with the exception, of course, of those who died in the struggle or who are incarcerated. Why is it that a little-known Leonard Peltier becomes mythic in the mainstream American perspective years after the facts of the event, but the heroes and celebrities well known at the time when movement events were occurring—Means, for example, or even Dennis Banks—are now seen as anti-heroic by much of America and even by many Indians? Is it because they are not historic but just part of the twentieth-century past? Is it because they have little or no contact with the national peoples, or the native public, and therefore are only personalized heroes of past decades? More important, will they become heroic with the passage of time? Or are there no heroes in native life at all, people simply moving through their lives in silence and obscurity? It is difficult to write Indian stories that the American mainstream wants to read if you don't have the kinds of heroes based on the stereotypes the public wants.

Chapter 14: Pte—Coming Back from Oblivion

The audience at this conference was comprised of the individuals who work for the Indian nations involved in the reclaiming of the Plains area for the raising of buffalo herds. Many notables were there, including the husband-and-wife team known as the Poppers, who have written plans for the economic growth of the Plains area in the coming centuries. Reference is made to a book that can best be described in the genre as colonial history, i.e., Ralph K. Andrist's *The Long Death: Last Days of the Sioux Nation* (New York: Macmillan, 1964). Judith Hebbring Wood, an instructor at the Lower Brule Community College in South Dakota, presented a paper entitled "The Origin of Public Bison Herds in the United States," which was subsequently published in *Wicazo Sa Review* 15:1 (Spring 2000).

Chapter 15: Native Studies Is Politics

The introductory material is taken from the Nations at Risk Task Force Report, available since 1990 from the Indian Education Office, Washington, D.C. This speech was presented at the Institute for American Indian Studies, directed by Dr. Leonard Brughiere. For further reading concerning the Momaday-Deloria exchange, see the original article in the *New York Times,* Oct. 22, 1996; a letter by Yale University Professor Jace Weaver, "Science and the Native American Cosmos," Oct. 25, 1996, p. A38; letters of Nov. 2, 1996; and Momaday's op-ed piece, Nov. 2, 1996, p. A15.

Chapter 16: Reconciliation, Dishonest in Its Inception, Now a Failed Idea

A major reference for background reading is the Wilkins's *American Indian Sovereignty and the U.S. Supreme Court* (cited in the notes for chapter 5). The William Veeder quotes are from an unpublished position paper in the author's (Cook-Lynn's) files. This speech was sponsored by the Peace and Justice Reconciliation Council of South Dakota, even though they were aware of my opposition to the reconciliation efforts, and first appeared in print in *Wicazo Sa Review* 14:1 (Spring 1999), an issue that was guest-edited by William Willard.

Chapter 17: American Indian Studies

This address was included in *Wicazo Sa Review* 14:2 (Fall 1999), an issue that was guest-edited by Jace Weaver and Robert Warrior. More readings in history are available in H. Aram Veeser, ed., *The New Historicism* (New York: Routledge, 1989), and Robert Warrior and Paul Chaat Smith, *Like a Hurricane* (New York: New Press, 1996). Those interested in "ethnic" studies should plan to read the forthcoming book *From Color Line to Borderlands*, ed. Jonella Butler (Seattle: University of Washington Press), especially the essay by Elizabeth Cook-Lynn and Craig Howe, "The Dialectics of Ethnicity in America: A View from Indian Studies." See also Cook-Lynn, "American Indian Intellectualism," *American Indian Quarterly* 20:1 (1996): 57–76; Cook-Lynn, "Who Stole Native American Studies," *Wicazo Sa Review* 12:1 (Spring 1997): 9–28; Winona Stevenson, "'Ethnic' Assimilates 'Indigenous': A Study in Intellectual Neocolonialism," *Wicazo Sa Review* 13:1 (Spring 1998): 33–51.

Chapter 18: Anti-Indianism and Genocide

Daniel Patrick Moynihan, *Pandaemonium and Ethnicity in International Politics* (New York: Oxford University Press, 1993). To be fair, Moynihan was really talking about global conflicts, but in true imperialistic fashion he predicts that ethnicity will be a potent and destructive force in the future. He says that somebody has to go ahead (and who else but America) and do something to make the world safe from ethnicity. Yet he says nothing about tribal obligations to humanitarian law and, like most Americans, has little or no experience or interest in Indian affairs. The reference is used here as an example of contemporary anti-Indian forces inherent in historical and political dialogues that do not make the distinction between the development of Indian nationhood and notions of ethnicity in America, and even when they do, they work to rid the world of both.

Chapter 19: Postcolonial Scholarship Defames the Native Voice

A version of this paper was first published in *Wicazo Sa Review* 15:1 (Spring 2000). Arnold Krupat, *The Voice in the Margin: Native American Literature and the Canon* (Los Angeles: University of California Press, 1989); see also Robert A. Warrior, "A Marginal Voice" (review of *The Voice in the Margin* by Arnold Krupat), *Native Nations*, Mar.–Apr. 1991, pp. 29–30. David Stoll, *Rigoberta Menchú and the Story of All Poor Guatemalans* (New York: Westview, 1999). Reasons for rejection of the manuscript at other presses turned on "intent": what was the intent of this scholar's work? Readers thought it was not a reliable deconstruction but rather a personal questioning of authority based on the author's political views vis-à-vis Menchú's. Stoll seemed not to be concerned with the scholarship and methodological requirements of contemporary oral history, which is based on the use of tape recorders to produce verifiable evidence. He used no tape recorders. He also avoided indentifying sources by name. There was a basic ambiguity (the readers thought) in what the author was trying to accomplish. Did he want to revise certain episodes for "truth" (not the function of the memoir, which cannot and should not be taken literally), or did he want to simply question Menchú's authority? He seemed angry (readers thought) that Menchú had "launched her career" with something that was not *her* story. It was the *people*'s story, and she had somehow usurped their rights in telling it. Some readers decided that such a counternarrative as Stoll's turns out to be just as "mythic" as the narratives we as scholars are deconstructing, which means that his work is unreliable, although it makes claims to scholarship and veracity and truth. Memoirs are by their nature mythic but scholarship is not, they said.

Dinesh D'Souza, "Illiberal Education," *Atlantic Monthly*, Mar. 1991; D'Souza, *The End of Racism* (New York: Free Press, 1995). D'Souza also wrote "The Myth of the Racist Cabbie," *National Review*, Oct. 9, 1995, in which he says that as racism declines as a social force in America, something called "rational discrimination" will take its place, and though he doesn't exactly define what that is, he intimates that it will be a good thing. Richard Hernstein and Charles Murray, *The Bell Curve: Intelligence and Class Structure in American Life* (New York: Free Press, 1994).

Patricia Limerick, *The Legacy of Conquest* (New York: Norton, 1988), 195: "The temptation is to overplay the significance of federal policy, for one, seductive reason: it makes things seem simple. Following federal policy is, in fact, the only route to a clear, chronological, sequential overview of Indian history. Step away from Washington, D.C., and you face a swirl of distinctive regional, tribal, factional, and personal histories in which origins in these varying groups defer to no definite chronological sequence. Most unsettling is the experience of reading an Indian autobiography and finding no mention of the federal policies that were supposedly the key determinants of Indian life." Limerick goes on to make the astonishing statement of confused analysis that federal Indian policy is "irrelevant to many aspects of everyday life," yet "shapes" lives. The same might be true of the Constitution, but that hardly means that historians and scholars can call it "irrelevant." In our Native Studies curricula we do not "overplay" its significance. Every schoolchild must learn its history. Federal Indian Policy is a core course in the discipline of Native Studies. Having said this, the whole episode concerning the "legacy" Limerick speaks of seems to give credibility to the idea that even "sympathetic" and "deconstructionist" historians are avowing and promoting what may be called anti-Indian scholarship.

Russell Means, with Marvin J. Wolf, *Where White Men Fear to Tread: The Autobiography of Russell Means* (New York: St. Martin's Press, 1995); David Hurst Thomas, *Skull Wars: Kennewick Man, Archaeology, and the Battle for Native American Identity* (New York: Basic Books, 2000); Steve Fiffer, *Tyrannosaurus Sue* (New York: W. H. Freeman, 2000).

Chapter 20: Contemporary Genocide

For further reading, see "Native Americans in South Dakota: An Erosion of Confidence in the Justice System," a report of the South Dakota Advisory Committee to the U.S. Commission on Civil Rights, Mar. 2000, available from the Rocky Mountain Regional Office, 1700 Broadway, Denver, CO 80290. Hundreds of Sioux Indians, including the author, attended the one-day South Dakota hearing held in Rapid City, a meeting that was scheduled from 8:00 to 5:00 but continued until nearly midnight. Many came away believing that the commission needed more than one day to hear all of the relevant testimony.

ELIZABETH COOK-LYNN, one of the writers of the twentieth-century Native American Literary Renaissance, is the author of three novellas, *From the River's Edge, Circle of Dancers,* and *In the Presence of River Gods,* published as *Aurelia* by the University Press of Colorado in 1999, and a collection of short stories, *The Power of Horses and Other Stories* (1990). She has written two poetry chapbooks, *Then Badger Said This* (1984) and *Seek the House of Relatives* (1986), and a full-length book of selected and new poems, *I Remember the Fallen Trees* (1998). Her collection of essays, *Why I Can't Read Wallace Stegner and Other Essays: A Tribal Voice* (1996), was awarded the Myers Center Award for the Study of Human Rights in North America in 1997, and a nonfiction work, *The Politics of Hallowed Ground: Wounded Knee and the Struggle for Indian Sovereignty* (1998), co-authored with Lakota attorney Mario Gonzalez, was published by the University of Illinois Press. Cook-Lynn is a member of the Crow Creek Sioux Tribe, Fort Thompson, and lives in the Black Hills of South Dakota. She is a recipient of an *Oyate Igluwitaya* award given by native university students in South Dakota, an award that refers to those who "aid in the ability of the people to see clearly in the company of each other." Since her retirement from Eastern Washington University, she has been a Visiting Professor and Consultant in Native American Studies at the University of California at Davis and at Arizona State University at Tempe, and a writer-in-residence at several universities.

Composed in 10.5/13 Minion
with Castellar display
by Jim Proefrock
at the University of Illinois Press
Designed by Dennis Roberts
Manufactured by Thomson-Shore, Inc.

University of Illinois Press
1325 South Oak Street
Champaign, IL 61820-6903
www.press.uillinois.edu